Michael Troughton has been an actor and writer for over 35 years. He started his career as an A.S.M. at the Arts Theatre in London. He has appeared in many film and television roles, most notably as Sir Piers Fletcher-Dervish in *The New Statesman* from 1987 to 1992. In 2005 after being fast tracked as a teacher he took five years out from acting to teach physics and drama at secondary school level. In 2010 he returned to his first loves – writing and acting. He lives in Suffolk with his wife Caroline. They have two children, Matthew and Sally.

PATRICK TROUGHTON

THE BIOGRAPHY OF THE SECOND DOCTOR WHO

BY HIS SON
MICHAEL TROUGHTON

HIRST
publishing

Patrick Troughton

By Michael Troughton

First Published in the UK in November 2011by Hirst Publishing

Hirst Publishing, Suite 285, Andover House, George Yard, Andover, Hants, SP10 1PB

ISBN 978-1-907959-47-9 (Hardback)

Cover design by Robert Hammond
Internal design by Tim Hirst
Printed and bound by Good News Books
With thanks to Colin Baker, Matt Smith and Phil Newman

Paper stock used is natural, recyclable and made from wood grown in sustainable forests. The manufacturing processes conform to environmental regulations.

www.hirstpublishing.com

Contents

People often ask me,
  'What makes a good Doctor?'
  My answer is simply,
  'Patrick Troughton.'
  He's peculiar, without ever asking you to find him peculiar. And *Tomb of the Cybermen* is an all-time favourite of mine, and so Pat became my Doctor. And he never asked me to find him peculiar.

- Matt Smith

Patrick Troughton Esq..

Introduction
'Life Depends on Change and Renewal'

November the fifth 1966 was a very special day for me. It was fireworks night, my girlfriend Vicky had just snogged me in the back garden – but best of all, my Dad, Patrick Troughton, was about to become Doctor Who. I was twelve and he was forty-six.

The previous Saturday, most of the family had huddled around our flickering black and white Cosser TV waiting for the end of the final episode of *The Tenth Planet*.

'This old body of mine is wearing a bit thin,' William Hartnell had gasped before collapsing onto the cold TARDIS floor. We had all shared in Ben and Polly's amazement as the old Doctor's face blurred, bleached white and finally regenerated (with the help of high-tech special effects!) giving way to a teasingly short glimpse of a very different man's features.

Now, as distant cracks from rockets and roman candles began to fill that Guy Fawkes evening air, I watched transfixed as the first episode of *The Power of the Daleks* was transmitted. My Dad staggered to his feet and lent heavily on the TARDIS control panel, raising his hands to his face and feeling his features as if they belonged to a stranger.

'Hold this. Tilt it!' he commanded Ben.

A man with a Beatles-style mop of black hair, penetrating dark green eyes and a pale putty-like face filled the screen. He starred childlike into an overly ornate silver framed mirror and declared

'Life depends on change and renewal'.

For Patrick, as for the Doctor, life was about to change beyond all recognition. However, unlike the Doctor, who embraced his change with light-hearted indifference my father found it very difficult to accept his new very public role. He had always been an extremely private man who believed that acting was like *'being a magician… if you can see the cogs turning and the man inside the disguise - the illusion will collapse'*. He would always come out with this saying, or something similar, whenever he was asked to do an interview or make a public appearance as himself. He felt that the actor and the role were two very different things and the audience should never confuse them. He would wrestle uncomfortably with this problem for all of his career.

My father was a complex man but one thing was very clear – he had to act. He once confessed me, while working together on an episode of the seventies TV nursing drama *Angels,* that acting was part of his being, something he had to do rather than had chosen. He likened the process of inhabiting another character in performance to *'a drug-like craving that seemed to keep my whole self in order. I can't imagine my world without it. It sparks me with life.'* This is completely contrary to the way he mischievously described why he chose acting as a career, during one of the few rare public interviews he did as Doctor Who,

'Oh… It's just a job like any other. I do it for the pennies of course – I have a large family to feed and educate!'

In fact life was a bit more complicated than Dad would like to admit in public or even to close friends and colleagues. He had two families by the time he did *Doctor Who.* The first included his wife Margaret with children Joanna, David and myself who all lived in a large cold rambling house in Mill Hill, North London and a second younger family consisting of his girlfriend Ethel, nick-named 'Bunny', with children Jane, Peter and Mark who lived in a bungalow in Kew, South West London.

I can't remember a moment in time during my early childhood where I first became aware that my Dad had left my mother and fathered three more children – my half brothers and sister. There must have been one – a moment of stark lonely panic which woke me in the night. A moment of sudden realization my life had changed forever. A moment when I fleetingly glimpsed my mother quietly sobbing to herself. But I don't think that moment ever happened for me. It never occurred to me at all. In fact I accepted the situation of shared affection without questioning anything – far more than my brother or sister ever did.

Perhaps this 'secret family' also fuelled Dad's obsession with privacy. It is a bizarre fact that his mother was never told about the family he lived with in Kew. We were all sworn to secrecy, visiting her with Dad and my mum every Christmas and Easter as if we were all still one happy family. I assume Jane, Peter and Mark must never have met their grandmother. She died in 1979 never knowing the truth.

Patrick lived through a time of many changes including economic depressions, a world war, the sexual revolution and the explosion of the television entertainment. Throughout his life 'change and renewal' were to feature constantly both in the artistic creation of characters for TV and in the complicated private life that he so wanted to keep secret.

Chapter 1
Mummy's Boy

Patrick George Troughton was born in Mill Hill, London on 25th March 1920. He was an ugly baby judging from the faded sepia pictures that lie crumpled in my mother's old pig skinned memorabilia suitcase in the attic. One photograph shows a baby in a black pram with dark spiky hair, a pinched forehead and very prominent pointed nose peering out of a starched white bonnet. I remember my uncle Robin always teased Pat by telling everyone how shocked people were when they took a look in his pram. But by the time he was four, pale smooth skin, hooded green eyes, ink black hair took control of his looks and he began to develop into a thin but handsome young boy.

His mother and father were a strange mix. Mr. Alec George Troughton was 'a nice old boy and looked a bit like a pirate but was actually a highly respected lawyer.' Mrs. Dorothy Evelyn Troughton 'had a distinct air about her and came over as rather grand – a bit of a ship in full sail, and probably of the battle variety!' She had been a teacher in a boarding school in Cheshire before coming to London and settling in Edmonton with Alec. They were married in 1915 and after the Great War, had settled in what was then the leafy and tranquil village of Mill Hill. Their house was a modest semi-detached property in Langley Park Drive close to the station. Neither of Pat's parents or relations had any professional connection with the theatre.

Pat was sent to nursery school at the age of five. A privately owned kindergarten close to Mill Hill Broadway run by a warm and friendly woman called Miss Webb. I think she must have been a failed dancer because most mornings were spent dancing and singing to music played on an old windup seventy-eight record player. She followed the style of the infamous Isadora Duncan that included free and natural movements inspired by the classical Greek arts, folk dances, social dances, nature and natural forces as well as athleticism which included skipping, running, jumping, leaping and tossing. This must have inspired the young Pat so much that he was able to talk his mother into having ballet lessons under the guidance of a friend of hers, the film actress and ballet dancer Pearle Argyle who would later star in the H.G. Wells film *Things to come*. She had studied with Rambert and Legat and made her debut in 1926 with Rambert's company. Later she would become the Principal Dancer with Vic-Wells Ballet 1935-38.

Pat's childhood home, Mill Hill Broadway 1930

Pat sang and danced on a number of occasions in the local village hall by Mill Hill church in front of an audience of doting parents. By all accounts he 'was rather gifted with a great talent for artistic movement' and had a voice that was 'clear and sweet.' This opportunity that Pearle provided was his first ever experience of the thrill of a live show and it must have enthused him so much that even from an early age a seed had been planted in his mind to become a performer of some sort.

Pearle Argyle was one of the few 'right sorts' of people that Pat's mother Dorothy desperately gravitated towards. They probably met at one of the many parties held by her husband's firm of shipping lawyers. Being from a lower middle class background Dot suffered dreadfully from an inferiority complex that tormented her all her life, unhappy with her social position and constantly trying to better herself. This restless need to drag herself and her family towards the upper middle classes was to have a huge influence on young Pat's early life. On many occasions she forbade him from playing in the park with the local working class children who he had befriended at nursery school. She obviously felt they were not the 'right kind of people' her son should be mixing with and feared that they would have some irreversible influence on him. She employed a live-in maid who it is alleged on more than one occasion sexually abused him in his bedroom. She encouraged strict dress code, especially at suppertime. But worst of all for him, she insisted that he followed the traditional education route of all 'properly brought up upper middle class children' and attended a prestigious private school. So at the age of seven with his carefree ballet days behind him he was packed off to a preparatory school in Bexhill-on-Sea.

My father never talked to me about this time in his life but I always sensed he could remember it all too clearly, young as he was. Bexhill-on-Sea boarding school must have been a lonely and frightening place for such a young child who had enjoyed a happy, secure and comfortable home life up until this point. In fact, he was so unhappy during his first year after three terms of desperate letters pleading to come home his mother finally relented and took him away from the school at Christmas.

He continued his education at Belmont preparatory school, which was in the grounds of Mill Hill senior school. The headmaster, Arthur James Rooker Roberts was an extremely compassionate man and had dedicated his entire life to setting up and running the school. He was a man with boundless energy and limitless vision, respected and adored by all his students including the young Patrick.

Belmont School 1930   Arthur James Rooker Roberts

Unlike Bexhill-on-Sea, this school offered just what my father needed. The children were encouraged to stretch themselves academically but also explore wider opportunities such as the arts and sport. The school was known for its family atmosphere and my father thrived in its loving and caring ambiance. It provided him with 'A true sense of belonging and encouragement on a consistent basis'.

In 1931 he became a weekday border at the senior school and around the age of fourteen he was 'bitten' by the acting bug.

'I heard a radio programme about Fay Compton and was interested in what she had to say. She was the daughter of actor-manager Edward. After drama school she was so successful that she became known as 'the actress who is never out of work'. She could play any role with utter sincerity, whether in Shakespeare, music hall, or modern drama. The life she described appealed to me, and I felt that I'd like that kind of life for myself.'

* * *

On holiday - Sister Molly, Mother
and Pat 1925

Pat, Molly and brother Robin
Bexhill on Sea 1929

After winning a number of public speaking and poetry prizes he
plucked up courage and auditioned for a school production of
HMS Pinafore. He was successful and was cast as 'Able Seaman
Dick Dead Eye'.

*'I had so much makeup on and this black patch over my eye. The wig was
too big and kept falling across my face so I could not see where I was going... I
kept bumping into everyone on stage. The audience loved it and this was when I
first realized how good it was to hear and feel that admiration from an
audience. That feeling never left me. It's like a drug. You get fixed on it and
you can't stop wanting it.'*

The following year he played the Pirate King in Gilbert and
Sullivan's *'The Pirates of Penzance'* and appeared as a 'wicked thief' in
the school pantomime. Many other school productions followed
and by the age of sixteen he had decided that his future career was
going to be as a performer.

'I just knew that is what I had to do. Robin [his brother] *was locked into a career with my father in the firm but I was lucky. I could choose my own way.'*

Patrick performing on stage at Mill Hill School in an unknown production

Patrick's mother and father seemed happy with his decision. However, they had all agreed that he must complete his education at Mill Hill in order that he had something to 'fall back on'. In later years Dad would say exactly the same to me. Although he had known that his father would back the decision to become an actor he was surprised that his mother had allowed him free rein and had not insisted on a 'sensible' profession.

18

I am unsure why my father found his mother's enthusiastic agreement strange. Perhaps he had never realized that he was his mother's favourite and would always remain so.

By the summer of 1938 he had sat and passed his London Certificate (equivalent to GCSE) in eight subjects and achieved a second division matriculation in four subjects at Higher London Certificate. He had also distinguished himself as member of Mill Hill School OTC (Officer Training Corp) showing 'good leadership skills and boundless energy' on an end of term field day.

In August 1938 he enrolled at the Embassy School of Acting in Swiss Cottage, which was then run by Eileen Thorndyke, sister of the actress Dame Sybil Thorndyke. He said she,

'Had an instinctive skill for teaching everything from Shakespeare to modern. She had been a professional actress herself and this brought a certain respect and truth to her teaching. Eileen was able to communicate an extraordinary love of the work, in both the emotional and physical sides to the training especially in Shakespeare classes.'

Pat was still able to live at home, which pleased his mother no end and reduced the costs of his training quite substantially. He commuted every day back and forth from Mill Hill to Swiss Cottage along the A41 and Finchley Road using the recently introduced new double-decker 113 bus route.

The Embassy theatre had opened in 1928, when Andrew Mather adapted the premises of Hampstead Conservatoire. After two changes of control and the establishment of a playgoers' association in 1930, the Embassy school of acting opened there in 1932. The school provided a modern but by now traditional course in acting based on the methods of the Russian practitioner and teacher Stanislavski. Classes took place in a studio attached to the Embassy and visiting lecturers included some of the top London actor and actresses of the period. At the same time commercial productions were produced at the theatre that enabled my father to 'learn by watching' other professionals.

'It was a real treat to see and be able to talk to such actors as Michael Redgrave, Constance Cummings, Glynis Jones, Sybil Thorndike and Mabel Love. It felt like we were being taught by the best and that really excited us into committing ourselves to the work.'

Patrick, aged 16

Patrick kept a detailed diary during 1939 of his last term at the Embassy School. Every rehearsal, movement class and singing lesson was recorded and duly commented on. He began the new term rehearsing a play called *The Boy David*.

Monday 2nd January 1939

'Got my copy of play and maybe more than 7/6 – ask father to help. Rehearsals this afternoon were very long and my cold is worse – hoarse voice. Going well though, learnt my words more quickly than ever before. Finished at 4.30 and went to see 'The Lady Vanishes' with Robin and Peggy. Extremely good!'

Tuesday 24th January 1939

'Tatty dress rehearsal. Too slow on Q's. Luckily Miss Thorndike mentioned it to me after first Act – I benefited from it and picked it up. I think I shall be good. Costumes are superb. Grand makeup. Miss Thorndike is getting me a letter of introduction to Tyrone Guthrie!'

Tuesday 14th March 1939

'Richard II went very well. Best thing I have ever done yet. Eileen pleased. I've found the way to be emotional in a pleasing way. Before it was all horrid. 'Emotional memory' is the right way to get feeling. Eileen wants father to see her. The possibility becomes probability – America!'

Tuesday 4th April 1939

'First night of 'Black Eye' – COLOSSAL SUCCESS! Carried it off 77 times better than I could ever have imagined and in front of all my friends and relations. Everyone. And in the face of awful odds – the weather, my cold, violent nose bleed beforehand.'

My father began to shine in the many productions at the school and started to get the reputation for being able to play older than his age. Shaun Sutton, who was later to become Head of Serials at the BBC during Pat's time on *Doctor Who*, was also a student at the

21

Embassy in 1938. They became firm lifelong friends. Shaun described Pat's looks in those days:

'I had actually been a drama student with Patrick Troughton many years ago, before the war. And even back then, Patrick had those deep lines on his face, he had the look of a thousand-year-old leprechaun, and I remember saying to him once… Pat, you have the secret of eternal age.'

Pat also met his first girlfriend Cynthia, at the Embassy. She was a fellow student and lived in Totteridge, quite near to Mill Hill. She features quite heavily in his diary entries.

'Cynthia sent me her photograph today. She is really jolly pretty. She phoned me yesterday to say she had got an audition for Windsor.'

'Cynthia phoned soon after breakfast to thank me for her birthday telegram. I am taking her to lunch tomorrow and then to a film!'

'I kissed a girl for the first time today – my Cynthia. We both laughed afterwards. I think I am in love'

'Auditions for last play today. Hope Cynthia and I get good parts.'

The final production of the term was *A Midsummer's Night Dream* and Pat was cast as Bottom. I remember him explaining that he had a very heavy head cold during the short run of the show and unfortunately they had insisted that he wore an extremely close fitting and heavy ass head for the scenes with Titania.

'Every time I came off I had to literally drain the mask. I could have drowned in my own snot if I had left it. The whole head just kept filling up because of my streaming cold!'

Pat remembered being disappointed on the last night that his final scene had not gone so well – the famous Pyramus and Thisbe scene that is supposed to bring the house down. On this night however the audience was particularly subdued and Pat had felt a little depressed with his performance blaming himself for the lack of reaction. In the audience that night unbeknownst to him was a director of the American Leighton Rollins Studios who was scouting for students from England to complete a summer scholarship at their John Drew Memorial Theatre in East Hampton, Long Island, New York.

The following day he was contacted by Eileen to say that he had been offered a chance to audition for one of the prestigious limited places. My father leapt at the chance and quickly began preparing a couple of speeches. From Shakespeare he chose Hamlet and the famous speech where Fortinbras arrives to greet King Claudius but encounters the deadly scene: Gertrude, Claudius, Laertes, and Hamlet are all dead. Horatio asks to be allowed to recount the tale to 'the yet unknowing world,' and Fortinbras orders Hamlet's body borne off in honour. There is no record of his second piece.

In a letter to his mother and father he described the audition and how his nerves almost got the better of him,

'When my turn came I literally could not stand up. My legs felt numb and my throat was dry as a brush. I staggered to the centre of the stage and stared into the glaring working lamps. Somehow I just began. I don't know how, but it was like being outside my body. I suddenly felt calm and in control and I hummed through that verse without a single fluff or quaver in my voice. It must have been good because when I had finished everyone in the theatre applauded loudly but I can't even remember acting it. It's a complete blank.'

Pat won the summer scholarship and went out to America the following month.

* * *

Patrick playing 'Bottom' in *A Midsummer's Night Dream*
at the Embassy School of acting

Leighton Rollins was Boston born and bred and very much of the old school of theatre. His staff also came out of that mould, the classic theatre, actors and actresses that meant something then but have disappeared in to obscurity now. It was a dedicated group that in some ways was way ahead of its time. Rollins had started his career as an English teacher but quickly discovered that theatre was his calling and he joined the Repertory Theatre of Boston where he became the director's general assistant.

Aged 26, Leighton moved to New York and became a P.A and drama lecturer. While there, he saw many young struggling actors, so in 1929 he founded one of the earliest summer festival theatres in the United States. In 1934, he opened and ran the theatre school for ten years called 'Leighton Rollins Studio' in East Hampton, NY.

My father described his time during the summer of 1939 as a 'as a happy and wonderful experience.'

'We did a lot of plays there, as well as a lot of hard work in our studies. I had a wonderful time.'

24

However, these eight weeks were more than just fun and hard work. They were to have a profound effect on my father as an actor. Here would be the foundation on which all his ideas, techniques and philosophy of acting would blossom and develop - the beginning of a process that would continue throughout his life. The school had a number of very experienced teachers but the one my father gravitated towards was a Russian called Leo Bulgakov, a former director and actor of the Moscow Art Theatre. He had worked under Stanislavski on many occasions and his teaching reflected the methods that this famous practitioner had developed.

On the first day at the Long Island studio my father was posed the question,

'I am an actor. My job is to appear to be someone else. But I cannot actually be someone else… so, if I can only be myself, how do I create and present a character whom an audience accepts as fully rounded, but who is not me?'

In order to answer this, Pat would be introduced to 'the system' – a collection of ideas and techniques set out to solve the problem through a study of acting, actors and real life. More than any other influence on his career, this was to be the most vital. The moment in time that would form the basis for his strengths as a deeply emotional actor. An artist who could work effortlessly from the emotional inside of a character to the physical outside. An actor who listened, reacted and appeared at all times real. He would learn to move from the 'Real I' to the 'Dramatic I.'

In later years, my Dad always made light of the 'creative process' of acting saying that there was nothing to it but 'saying the lines and not bumping into the furniture.' The most important thing he told me was to make sure before you went on your checked your flies! He always skirted around the process of rehearsal with the comment,

'I just do it. I don't know how and I don't want to. If you think too much about it, you destroy the illusion for yourself and thus the audience.'

He would never admit it, but those instinctive rules he worked with had been instilled in him during that summer of 1939. His diary entries reflect how happy he was at this time,

'A most perfect day. Leo and Mrs Pole have told me grand things about my acting. From them its compliment indeed. Working all day. Act five tonight. Was ever a boy as happy as I – happy because he was, to his surprise doing a job well.'

'My play 'Fashion' is a roaring success! I was clapped on exit for the longest time ever last night. Mr. Leighton and Shirley were very pleased with me. Shirley says I'm a second Claude Rains. They are hinting about jobs and there may be a contract.'

'Rehearsals for Pygmalion went well today. Leo says I have a very good line on Doolittle. Must know Act II by tomorrow if I have to stay up all night. Talked to Leighton. He criticised me for being too much of my own mind about things. Am I. He did say though that he had seen 12 'Bottoms' at the school and he had liked mine the best!

'Doolittle - Best job I've done!! Got laughs on nearly every line because I didn't force it. Eileen saw it and said it was my best job yet. I have now a succession of successes as a backbone. I ought now to go ahead from here if I am careful. I was good tonight because I just didn't care.'

The course was very hard work but every Sunday was free and Pat was able to explore the local area. The coastal strip had been badly affected by a powerful hurricane the year before and evidence of its destructive force was everywhere especially in East Hampton where the reconstruction of local houses and sea defenses were still not complete. Pat spent many afternoons walking along the huge East Hampton sand dunes and was invited by a newly acquired American friend at the studio to play golf for the first time at the rather exclusive Maidstone Golf Club. By all accounts his first encounter with the game was not particularly skillful but a lifelong love of the sport obviously stuck. Life was good and Pat was very happy but then darkness fell across Europe.

The day we broke up we listened to Neville Chamberlain announcing that we had declared war on Germany. I just couldn't believe it. It all seemed so far away.'

Pat immediately contacted his father by telegram insisting he should come home at once and cancel the arranged three weeks holiday exploring the east coast. His father agreed and managed to obtain a ticket for him through his New York office aboard the Belgian cargo ship 'Alex Van Opstel' sailing on 6th September 1939 to Antwerp.

The 'Alex Van Opstel' that belonged to the Maritime Belge had a crew of forty-nine and only eight passengers on board. Its planned route included an unscheduled stop at Weymouth for a routine inspection and my father had asked to be put ashore at that point. The cargo vessel only had a top speed of sixteen knots which made the transatlantic voyage longer than usual. During the journey he befriended a Belgian woman called Madame Andre who tried to teach him a variety of card games.

Pat wrote,

Thursday 7th September 1939

On the high seas. Glorious day. I have bathed in the canvas swimming pool. Sea porpoises, sea turtle and a whale. I listened to the news from the BBC. Heard that German submarines were sinking British shipping. Oh it is good to rest for a while after such hard work. Spent the evening as night fell watching the stars come out at stern.'

Saturday 9th September 1939

There is a big swell today. I played shuffleboard and bathed. Feeling a bit dull and tired. Played chess with the Commander. He beat me. I played well though. Ran into fog'

Sunday 10th September 1939

Making 16 knots. Very large swell. We are rolling and pitching a great deal. I hope the Belgian lady is better. She was very seasick. Had party tonight and I turned in at about 12.00 a bit tight. Others carried on until 4.30 and made such a racket.'

Monday 11th September 1939

We are half way across. The Belgian lady is well again and is at this moment talking to old 'How-De-Do' [Texan man]. *Played chess with the captain. Won a game. Had beer and went to bed tight again!'*

Wednesday 13th September 1939

Feeling better today. Played bridge with Madame Andre.

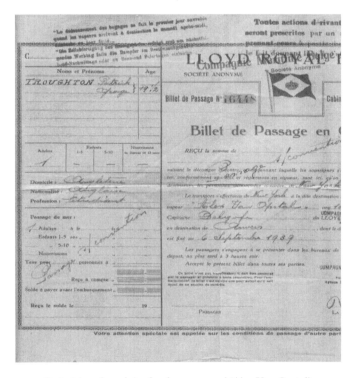

Pat's ticket aboard the fated cargo vessel 'Alex Van Opstel'

By the 15th September 1939 the ship had arrived just south of Portland when at 5:55pm, there was an explosion near the number two hatch. She lifted 6-7 feet out of the water as a result, fell back and broke her back between the front of the bridge and the number three hold. It is thought that she hit a mine. My father kept the newspaper report of the sinking which makes dramatic reading:

'Captain Delgosse said that seven people were injured and are in hospital. The ship was blown up and sank about 6.40pm. The passengers and all the crew were taken off in the lifeboats, and the Greek steamer Altanticos picked them up. A seaplane came over and reported their position, and boats afterwards came out and took both crew and passengers off the Atlanticos. First aid was given on board one of the boats, and then another boat came along side with a doctor and stretchers. Everyone had been put ashore before midnight.' Asked if he had seen any submarines the captain said,

'We saw nothing. All I know is there was a terrific explosion near number 2 hatch, and the ship broke in two in front of the bridge. The sea was rather rough with a northerly wind, but visibility was good. One of my passengers Madame Andre, a Belgian woman from New York, was among the injured, and is in a hotel with one of her ribs broken.'

The assistant engineer on the vessel, Alfred Thorne said,

'I was in the engine room when there was a fearful crash. We were plunged into darkness, and fuel oil began spurting all over us. There were shouts that we had been sunk. We went up on deck and found the ship had been cut clean in two. We got into the lifeboats and pulled over the Greek ship. We understood from the Greeks that they had seen a submarine. We escaped in what we were standing in and the passengers, like ourselves, lost everything. Several of the crew were injured, including the radio operator Gielen, who is in hospital with a broken leg and arm. Our best cargo boat on the Antwerp-New York service has gone. She had only been running two years.'

My father was uninjured but badly shaken up by the incident. He had been in his cabin when the explosion occurred and witnessed the whole ship lift out of the water. One of the crew members had banged loudly on his door and had bellowed to get out on deck to muster stations. After the rescue, he stayed the night at a Weymouth hotel thankful that his life had been spared but having lost all his possessions - everything but the wet clothes on his back.

It turns out that he had been rather the hero that evening, helping the injured Madame Andre into a lifeboat and going back to assist other passengers before clambering aboard himself. He sustained a nasty gash to his forehead as he was thrown to the cabin floor during the explosion but managed to stop the bleeding with his handkerchief and a pair of underpants, which he had tied securely around his head.

The sinking was big news at the time and the Belgian magazine 'Ons Volk' ran it as their front cover. Dad used to look at this front cover that hung as a poster in our upstairs loo and swear blind that the front passenger in the brown blanket looking very heroic was him. I was never sure whether he was telling the truth or just pulling my leg.

It is clear however that my father only just escaped with his life and if the Greek steamer had not been within hailing distance things could have been a lot worse.

Pat's diary entry for that fateful day reads,

'Torpedoed off Portland! Took to boats, Greek steamer stood by and took us on board. Then taken ashore by paddle steamer. All saved including 'Blackie' (captain's dog). Some of the crew hurt badly. Admiralty treating us to hotel for the night. Phoned Dad. Mother meeting me tomorrow at Waterloo. Ship sank.'

The next day he wrote,

Rather a restless night. Limbs ached and head hurt. Staying at hotel in Weymouth. Very hungry. All my money safe. All else gone. Had superb breakfast of bacon and egg and English tea. Lloyd's called and saw I was

ONS VOLK

N° 40

Weekabonnement 1 fr. 60.
Per nummer 1 fr. 75.

DE ONDERGANG
VAN DE «ALEX VAN OPSTAL»
naar de teekening van Luc. De Decker.

Weekblad. – 1 Oct. 1939.
Jaargang XXV. – N 40.

OK. I caught the 11.10 after wiring home – We are at Southampton. I am in the guards van. We get in at 4.10. Very weary. Want food when I get to London.'

When Patrick returned to Mill Hill, he immediately announced to his father that he intended to volunteer for the navy. His father was delighted at the prospect of his son following the family's traditional route of going to sea at time of war, but he had to explain to the enthusiastic and patriotic Patrick that he was too young to qualify for a place at that time. On the outbreak of the Second World War, Parliament had passed the National Service (Armed Forces) Act, under which all men between 18 and 41 were to be made liable for conscription. But the registration that was to begin on the 21st October 1939 was only for those aged 20 to 23. Pat was going to have to be patient and wait for his call up papers. He was bitterly disappointed.

However, in late November he auditioned and was accepted for a season at the Tonbridge Reportory Theatre under the direction of the famous playwright Christopher Fry. It was a semi-professional company called the 'County Players' situated in Avebury Avenue where a health club now stands. This was Pat's first ever paid acting job and it went some way to taking his mind off the sense of futility that everyone shared in - that nothing was going to last very long.

'I feel like a proper actor for the first time in my life.' he told his mother. *'We are doing a wonderful play by John Willard called 'The Cat and the Canary'. You should come and see it with father. It is a mix of comedy and horror.'*

But by December Patrick had suddenly started to question his love of the stage. In his diary he writes,

'I intend giving up the stage. It is too much of a strain on my nerves. And it obliterates family life, which is very dear to me. I shall give a fortnights notice. No more acting for me. I do love it but I am not prepared to make it my life's work. I think I am satisfied that I have shown I no longer fear

acting after my big dry. But no more. My next job in hand is fighting the war.

Despite penning these thoughts, all through the spring and summer of 1940 Pat continued to perform Shakespeare, modern plays and a number of productions written by Fry, all in fortnightly repertoire. It was hard work but it offered the opportunity of playing parts that Patrick would normally never have been offered such as Hamlet and Romeo.

Although these rewarding and challenging parts helped quell his impatience to fight for his country, the war was never far from his mind and in late September he experienced it's terrifying reality for the second time when a solitary German bomber released a carpet of 44 bombs over Tonbridge in a straight line from Connaught Way to Great Culverden Park and then again from the hospital to Grosvenor Road. Twelve people were killed that night and 16 were injured. Hundreds of houses all over the centre of town were damaged; the hospital was hit too with its casualty ward being put out of action. Pat had sheltered in the basement of the theatre during the attack but a number of the cast were injured, one seriously.

The season ended in August and the theatre closed for the duration of the war. Fry proclaimed himself a pacifist and spent the war first as a fireman and then clearing out sewage from the docks in Portsmouth. One of the Tonbridge repertory actors was arrested by the police and taken away as a suspected enemy alien. He was never seen again. Patrick returned to Mill Hill to await his call up.

It was November 1940 when Patrick met my mother Margaret Dunlop for the first time. A friend of hers explained,

'Margaret was tall and slim with bright blue eyes and shoulder length hair – a picture of health. She was a 'golden girl' and extremely popular amongst her group.'

'Although we lived near to each other in Mill Hill, I think I first met Pat at the time he began to court Margaret, to use a very old fashioned term. Margaret was a near neighbour of ours and a great friend of my older brother Michael. They were both part of a group of young people who had formed their own social circle and who enjoyed energetic outdoor activities such as cycling and swimming. Certainly in Margaret and Michael's case they also enjoyed going to the cinema and whenever possible the theatre.'

'In the winter of 1940 after the war had started, Margaret and Michael threw a party for their friends shortly before they would be called up to serve in the forces. The dance was held in the hall of my school, Goodwyn in Mill Hill, where Margaret would later become a temporary teacher. They had laid on a buffet, a pianist and a gramophone with records of all the latest dance hits. It is not clear who had invited Patrick to the party but I don't think before then he had featured much in the lives of the group. Most of them had been to UCS school and Pat had of course been to Mill Hill. He was in any event rather different – a flamboyant loner, rather wary and a touch sardonic, three or four years older than them and already out in the world… and with saturnine good looks as well! An intriguing character all round.'

'Sometime after the dance I remember Michael coming back from visiting the Dunlops and reporting that Pat Troughton had been there, sitting at Margaret's feet reading poetry to her… Michael was rather put out by this turn of events, especially as Margaret seemed to be enjoying it! Pretty soon we all realized that Pat was a now permanent fixture in her life.'

The New Year saw Patrick visiting the Dunlop household on a regular basis with more poetry, visits to the theatre or cinema and country bike rides. My mother described those few early weeks of courting as 'a truly idyllic and romantic time that neither of us wanted to forget.' Pat and Margaret were to become firm friends and lovers over the months that followed, marred only by the darkness of war that began to close in all around them.

Margaret Dunlop, 1940

Chapter 2
Duffle Coats and Tea Cosies

On a buff brown card with bold black heading proclaiming 'National Service Armed forces Act 1939 Medical Registration Card' were the words that Pat had been waiting for so patiently but his girlfriend Margaret had been dreading:

> 'Mr Patrick Troughton whose address on his registration card is 26, Langley Drive, Mill Hill, NW7 London was medically examined at London Medical Board 4 and placed in Grade 1.'

Across the bottom where the signatures of the doctor and the chairman of the board had been scrawled in blue ink, was a red box stamp exclaiming 'Fit for duty 15th March 1941'.

Pat and Margaret's last evening together was spent at the Dunlop's home in Woodland Way, Mill Hill after an afternoon at the 'pictures' in London. The Dunlop's household was usually a very happy place with a wonderfully welcoming atmosphere. Mr. Dunlop was a kindly, lanky, humorous man who puffed his pipe and watched on benignly while Mrs Dunlop, who was small and determined, reigned supreme in her 'salon'. Margaret's friends and especially Patrick adored her mainly because she took young people seriously and listen to what they had to say – quite a rare gift in those days. However, this particular evening was tainted by a rather gloomy atmosphere as my mother's diary reveals,

> 'When will the war end? We asked ourselves that question tonight. Mummy says next September. Pat says August 1942. Daddy - November 43. I say in about a year and a half. But God... I wish it were sooner. I am so afraid. We all are deep down but none of us want to show it.'

'There was the biggest fire ever, over in the city direction tonight. There was a brilliant glow, starting as somber yellow, deepening to a blood red orange, as it merged with the black sky. It seemed to start soon after the sirens, and until ten o clock it gradually spread across the horizon. Looking out from our back windows, as we all did more than once, it was well to the left of us. The trees in Bunns Lane stood out silhouetted a dark blue against it. We could see the smoke and flames reflected on the clouds, which were low, and from here we could have believed all of London was alight. Coming as it did directly on our return from the West End it seemed so unreal. London had looked so serenely grey and unconquerable when Pat and I left it. The streets were full of queues outside all the cinemas, and people were still going into the restaurants. London certainly can take it.'

The following evening after Patrick had left for training, Margaret wrote,

'The city is still smoldering. Five churches have gone. The Guildhall is a shell; St Paul's surrounded by blackened ruins, but unharmed. Malcolm (her brother) saw the tired firemen coming home along the Finchley Road, their heads bandaged, their hands gashed, while in the opposite direction water pumps were still being rushed to reinforce the failing water supply. There was ice on the water bucket today. We threw stones and cracked it, and it lay on the path like a broken milk bottle. The wind swept around my skirts, whirling and curling them. As we walked towards the station for our goodbye, the street was white with cold, bleak trees, bare pavements, blue figures crouched down the road, noses were red and faces ripped. Life seemed frozen.'

Patrick had been accepted for officer cadet training at HMS King Alfred in Hove, East Sussex. He qualified under the 'Y' scheme

38

which recruited public school educationally qualified (School Certificate holders) young men who were at or had just left school and were 'potential officer material'. He had his father to thank for this opportunity. It was he who had been so adamant about Pat staying at school to get good qualifications and it was he who had encouraged Pat to become a member of the junior OTC at Mill Hill School.

The Royal Naval Volunteer Reserve Officer training establishment had been set up at the beginning of the war to increase the number of men who would be needed for the rapidly expanding wartime fleet. 'Y' scheme cadet ratings like Patrick comprised a large percentage of the trainees to pass through HMS 'King Alfred'. They were not afforded the title 'officers under training' until the final two weeks of the 12-week course although they were given similar privileges.

Patrick arrived at Hove in Mid-March 1941. Under the training programme the officer cadets passed through each of the three 'King Alfred' training sites in turn; beginning with a two week initial training, evaluation period at Mowden School then on to six weeks at Lancing College where advanced subjects were taught, including communications, seamanship and navigation skills. The final stage of training was at 'King Alfred (H) where the course was to be completed.

Basic training at Mowden came as quite a shock to Pat. He had been billeted to a family in Ferndale Road, Hove who on first meeting seemed rather surprised and put out by his arrival. They weren't at all friendly at first and seemed to resent him staying with them. His first day included yet another medical inspection, a number of talks regarding the subject of achieving and maintaining a high level of OLQ or officer like qualities and a six mile run around the outskirts of Hove. Basic training began with some drilling and use of simple weapons. He was also introduced to 'the joys of morning divisions' on the old playing fields along The Droveway. At 7.00am sharp every morning regardless of the weather he would join his Jellicoe division named after the famous naval admiral and standing to attention witness the raising of the

White Ensign generally accompanied by some form of band or bugle. He was pleased when these two weeks had come to an end. As he hastily wrote to Margaret on the back of a sepia tinted postcard of Hove,

'I am absolutely exhausted. The training here is relentless and they do not allow you to make any mistakes. I will be pleased to get to Lancing! Basic training is torture. I do hope you are not missing me as much as I. I so long to hold you again my darling. Will try to get some leave ASAP. All my love Pat.'

Pat could not have known how much my mother had been missing him. The first night away from him she had written in her diary,

'A sickly time. The night swam when I woke up, the pillows twisted and turned in quick succession. They were as hard as lead and the folds stuck into my head. They cut into my whirling brain – over and over the pictures in my head were of a dead Pat lying helpless at sea. His head face down in a salty suffocation. My glass of water jangled against my teeth, and gurgled as it lay in my stomach. My feet were hot. The dog lay on them. I won't be sick… I can't be sick. The family snored on. One great effort to stop the pillows, to stop the nightmare in my head…One feeble 'I won't.' And then I was sick.'

By the end of the two weeks Pat had endured physical exercises, marching, teamwork, firefighting, weapons handling and general naval training.

He now moved onto six weeks advanced training at Lancing under the care of Commander Hugh McClean. A letter to Pat's mother reveals the complex nature of some of the skills he needed to acquire and the often rather comical ways some of the practical skills were taught,

'I have just begun brushing up on my trigonometry. When I was at Mill Hill I never thought I would ever see that blessed nonsense again. How

wrong! As I write this I am deep in the pages of a manual entitled 'Solutions of triangles as a means to navigation'.

I have also been to a talk on navigation lights and buoys in the library today... so many I don't know how I am going to learn them all. We 'played' with model vessels in the Ship Handling Tank yesterday just as you said Father. I have been out in the field all today practicing with navigation instruments lashed to a three-wheeler bicycle pulling a wheeled platform. It is quite the most ridiculous thing I have ever done, pretending to steer our 'vessel' around a sea of grass and calculating the correct bearing to intercept the enemy. To an onlooker we must look the most amusing sight.'

On May 29th 1941 His Majesty King George VI visited HMS 'King Alfred', and is known to have inspected the Lancing and Hove sites. While at Lancing he inspected several Divisions of Cadet Ratings on the 'Quad' but it is unknown whether my father was present.

At the completion of their six weeks at Lancing the entire division transferred to the main site at Hove for the final stage of their training. My father was relieved to leave his billet in Ferndale Road and transferred to a hotel on the front, luckily avoiding having to stay on base in a communal dormitory converted from an underground car park. Hove was a very different place - strict and more naval than he had experienced in the previous eight weeks. Before his final exam, my father was instructed to visit one of the many naval tailors that had sprung up in the town and to order his uniform which he would pay for if he obtained his passing out certificate.

Pat successfully completed his exam and duly donned his 'wavy navy' uniform. The passing out certificate reads,

'H.M.S. 'KING ALFRED'

'PASSING OUT CERTIFICATE'

of a SPECIALLY SELECTED RATING examined for the rank of

ACTING SUB LIEUTENANT
TEMPORARY SUB LIEUTENANT
MIDSHIPMAN

This is to certify
that at an examination held in
H.M.S.KING ALFRED

Patrick George Troughton
obtained 920 marks out of a maximum of 1000 and is awarded a

FIRST CLASS CERTIFICATE

Pat had two days leave before he was sent up to the Scottish Highlands at Loch Ewe where along with four other 'Tempy' commissioned officers, he completed a further three months training aboard a destroyer that would later protect the Russian convoy routes.

By September 1941 he had transferred to a destroyer on the East Coast convoy working between Rosyth and Sheerness. All during this time Pat continued to keep in contact with Margaret and although leave was very rare their relationship continued to blossom through rather poetic but mundane weekly letters,

'Pat, my darling, Today was the shortest day of the year, yet when mummy and I came out of the cinema at 6.30 it was still lightish. London in the gloom looks slightly sinister. The dimmed lights, the blue-grey atmosphere, the cross of the traffic lights, the dim cars. We headed out of London. The road swished past. At Finchley Road it was darker, yet the sky was still a pale blue. The yellow wallpaper on the tall, bombed houses, stood out bright against the air, flapping like skirts in the cool breeze. Chimney openings hung hopelessly. At the Vale, the 'warning' went. The lights in the bus went out. Across the skyline, the guns flashed orange. In space a star burst and then another. Scurrying across the darkened park we heard the booms and then home to the fire and Freckles [her dog].

By the spring of 1942 Pat had completed six months of nearly continuous convoy duty. He was due two weeks leave but just before he took it, a communication arrived aboard his vessel commanding him to report for Coastal Forces small craft training.

Pat rushed back to Mill Hill with the news. Margaret wrote,

'Two whole days! It was absolute heaven. Mummy said we didn't stop holding hands for the whole time. And yes…he did and I said 'of course' and that was that. No knees or poetry but a beautiful ring with the clearest of diamonds. The date is set for next year but things may change. None of us knows what is going to happen.'

Pat left for small craft training which involved three weeks at HMS St. Christopher, Fort William, Loch Linnhe, in Scotland, followed by three at Ardrishaig, on Loch Gilp, an inlet of Loch Fyne. He traveled to Chatham docks and caught a train that took two days to get to Glasgow. The journey from there to Fort William seemed even longer,

'My dearest Margaret, an early start. Arrived Fort William midday. It's still raining and I am bitter frozen. The station is a mass of people. Refreshments laid on with tea served in old jam jars. It is most welcome. When I know where I have been billeted I will forward the address. Only six more weeks until we see each other again. My dearest, all my love Pat.'

H.M.S. St. Christopher had been established to train new crews for a variety of different inshore patrol craft. At a floating dock at Corpach in Loch Linne there were around eighty to ninety craft

43

including nine motor torpedo boats, thirty seven motor gun boats, fourteen high speed motor anti-submarine boats, and a number of motor launches, many of them of the B Class Thorneycroft-Fairmile design that my father would come to know well.

The training was very practical generally involving setting off each day in one of the ML's down the Loch and into the open sea. Lessons would begin off the Isle of Mull including, semaphoring, engine room operation, depth charge setting, helm control, lookout identification skills and gunnery practice. On their return they would practice coming alongside a buoy thrown overboard in the middle of the loch to prevent any damage to the precious ML's. The instructor would then steer the vessel back to the floating Loch.

On completion of the training there, Patrick went on to the anti-submarine School at Ardrishaig, where he took a course utilizing a very old prewar submarine which was kept in the loch.

On 22nd June 1942 Pat was posted to H.M.S. Midge (Yarmouth). He would remain stationed in Yarmouth for the rest of the war under the command of Coastal Forces. These naval bases that were strung along the east coast of England were named after insects. Thus Great Yarmouth became H.M.S *Midge,* Lowestoft *H.M.S. Mantis,* and Felixstowe H.M.S. *Beehive.*

Patrick's first commission was aboard M.G.B. 603 as a First Lieutenant under the command of Lieutenant Lightoller whose father was Commander Charles Herbert Lightoller, surviving second officer aboard the fated Titanic.

Dad and his crew were involved in many fierce close range attacks by the Germans in the so called 'E boat ally' off Great Yarmouth. Their main job was patrolling the shipping lanes and offering protection to the convoys of coal carrying merchant ships.

M.G.B. 603 was a very vulnerable craft. Built of thin wood and fuelled with highly inflammable high-octane spirit, its big plus was the powerful engines and maneuverability. Patrick's nickname for the engine room was the 'hell hole'. He always remembered it as the worst place on the boat because of the ear splitting noise and the unbearable heat from the powerful twin motors.

Going into the attack, Pat remembered,

'… *was an experience he could never forget. Terrifying streams of bullets and shells would buzz past you. Lines of tracer and incendiaries too, all directed at your fragile 'little ship'.*

However, apart from these short adrenalin filled moments most of the work of the Coastal forces was rather boring and uneventful.

'*Most of the time we would sit night after night stopped and rolling helplessly in the trough of a moderate swell awaiting orders to stations but generally we would return having seen absolutely nothing. All of my work was done under cover of darkness because of the enemy aircraft threat and the fact that the German E-boats were almost always nocturnal. It was monotonous, exhausting work most of the time drenched through with rain and sea spray. On some occasions the winter weather was so bad all we could do was lay idle alongside the jetty and wait for the weather to break. In the summer the days became longer and our patrols became shorter.*'

'*On those rare occasions when the lookout did call 'enemy sighted'… even then things didn't happen that quickly. It was more a game of 'cat and mouse' where you tried to sneak undetected as close to your enemy as possible before opening up with everything. Quite often you would be spotted and the enemy would cruise off at high speed without even engaging. That happened to us countless times… very frustrating.*'

One such occasion occurred on the night of 28th March 1943. A sortie of E-boats had come over with the intention of attacking a southbound convoy at a location called Smith's Knoll close to my father's patrol area. MTB 603 was amongst a number of forces sent out that night waiting for just such an enemy attack. An entry in his log describes his frustration that night,

45

'We sat for hours in the dark listening for those engines but we heard not a dickey bird. I got back around six and was told Donald Bradford had engaged the enemy south of Smith's - lucky bugger. Apparently he rammed one of the S's [E-boats] and sank it!

MTB 603 officers and crew – Patrick sitting in chair to the left of Lt Lightoller who is also seated.

By the summer, preparations were well underway for Margaret and Pat's wedding arranged to coincide with two weeks shore leave starting at the beginning of September.

Margaret had been working as a stage manager at the 'Q' Theatre opposite Kew bridge station in London since 1942 and had taken a number of successful productions to the West End. They included *Jupiter Laughs* at the Wyndam's theatre with the Hollywood actor James Mason and *Children to Bless You* with Sylvia Sims. However, now her career in theatre was put on hold as she prepared for a life with Pat in Great Yarmouth.

A close friend of Margaret described her wedding preparations, which had to be on a restricted budget,

'I remember the preparations for Pat and Margaret's wedding, and Margaret shopping for her trousseau. She went to London to buy her wedding outfit, but this was wartime and 'austerity Britain' in a big way...with clothing coupons in short supply. I think she went to one of the big stores – Marshall and Snellgrove's or Debenhams and Freebody's would have been the main choices. She was directed to the 'Maids Department' that was nothing to do with domestic servants but a section between adults and children on the Ladies Fashion Floor, which catered for young slim girls. Eventually she found a very pretty pale blue costume and a little white hat.'

Pat and Margaret were married at Mill Hill in the Union Church on 3rd September 1943. Her friend wrote,

'I can still see Pat standing at the altar looking very smart in his naval uniform, and Margaret coming up the aisle on her father's arm, looking very flushed and embarrassed at having to play this starring role. Afterwards they had their reception in the upstairs of 'The Hunter's Horn', Mill Hill's poshest restaurant at the time, with lots of friends and family.'

After this they left by train for Tavistock in Devon to stay at the Bedford Hotel for two glorious weeks. Patrick had forwarded their bicycles by freight train so that they could explore Dartmoor and the surrounding countryside immediately they arrived.

Margaret's mother Mrs Dunlop wrote to them,

'Daddy and I were so happy when your card arrived this morning. You have not left our thoughts since Thursday, and we have talked incessantly about you, saying – 'I wonder where they are now?' – 'When shall we hear from them?' etc., etc... We are so happy Tavistock is a fairy tale town and that everything is so perfect. What did you think of your wedding? – Everybody I meet (and it is impossible for me to get back from the shops quickly since Thursday) says that it was the most beautiful wedding they ever attended. I loved every minute of it and was so excited and happy I did not hear one note of my beautiful 'Planets' on the organ. By the way, I am so sorry she was so bad – I could have done it better myself, although I can't play the organ. Dr. Watts was perfect. I usually hate wedding services but yours was beautiful.'

'By the way, did you hear the joke about grandpa (Mrs. Dunlop's father) He went up to Robin (Pat's brother) and said 'You've found a fine girl Pat.' Oh dear he must need glasses! We all went to the Brent Bridge Hotel on the wedding evening after you had gone. We had such a jolly time.'

'I have been talking to Pat's mother on the phone today about where you will stay when you return from Tavistock, and have said leave it to her. After all, I shall have Margaret but she will not have Pat for long, so she says she will put another bed in Pat's room and you can stay there for the few remaining days.'

'Well, I think I better close down… What can I wish you, dear children? Words are so feeble, but my heart is very full of love for you both my 'babes in the wood' – but thank God the wood is getting lighter, and you will soon be out in the sunshine. Daddy sends his love. He gets his teeth very soon – I hope he won't bite me! L of the D's, MUMMY.' (Love of the Dunlops)

When they returned from their honeymoon Pat and Margaret had come to a decision. They did not want to be separated from each other anymore – Margaret had agreed to live with Pat on the base at Great Yarmouth. So by the end of the two weeks leave not only did Mrs Troughton lose a son but Mrs Dunlop also had to wave goodbye to her daughter.

The new Mr and Mrs Troughton now took lodgings in Dagmar House, Albert Square, Great Yarmouth on the sea front close to Wellington Pier for which they paid the princely sum of £1 and 5 shillings per week. She remembered the flat well,

It was a semi-detached three-storey Edwardian house and we had a small sitting room, bedroom, and shared kitchen. I recall that we slept downstairs in the coal cellar on many occasions when the raids were on.'

Dagmar House, Albert Square, Great Yarmouth 1943

A large number of people in Great Yarmouth had left their homes due to the threat of bombing. The coastal belt had become a no-go area for visitors and only official vehicles were permitted on the streets. A large proportion of shops, hotels, and B & Bs had been boarded up. It was a lonely but beautifully empty place that had the feel of a ghost town my mother remembered.

'Of course one couldn't go walking on the beach or sand dunes because they had all been mined. It was a bit claustrophobic at times but one got used to it.'

Their social life was centered round the Regent cinema in Regent road, but Sunday lunch was the focus of week.

'The ship's cook would prepare a fantastic lunch aboard the M.G.B and serve it in the tiny ward room to the officers and their wives. There was no rationing at the base and everything was duty free. We would all eat, drink, and smoke far too much. It was a real knees-up!'

Margaret used to wave Pat off from the harbour entrance as M.G.B. 603 went off on a night patrol. She recalls 'the eerie fluorescent, white foaming wake and uplifted prows of the departing boats' and also remembers 'the dreadful private thoughts that maybe he would never come back.'

These 'thoughts' were almost realized when on the night of the 24th October 1943 my father engaged the enemy in a vicious and fierce firefight.

It was a calm moonless night and perfect conditions for hunting the enemy. Pat's MGB 603 and another motor gunboat commanded by Lt. R. M. Marshall had been on station for three hours waiting for the sound of approaching engines. Around thirty E-boats had been reported to the north of their position engaging a convoy near Smith's Knoll. Soon after two o'clock four E boats were heard approaching my father's position. A few minutes later MGB 603 fired a star shell and illuminated the startled enemy who had been completely taken by surprise. Patrick recalled,

'Marshall shooting up S.88 and setting it ablaze and then ramming a second E-boat amidships at almost full speed. As we went in to pick up survivors S.88 exploded into a huge 200' column of burning debris which rained down on us.'

Pat's boat rescued 19 survivors that night but five of his crew was dead, six were injured and a close friend of his was blinded. Pat was mentioned in dispatches for bravery under fire and received the bronze oak leaf. He was also promoted to Lieutenant and became Lightoller's 'number one'.

On 21st June 1944, fifteen days after the invasion of Europe, Pat was given command of his own vessel, R.M.L. 514 (Rescue Motor Launch). The job this time was to patrol the coastal strip and rescue airmen who had been shot down over the North sea. His wife can remember how relieved she felt at the news of Pat's promotion to Captain of the R.M.L.

'Although the R.M.L. was still very dangerous work, at least he was away from those dreaded E-boats.'

The 60th RML Flotilla was also based in Great Yarmouth under the command of H.M.S. Miranda which was very convenient for the newlyweds who could continue to rent the Albert Square flat.

By the winter of 1944, the United States Air Force was increasingly adding weight to the ongoing RAF offensive both during daylight hours and at night. My father's R.M.L. 514 was on duty round the clock often at sea for days at a time waiting to rescue ditched bomber crews. He would station his vessel at a specific point in the North Sea beneath the allied bombers' flight path and remain there whatever the sea condition until the appropriate command had assessed details of aircraft safely returned from their sorties. Where a ditching had occurred a radio message from HMS Miranda would be relayed to the nearest RML and they would begin searching the area with the aid of a Vickers Warwick aircraft.

One of the many entries in my Dad's naval logs typed by hand on gossamer thin paper describes a typical day of work,

To: HEADQUATERS H.M.S. MIRANDA

'Sir,

I have the honour to submit the following report on Air Sea Rescue affected by R.M.L. 514 on the 12th December 1944. R.M.L. 514 slipped in accordance with orders form H.M.S. Miranda command F.O.I.C. and proceeded to rendezvous position, namely East Barnard Buoy. At about 14.40 a B24 Liberator aircraft 'N' for NAN was heard over the VHF radio to be in trouble and she believed she would have to ditch before reaching the coast. Radar operations informed 'N' NAN that she was about 8 miles off the coast and asked her to try and make it. Radar operations was then heard to call Teamworks 45 and 46 (Warwick Aircraft) telling them to rendezvous with 'N' NAN and also to contact Seagull 25 (Air Rescue Launch) and R.M.L. 514. Our engines were started up at this point and the rendezvous buoy closed to ensure accurate departure.

At 15.07 'N' NAN was heard to say she could see the water close below her and that she was ditching. At 15.09 Radar operations lost contact with 'N' NAN on VHS and called Seagull 25 in the hope that she could hear – telling her to steer 180° for two miles. Almost at once the Teamworks announced they had found wreckage of the plane 'N' NAN and were orbiting.

R.M.L. 514 now set course of 180° at 18 knots when signal was received. Contact was then made with Teamworks aircraft on VHF. When R.M.L. arrived at the given position there was no sign of either wreckage or aircraft. Visibility was one and a half miles but a trawler was observed bearing N 65°E lying stopped. Course was set to her and eventually the Teamworks were seen orbiting her. Speed was increased to full ahead.

We approached the wreckage from the south and took two survivors aboard straight away. We found a body that we engaged in picking up and a further possible survivor who appeared to be drowned. I ordered artificial respiration to begin immediately with the help of NOVAX. Two other men were found; one was badly injured to the head and given morphia.

A doctor's assistance was required in the opinion of my Sick Berth Attendant so R.M.L. 514 set course at 18 knots for harbour. A signal was made requesting doctor's assistance and giving brief details.

Artificial respiration was continued without break on the apparently dead drowned man until the medical officer took over. My S.B.A. should be mentioned for his great energy and efficiency in dealing with the causalities, and members of the crew detailed to work very hard to bring the drowned man round.

At 16.40 R.M.L. 514 berthed at H.M.S. MIRANDA Grt. Yarmouth and handed the casualties over to the Medical Officer.

REMARKS: It is considered that B24 'N' NAN hit the water out of control and did not have time to ditch. The character of her VHF transmissions, just before they faded out, and the small number of men *picked up (and their condition) seem to point to a catastrophic entry into the sea.*

I have the honour to be, Sir,
Your obedient servant,
Lieutenant R.N.V.R. Patrick Troughton

My father with his crew, R.M.L. 514

Patrick became very close to his crew of fourteen men aboard R.M.L. 514 not simple because they had to spend so much time at sea together but because of the absolute commitment they showed while under extremely stressful situations. He commanded a crew of fourteen that included his 1st lieutenant, cox'n who was a senior rating, a motor mechanic, two assistant mechanics called 'stokers', two telegraphists, the Sick Birth Attendant, a cook and five ratings who manned the guns.

My mother remembered how the crew looked up to Dad,

'They were all devoted to him. He was strict but fair and would treat them all as individuals. He took the time to find out if any of them had problems at home and would do his best to sort them.'

'They had a nick name for him – Lieutenant 'cosy'. This was because at the start of his command it was very cold. I kept telling him he should buy a bobble hat. He already had a duffle coat and full oils but refused to wear anything on his head. Then one morning after I had complained to him yet again about him catching cold with no hat he suddenly grabbed the tea-cosy on our breakfast teapot and pulled it over his head! From that day onwards he always wore that dirty tea-cosy as a hat. It's my fault really; I should have just bought him a hat.'

Pat on the bridge of R.M.L. 514 wearing his famous tea-cosy hat

This may well have been the beginning of his famous preference for rather unusual and eccentric clothes that would be such a well-known trademark of Patrick as an actor and would be affectionately remarked upon on by his friends time and time again in later years.

When he was commissioned as a C.O. it had been made clear to my father that the R.M.L.'s primary purpose was a humanitarian role. There was to be no discrimination between friend or foe if they were found to be in distress and on many occasions the rescue launch was able to pull German pilots from the cold North Sea. However, the motor launch was equipped with a 2-pounder pompom gun, a number of machine guns, anti-submarine depth charges and a smoke making machine. It had been made perfectly clear that if enemy patrol boats or aircraft were spotted, they were to engage without question. In fact the previous vessels had been painted yellow to identify them as rescue vessels but the Nazis ignored the signal and destroyed a large number until the practice was stopped. This aggressive behaviour only hardened the crew's attitude to pursuing enemy vessels, engaging enemy aircraft or depth charging enemy submarines whenever the opportunity arose.

Early spring 1945 the work of my father's R.M.L. was vividly described by a 'Daily Sketch' Air correspondent aboard a Vickers Warwick air rescue service aircraft.

Coastal Command had employed these aircraft because they were capable of carrying the Lindholme rescue package and lifeboat that could be dropped on three parachutes. The Lindholme gear included a dinghy, and several containers with food, water, and survival equipment.

'FLYING LIFEBOAT SAVES AIRMAN – above the North sea.

Hundreds of feet below, a tiny yellow speck gleams in a vast expanse of sea. It is a rubber dingy, and in it is the crew of a ditched bomber.'

'Their lives depend on the RAF's newest air sea rescue device and the brave crew of R.M.L. 514.'

'From my plane I watch as we make a last run at 700'. A lever is released and a complete power driven lifeboat sails gently down under a canopy of six parachutes.

As it strikes the sea the impact makes two rockets fire from the boat and 175' of life lines shoot out either side.'

Soon the ditched men clamber aboard the boat, start up the 4hp motor and head off...'

'R.M.L. with Lieutenant Patrick Troughton commanding comes along side and takes all crew aboard safely.'

On many occasions my father and crew received letters of thanks from airmen who had been rescued by them. One letter reads,

To: The commanding officers of H.M. R.M.L. 514

Dear Sirs,

On behalf of my crew and myself, I would like to take this opportunity to express my deepest admiration for the officers and men who saved our lives in the North Sea on the morning of the 4th March 1945. Due to adverse sea and weather conditions, the courage and determination displayed by the rescue launch, along with the rescue aircraft, will long be remembered. We sincerely thank each and every one of the officers and crew who participated in one of the most daring rescues on record.

We remain,

Lt. John V. Lapenas (First pilot)
Lt. Theadore J. Langan (Co-Pilot)
Lt. Charles V. Buffington (Navigator)
Sgt. William Dotson, Engineer
Sgt. James McMullin Radar Op.
Sgt. Daniel Hochstatter Radio Op

Dad remained C.O. of R.M.L. 514 until the end of the war in Europe. V.E. day had mixed emotions for both Margaret and Pat. My mother wrote,

'In the evening as the sun set, Pat and I sat together on the front watching the lights of Yarmouth switch on for the time since 1939. We could hear bells ringing and on the autumnal breeze the sound of laughter and parties. Beautifully reassuring sights and sounds, but deep down we both know the war in the east will soon part us. Pat is to be stationed out in the Pacific somewhere and I will have to return to a life I have grown out of - back in Mill Hill. I feel sick at the prospect. I have changed so much. We all have. The war has changed us… maybe for the better or possibly not? I seem harder and so does Pat. Perhaps if we can survive until the end things will mend.'

As events were to prove their worries were unnecessary with the early surrender of the Japanese. The order to cease hostilities is stuck in my mother's scrapbook. It is a fairly brief statement on cheap pink paper from the admiralty – a bit of an anticlimax.

TO ALL SHIPS & ESTABLISHMENTS – most immediate
(1) H.M. Government has announced that the Japanese have surrendered.
(2) All effective operations are to cease forthwith.
(3) Some time may lapse before the instrument of surrender is signed and before it is clear Japanese forces have received and intend to carry out instructions of their High Command. Accordingly danger of attack by individual enemy surface craft, U-boats and aircraft may persist for some time.

My father had written in his diary the famous short speech US General Macarthur made at the end of hostilities – I think Pat wanted to make sense of what he had gone through; what he had endured; what he had lost; but above all it was a speech that made him feel he could answer the question so many people were asking – why?

'It is my earnest hope and, indeed, the hope of all mankind, that from this solemn occasion a better world shall emerge out of the blood and carnage of the past; a world founded upon faith and understanding, a world dedicated to the dignity of man and the fulfillment of his most cherished wish, for freedom, tolerance and justice.'

Chapter 3
All That Shouting in the Evening

By October 1945, Pat and Margaret had temporarily moved from Great Yarmouth back to his mother's house in Mill Hill. They were both determined to remain independent after being 'demobbed' and hastily began to look for somewhere to live. My father was a very proactive person. He spent the whole of October and November relentlessly searching for a flat. These were in very short supply after the war not only because of all the bomb damage but because so many other people were trying to pick up their lives from where they had left them in 1939. Competition for accommodation in London was very high and it meant either paying over the odds or putting up with fairly sparse conditions. My mother told me that,

'Pat would not take no for answer. He walked for miles and miles around London every day banging on doors and asking if anyone had rooms to let. It was inevitable he would finally be successful. He was like a dripping tap or a dog that would not give up his bone! I loved him for that.'

Finally in December he managed to persuade the owner of a large dilapidated building on the Finchley Road in London to rent him two rooms. A friend of my mother describes it well,

'After the war they rented a flat in Swiss Cottage on a stretch of the Finchley Road opposite the old Odeon and close to the famous pub. In those days there was a row of substantial detached houses, each with what had been stables, but then converted into garages with flats above. I remember a very rickety staircase inside the garage up to the flat, and the intriguing fact that the bath was in the kitchen, with a large wooden cover serving perfectly as a table during the day. I envied them living there so close to the bright lights, and the fact that they had such a relaxed 'bohemian life style' which included going out for breakfast when they felt like it!'

My mother had managed to get a job as stage director at the Westminster Theatre in the West end of London on a production of *The Sacred Flame* by Somerset Maugham. The plan was that her salary would support both of them until Pat was able to reestablish himself as an actor. This was a lot sooner than either of them had anticipated.

A friend at the naval base in Great Yarmouth had suggested to Pat that he contact the artistic director of the Amersham Repertory Theatre. This company was a fairly progressive setup, well ahead of its time, and was managing to produce good quality productions even with the meager resources of those austere days after the war. The Amersham Playhouse, then Buckinghamshire's only theatre, opened in 1936 in the old Bijou Hall in Station Road. It seated 240 people and was headed by Sally Latimer, leading actress, and Caryl Jenner, her producer. The range of plays was very progressive and innovative, including a lot of new writing. By 1946 there was an exchange system with Guildford Repertory, so that every production played a week in each Theatre. Amersham was so well regarded that Picture Post photographed the Players in 1946 in a feature called *Small Town Theatre*.

The Cast Works Out a Difficult Scene
At rehearsals, the players argue out the best way to interpret difficult phrases. Sally Latimer usually wins.

The Producer Talks it Over with the Cast

Amersham – *Small Town Theatre* article in Picture Post

Patrick auditioned for Sally and Caryl two days after the 1946 New Year celebrations and was cast in two productions for an initial four-week contract. He began rehearsals on 18th January, which meant my father had only taken two weeks to find work.

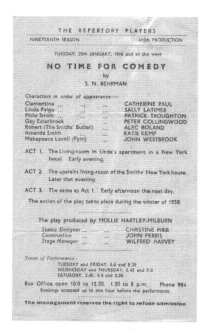

Amersham Repertory Players programme for *No Time for Comedy*

*'**PHILO**: Yes. It is incredible to me also. And yet I went to sleep—thinking of you. I awoke—thinking of you. I am forty-eight. That in itself is absurd. And yet—after two unsuccessful marriages—after so many years of rigorous discipline—after a long renunciation of any idea of personal happiness—I tremble before you.'*

These were the first lines my father spoke on stage since having been forced to put his acting career on hold. It was a play called *No Time for Comedy* by American playwright S.N. Behrman and was

61

later to be made into a Warner Bros film starring James Stewart and Rosalind Russell. My father played a character called Philo Smith. The casting could not have been stranger. Here was a twenty six year old man with fresh completion, jet-black hair and youthful energy playing a middle-aged graying rather nervous, pompous and introvert American banker. Sally Latimer must have seen Pat's raw talent right from the start to have the confidence to cast him in such a mature role. In fact both Sally and Caryl were to play a big part in furthering my father's career.

The second play was *This Land of Ours* by Lionel Brown. Both these productions played one week at Amersham and then one week at Guildford.

Patrick aged 26, on stage in a production at Amersham Repertory Theatre

Pat was contracted to do further productions at Amersham including a play called *The Drunkard* with Denholm Elliot. He was pleased to have become a regular member of the company. However, unbeknownst to my father, Sally Latimer had been talking to Hugh Hunt who had just been appointed artistic director of the newly formed Bristol Old Vic Company. She had been to see his production of *The Beaux Stratagem* and in conversation had mentioned her 'new talented find' – my father. As my mum described it,

'Sally had shot herself in the foot really. She had given Pat a chance at her own expense. She promoted Pat knowing she would lose a gifted actor from her own company. A selfless act for which Pat was forever grateful.'

Dad joined the Bristol Old Vic Company in March 1946 for the entire season. He had already missed the first production but was immediately cast in a new play based on a short story by J.B. Priestly called *Jenny Villiers*. The programme notes that Pat played two characters – the Mayor of Barton Spa and Jacob B. Mangles.

It was a ghost story about an old Theatre Royal full of traditions, in which great actors and actresses of the past had played. A modern repertory company has come to this theatre to put on a new play. The author left alone in the green room, sees the ghosts of a company who played there in 1840 and learns from the young leading actress the lesson that the theatre never dies, but has in its self the seeds of its own regeneration.

In the company with Pat was a young Kenneth Connor who was of course later to become famous for appearing in many of the Carry on films. A few weeks after the war had finished, Kenneth had received a message from William Devlin who was a director/actor, asking him to join him in the newly formed Bristol Old Vic. He jumped at the chance and when he arrived at the theatre, he was on stage before he had time to unpack. Kenneth always looked back with affection on his three years at Bristol, playing classic roles and modern plays. He thought of it as one of the most satisfying periods of his stage career. I was later able to talk to him about his experiences and friendship with my father because I went to school with his son.

He remembered 'how all the ladies swooned over Pat as he was an incredible good looker' and 'the very nervous nature to his acting which made him burn so bright on stage.'

Pat appeared in six productions during that first season. They included, a comedy called *Keep in a Cool Place* which according to the critics 'wouldn't they feared, keep for very long!' *Twelfth Night*, which had mixed reviews and accused Hunt of asking the question, 'Now by what new twist can I jazz up this old play.' *Macbeth*, with Faith Brook as Lady Macbeth and Kenneth Connor as the Porter and *Weep for the Cyclops*, a true history of Dr Jonathan Swift.

However, it was in Chekhov's *The Seagull* in which my father made his biggest contribution and impression as Konstentin Gavrilitch, the dreamer and compassionate soul who fills the void of affection in his life with self-doubt. The press wrote,

'Hugh Hunt's production fluctuates between success and failure. Miss Sherwood reminded us more of Judith Bliss (Noel Coward Hay Fever) than Irina, but the emotion flowed naturally from Yvonne Mitchell and Patrick Troughton. The subtlety of Konstentin's touch at his previous scar as he goes out to kill himself was pure brilliance.'

'Miss Yvonne Mitchell's Nina and Mr Patrick Troughton's Konstantin were worthy of special praise. These two players were playing their first important parts with the company last night and fully share in the success.'

'Mr Troughton's Constentin was his best work so far and showed a good depth of emotion.'

These reviews and the success of his performance attracted the attention of Laurence Olivier who came down to watch the show. The season ended with *Weep for Cyclops* on 6th July 1946 but the company played a further two weeks at the Arts Theatre Cambridge.

The original programme for *The Seagull*, performed at the Theatre Royal in Bristol on 30th April 1946

During August, Pat and Margaret decided to celebrate their wedding anniversary early and to take a holiday in Norfolk. They hired a two-birth sailing boat called 'Mongoose' from the George Applegate Boat Yard at Potter Heigham on the Broads. The next two weeks was spent sailing the network of rivers and broads, stopping at pubs and enjoying the solitude of the country. A postcard from them both sent to my grandmother describes the idyllic postwar emptiness of this stretch of the country.

'To Mother and Father, Just moored a little outside Horning. Sun is a golden splash across the pond still water. I am fishing and Margaret is lounging by the tiller reading a book. What a beautiful place this is. Don't ever want to come back to London and the worries of finding work! We both send our love, Pat and Margaret.'

Pat and Margaret had a strong bond with Norfolk and thought more than once about moving out there. I think they both felt they needed to continue links with Yarmouth and especially the Broads having spent the war years there. In fact during the sixties Pat purchased a riverside chalet near Potter Heigham which both families were able to use. In later years Margaret agreed that their wartime memories had forged an unbreakable link with this precious area.

Pat returned one day early from the holiday because he had received news that Fanfare Productions Ltd wanted to meet him to discuss a part in the new Robert Donat production of *Much Ado About Nothing*. Donat had seen a production of *Henry V* directed by Fabia Drake and immediately had asked her to undertake the casting and direction of his postwar season at the Aldwych Theatre in London. Fabia Drake was an actress and director of considerable experience who happened also to be a close friend of Lawrence Olivier's. Although not documented anywhere, it seems reasonable to assume that Pat was asked to join the company after Lawrence Olivier had seen his performance in *The Seagull* and conveyed his enthusiasm to Fabia.

The production opened in Manchester on 23rd September 1946 and played for six nights before coming into London. Unfortunately, the production was not a happy one with Fabia Drake and Robert Donat constantly at odds with one another. The critics did not like it either,

'…the principle artists are not ideally fitted to their parts. Robert Donat seems to the writer to be very heavy in manner and at the same time too exaggerated in gesture to satisfy one's conception of Benedick. The part demands a generally lighter and more spontaneous touch.'

My father was cast as The Messenger but half way through the run had to take over the role of Claudio. Andrew Cruckshank who normally played the part had become ill and could not continue. Although this enabled my father to take on a weightier role, the critics were rather cruel,

'Patrick Troughton's Claudio lacks romantic grace…'

However one of the first fan letters that my father received, from a lady called Janet Wallis who lived in Hornsey, London N8, totally disagreed with them.

Much Ado only had a short run as audiences dwindled and it closed before Christmas. Donat made substantial losses on this season, which he had initiated so optimistically.

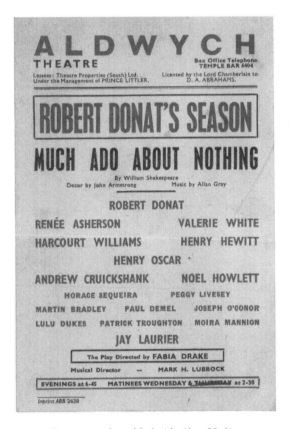

Programme from *Much Ado About Nothing*

Patrick did not let himself become disheartened by the early closure of the run or the unkind reviews he had received. As he always retorted after reading bad criticisms of his own work, 'It will be fish and chip paper tomorrow!'

Neither did he get depressed waiting around the flat all day for the phone to ring or a telegram to arrive. Instead he started an assault on BBC Broadcasting House in order to break into the lucrative area of radio drama. He sent letters, made appointments to see producers, introduced himself to writers and generally hung around the foyer area hoping to meet potential casting producers. As with his flat hunting, his patience and tenacity paid off the week before Christmas when Felix Fenton cast him in *Christ's Comet*, which was to be broadcast on the Home service on Christmas day at 9.10. This was a play all in verse by Christopher Hassel and had first been performed in Canterbury Cathedral in 1938. It stared Robert Harris and Robert Farquharson. Pat played Nicholas of Damascus, Herod's biographer.

Two week after Christmas Margaret told Pat the good news that she was pregnant. The doctor's hand written letter pasted in her scrapbook reads,

'I certify that, in my opinion, Mrs Patrick Troughton is about seven weeks pregnant. 11th January 1946.'

There were no pregnancy test kits in those days - only considered opinion! My mother told me they had been trying for a baby ever since the holiday in Norfolk and that when she told Pat he rushed out into the Finchley Road and bought her the largest bunch of flowers he could find. He was absolutely delighted. My mother also remembers,

'...being really excited not just because of the pregnancy but because I would be able to apply for a pregnant woman's ration book! All those extras like tea, sugar, cream, butter, meat, eggs, cheese, clothes, jam, sweets were all rationed at the time.'

That same day Pat was contacted by E. Martin Brown, who was starting a season of new plays by poets at the Mercury Theatre in Ladbroke Road, London. Pat was offered the part of the Third Priest in T.S. Eliot's *Murder in the Cathedral*. Initially, it was to be around a week's work with only expenses of £5, but more had been promised.

Ashley Dukes had set up the Mercury Theatre in 1933 for the production of new drama and as a base for Ballet Rambert run by his wife Marie Rambert. It was an intimate and well-equipped small space with around 150 seats.

Patrick continued to work with the Pilgrim Players, as the company had been named, throughout most of the spring performing at various venues big and small including the Lyric Theatre in Shaftsbury Avenue. Performances alternated between *Murder in the Cathedral* and *The Family Reunion* another of T.S. Eliot's plays. The latter included in the cast his old teacher from the Embassy School, Eileen Thorndike.

Patrick as the Third Priest in *Murder in the Cathedral* at the Edinburgh Festival

In the summer both plays were taken to the Edinburgh festival and received well. The Stage reviews for both plays were very good but did mention my Dad's vocal weakness in *The Family Reunion*,

'The dominating mother is excellently played by Eileen Thorndike. The intense, unhappy son, Harry, is played by Patrick Troughton with powerful confidence, but at times he is scarcely audible.'

Pat was in his last week at Edinburgh when Margaret gave birth to their first child, Joanna. The telegram he sent read,

TO MRS. TROUGHTON AT ANNIE ZUNZ WARD MIDDLESEX HOSPITAL LONDON. YOU CLEVER CLEVER WOMAN STOP I ADORE YOU STOP KISS JOANNA FOR ME STOP I AM BURSTING FOR FULL DETAILS STOP ALL MY LOVE - PAT

A friend of my father's described the moment when they saw her for the first time,

'She was born on September 9th 1947. I saw Jo in her crib in Woodland Way soon after Pat and Margaret had got back from the hospital. After his last performance at the Gateway, Pat had rushed down through the night on a milk train that stopped at every station to be with Margaret as soon as possible. He didn't look tired. He was grinning from ear to ear and looked the happiest I had seen him in years. Joanna was lying on her side in her crib, a lovely baby who looked like a tiny image of her father, with her little straight nose and dark hair.'

Pat and Margaret had decided that they really needed to rent a 'proper house' now Joanna had arrived. The 'bohemian flat' that had served them so well for a couple of years was fast becoming too small to bring up a new family in. They were also concerned that London was not very good for the baby's health and so after searching the local papers they moved out to the suburbs. They found a cottage with a garden in Old Church Lane, Stanmore close to Mill Hill.

Proud parents of baby Joanna

By late autumn 1947 Dad was working hard not only with the 'Pilgrim Players' but also rehearsing for a major new TV version of Hamlet. George More O'Ferrall had cast Patrick as Horatio not only because of his skill as an actor but also because he had experience of working in the new often complicated area of television. He had played Baldock in a short TV version of *Edward II* earlier in the year and had impressed everyone with his studio acting abilities.

Many actors were wary of a medium that was surrounded by technical uncertainty. Patrick embraced it whole-heartedly and seemed to relish the opportunity to perform to the camera. This lack of fear and suspicion of a medium the film industry had cynically labelled 'instant movies' was to prove a real asset in directing his future career.

Rehearsals began at the beginning of November with around forty-eight actors, including John Byron as Hamlet, Muriel Pavlow as Ophelia and Sebastian Shaw as Claudius. At the read-through they were shown scale models of the sets and a plot of quick change areas, set transfer routes and camera positions so that they could orientate themselves right from the start and would not be taken by surprise during the two live performances. The costumers Morris Angels of London, and Foxes, had designed a number of cloaks and tunics for the performance not in the usual solemn blacks but in TV camera friendly dark green, which on the studio floor looked rather garish, but on the screen worked very well.

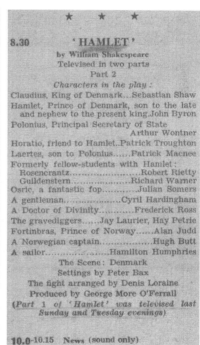

★ ★ ★

8.30   'HAMLET'
by William Shakespeare
Televised in two parts
Part 2
Characters in the play :
Claudius, King of Denmark...Sebastian Shaw
Hamlet, Prince of Denmark, son to the late
     and nephew to the present king.John Byron
Polonius, Principal Secretary of State
                            Arthur Wontner
Horatio, friend to Hamlet..Patrick Troughton
Laertes, son to Polonius......Patrick Macnee
Formerly fellow-students with Hamlet:
    Rosencrantz.......................Robert Rietty
    Guildenstern.....................Richard Warner
Osric, a fantastic fop...........Julian Somers
A gentleman....................Cyril Hardingham
A Doctor of Divinity...........Frederick Ross
The gravediggers......Jay Laurier, Hay Petrie
Fortinbras, Prince of Norway......Alan Judd
A Norwegian captain.................Hugh Butt
A sailor......................Hamilton Humphries
The Scene: Denmark
Settings by Peter Bax
The fight arranged by Denis Loraine
Produced by George More O'Ferrall
*(Part 1 of 'Hamlet' was televised last
Sunday and Tuesday evenings)*

10.0-10.15   News (sound only)

My father remembered rehearsing for around five to six weeks and being unable to use the set until just four days before the live telecast. My mother remembered Dad telling her,

'That production was a real milestone in telly, although I didn't realise at the time… before Hamlet, drama had not been taken very seriously. This was a two part three hour show… George did a brilliant job with it.'

George O'Ferrall won one of the first TV awards for his production and it has been suggested by many people including my father that Laurence Olivier took some of his technical ideas and used them to great effect in his filmed version of Hamlet.

Christmas came and went with Dad noting in his diary,

'Had first Christmas stocking for many years. Oh what a joy to have Joanna. Margaret and I are so happy. Spending Christmas Day with the Troughtons and Boxing day with the Dunlops.'

Before the New Year began Pat was back at the Mercury Theatre rehearsing two new plays that had been specially written by James Bridie who was the founder of the Citizen's Theatre in Glasgow. Both plays showed their author in entirely different moods. In *The Dragon and the Dove* there was a fight for good over evil told in the style of *Jonah and the Whale. A Change for the Worse* was described as a mock morality and showed how much good could come out of the miscarriage of evil.

Pat had also been asked by Laurence Olivier to appear as the Player King in his film of *Hamlet.* This was the first time Pat had worked on a major film with big stars. They included Jean Simmons as Ophelia, Peter Cushing as Osric, Stanley Holloway as the Grave digger, John Laurie as Francisco, Eileen Herlie as Gertrude and Terence Morgan as Laertes. However, he didn't get much time to meet many of them as his filming at Denham studios took only a week to complete. Patrick had no dialogue as the whole sequence was done as a mime.

I don't think that Dad realized at the time how big that film was going to be. It went on to win two major academy awards for best film and best actor.

Hamlet

March 1948 saw Pat cast in what is thought to be the first ever science fiction programmeme on British Television called R.U.R. - short for *Rossum's Universal Robots.*

The production was based on Karel Capek's stage play first performed in 1921 that envisaged a world of android helpers and robots that could think for themselves – a concept well ahead of its time.

A Radio Times article that my father kept in his scrapbook gives a vivid and fascinating description of the live ninety-minute shortened televised adaptation.

The television revival of Karel Capek's drama of the Revolt of the Robots.

'The word 'robot' was introduced to the English language by Karel Capek in his classic drama of a world dominated by mechanized helpers. Not, mark you, mechanical in the accepted sense of the word with steel hands, jointed with nuts and bolts and photo-electrically operated reactions, but molded in the true form of man from synthetic protoplasm, with heart, liver, kidneys and a brain made to order in accordance with the commercial task in hand.

As the general-manager of the R.U.R. factory explained, 'immediately they are born – or, rather, manufactured, complete with ready-woven nerves and veins and miles of digestive tubes – they are put to work and they learn to speak, write, and count. They've astonishing memories you know. If you were to read a twenty-volume encyclopedia to them they would repeat it with absolute accuracy. But they never think of anything new. Then they are sorted out and distributed – 15,000 daily, not counting a regular percentage of defective specimens which are thrown into the stamping mill...'

No wonder these robots had no souls. They cost £15 a piece – that was in 1923 of course – and had they been used as labour-saving devices to wash up, run errands and make the beds all might have been well; but Mars (professor) started his insidious work and first one country and then another ordered job lots of thousands at a time to train as soldiers. They were cheaper than proper soldiers and better, because they didn't think, and they had no souls. Had these armies been made to fight each other, well and good, but experiments were made with super robots. Robots began to think. Then they began to fight, and Capek, disciple of Wells and adroit preacher of sermons, pointed his moral by making them fight side by side until mankind was annihilated.

They took the precaution of sparing one human being, but they chose the wrong one, because he didn't know the secret of robot-making, and robots like humans don't last forever...

Capek placed R.U.R. in his future in the 1950-60 period, but as that is now uncomfortable close, Jan Bussell, who is reviving it in television this week, has given us another thirty years grace – 1990's. He is also making a number of minor but important changes because of the events of the past twenty-five years. 'Several apparent anachronisms have had to be put right,' he says. 'For example, in the original the use of radio is ignored, and certain scenes could not occur in the light of modern science.

In the cast are quite a number of names that are familiar to viewers. Pamela Stirling, whom many will remember last year in *Victoria Regina*, plays the part of a girl who contributes largely to the success of the robots' revolt because of her humanitarian attitude towards them. Patrick Troughton plays the part of Radius, a robot who goes mad but is saved from the stamping mill through the girl's efforts, only to become the leader of the revolt.'

Photographed TV shots of my father's live performance in R.U.R.

Patrick Troughton   Pamela Stirling

As the professor's daughter who seeks to discover how the robots are made, and Radius, the 'intelligent robot' who leads the revolt, in Karel Capek's drama, 'R.U.R.'

It is apparent from this article that by 1947 Pat had become a regular name to be associated with BBC TV. This 'groundbreaking production' as it was described in another article and the enthusiastic response from the viewing public only cemented the fact that Pat had become one of the few actors capable of producing successful performances in this infant medium. A fan letter for R.U.R. shows the affection and praise for his performance as Radius,

Dear Mr Troughton,

I don't know how to begin but I have a whole list of nice, praising adjectives lined up before me. One of them is <u>realistic</u>. I believe you made the perfect Radius because of the realism you put into your character. Radius was neither entirely human nor entirely robot and I had the feeling that you, Mr. Troughton, caught just the right happy medium.

The next adjective is <u>powerful</u> – not in looks or actions but in character; almost domineering. The next is a noun – <u>artistry</u>. There was plenty of artistry in Radius as you portrayed him – just the right tones and no over acting. And your artistry is not just confined to Radius. Those fine qualities went to make your brilliant 'Horatio' in Hamlet so moving to watch. Your final scene was beautifully done and final speech beautifully spoken. I shall look forward to seeing you in your next television play or

hearing you on the wireless. I will probably write before the performance because I can always be sure to see a good performance from you.
   Yours sincerely,
   Brenda Ahilafia

My mother remembered watching R.U.R. with her best friend Jill round at Mrs Troughton's house. They had the distinction of owning one of the first television sets – a Pye B6T enclosed in a wooden cabinet.

   'I remember peering along with the assembled audience, at Pat in R.U.R. Vague misty shapes floating about on a tiny screen surrounded by a vast edifice of polished walnut. It didn't help that there were a number of robots that all looked alike! It was magic all the same. You could really only identify who the flickering image was by listening to their voice. We watched it twice because it was repeated the next day.'

After R.U.R Pat took the part of a Shepherd called Jim in a film entitled *Escape* directed by Joseph L Mankiewicz. It starred Rex Harrison, Peggy Cummings and a future Doctor Who, William Hartnell. This was another role that Pat engineered after knocking on office doors in Denham studios while filming Olivier's Hamlet.

By April 1947 Patrick had returned to the stage and was appearing in *Lucrece* at the Boltons Theatre club in South Kensington, which was a highly fashionable fringe venue.

   The theatre had started life after the war when John Wyse and Denise Blanckensee took over a derelict cinema in Drayton Gardens, and with a lot of volunteer help, converted it into a Club Theatre. Its policy was to present only new plays—no revivals—and, where possible, to cast ex-servicemen and women to help revive careers stalled by the War.

The play was based on *Le Viol de Lucrece* by the French playwright Andre Obey, who in turn was inspired by Shakespeare's poem *The Rape of Lucretia*.

 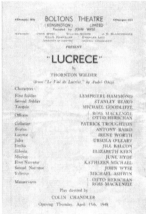

Patrick as 'Collatine' in The Boltons Theatre production of *Lucrece*

In July, Patrick was back in TV and cast as 'Lord Lebanon' in an Edgar Wallace crime mystery called *The Case of the Frightened Lady* starring Gordon Harker and Cathleen Nesbitt. At the same time, he was working on *The Rose without a Thorn* set in the court of King Henry VIII. Pat played 'Culpeper', Kathryn Howard's lover.

During the autumn of 1948 my father notched up a large number of TV roles including *Nurse Cavell* about an English nurse arrested for aiding allied soldiers in Belgium during the war; *At the Villar Rose* in which Pat played a waiter; *Celestial Fire*; *Land of Hearts Desire*, a theatrical lament on age and thwarted aspirations; *Murder Over Drafts* and a TV version of *Lear*.

Photographed TV shots of Pat playing Culpeper (Kathryn Howard's lover) in
A Rose without a Thorn

Victoria Road
Back - Pat's father and Margaret
Front – Pat's sister Molly with Pat and Joanna

Although payment for TV and radio was fairly low compared with present day levels even taking into account the difference in the value of money, my father was doing so many jobs at this time that he was now in a position to be able to purchase a house.

Margaret, Joanna and Pat moved to Victoria Road, Mill Hill, London NW7 in the spring of 1949. It was a small semi-detached house close to both their parents and had the space they wanted for a larger family.

Patrick in his new garden

Jill Taylor, my mother's best friend remembers being so excited at the prospect of having them back in Mill Hill and gives a vivid insight into their early life at Victoria Road.

'They moved into Victoria Road in 1949, a little house that they loved. They worked on the inside, and Pat made a lovely garden – I remember being there during the next few years, and so much went on in our lives during that time. Pat was occasionally in what appeared to be pretty black moods. The 'artistic temperament' as

Margaret called it, but normally he was warm, friendly and affectionate. I think some of this was probably related to the ups and downs of his career and his anxieties about how it was going. He was intensely ambitious and impatient to move forward – but also conscious of his obligations and responsibilities as a family man. This must have been a worry for both of them in such an uncertain profession.

They themselves seemed very happy, very companiable. I remember Pat's habit of suddenly sweeping Margaret into his arms and dancing madly around the room with her laughing and protesting and Jo toddling after them. They would finally collapse in a heap on the sofa, with Jo climbing up and clamoring to join in.

Pat was always very demonstrative, all females were tenderly embraced and frequently invited to join his imaginary 'dream harem' – an offer which I don't think was taken very seriously by anyone in his Mill Hill circle.

Pat was certainly highly domesticated and a loving father. Very creative, clever with his hands, and excellent at DIY. He was artistic and enjoyed painting, as did Margaret. Pat enjoyed cooking, which Margaret certainly didn't and he specialized in magnificent fry-ups. I remember many a time, if I was there when he arrived home in the evening, him going into the kitchen and then popping back to say would I like to stay to supper, as there was plenty. They were both wonderful to me, and I of course adored being with them.'

1949 had begun with Pat feeling confident that he would be able to meet the financial burden of owning his own house and everything that entailed. January started well with the release of a low budget film he had completed the year before at Highbury Studios called *Badgers Green*. This was a remake of a 1934 comedy about some villagers who were up in arms over a business scheme to convert a cricket field to a commercial complex. Patrick played a yokel villager called Jim Carter. He also appeared in two other movies in minor roles. *Cardboard Cavalier* with Margaret Lockwood, Sid Field and Esmond Knight. This was a box-office failure but it didn't affect my father, as he was dressed all in amour and on horseback for most of the movie - completely unrecognizable. And a Hammer movie called *'Someone at the Door'* in which he worked with Richard Hurndall who later played Bill Hartnell's part in *Doctor Who - The Five Doctors.*

This kind of nationwide exposure in movies helped keep him in the 'eye of TV producers' as he put it. He later described to me how casting worked in those days,

'So much of who was cast as what in those days was down to making sure you got your face on the screen, big or little, who you knew, and the experience that you had in those particular mediums. I was a great one for taking every opportunity to write letters, bang on doors and call people. It was a bit like a TV/Film repertory company that producers could dip into for casting. It was an easy option for them and they knew they were going to get a performance without taking any unnecessary risks. The trick was to stay at the top of the pile by making sure you were seen and heard regularly.'

He also described why he had started to concentrate on TV parts.

'Television didn't necessarily pay more, but you could do more of them. If I was to get a stage play – that would tie me up for many weeks. With TV I could do one studio on one day then a day's filming another – it was more economical to work that way because in the end I got more money from doing TV than stage and I needed it to support the family. It was a real worry during 1949, I can tell you. Things got quite bad during the summer.'

In February he was asked to play Seyton in a TV production of *Macbeth* directed by George More O'Ferrell. All available space was needed at Alexandra Palace studios for yet again another ambitious production with huge sets and a large cast which included many of the members of the 'Hamlet' ensemble.

Dad remembered the rest of 1949 as rather a nightmare year for work. For the first time since the end of the war, castings became few a far between. Every interview and meeting was met with disappointment. He told me,

'The very thing I had dreaded was happening. I had bought a house and needed to support my family but work was drying up.'

However one successful casting happened at the end of March when Pat went to meet with Bernard Miles who had recently formed a film company called Pilgrim Pictures. They were doing a movie entitled *Chance of a Lifetime* which told the story of a small factory where the workers, discontented with the owner boss (Basil Radford), challenged him to surrender the management to them. He does so and, of course, their nominated leaders quickly discover that life in the office isn't as simple as it seems. By the time Mr. Radford returns to save them from disaster they are more than delighted to leave managerial headaches and a seven-day week behind and get back to their benches.

Bernard had managed to assemble quite an impressive cast together for such a low budget movie, which included Kenneth More, Hattie Jacques, Julian Mitchell, Geoffrey Keen, John Harvey and Josephine Wilson. My Dad played a worker called Willie Kettle and filming took place at a disused factory in Stroud.

When it was released in April 1950 the critics generally liked it mainly because it was a film that addressed topical issues.

'There is something in this parable to flatter every political persuasion. Conservatives can see it as a vindication of private ownership. Socialists can take it as an illustration of the principle of management and labour getting cozily together. Communists can point out that the socialised result was achieved only by an initial revolution.

To a film critic – luckily not forced to have any political inhibitions – it is a reasonably entertaining minor film: at times too naive, at others too intense, but at least trying to make dramatic entertainment out of important topical issues.

Bernard Miles who in addition to being producer, director, and part author, performs his familiar West Country act: that sepulchral cross between a lay preacher who has lost his notes for next Sunday's sermon and a ploughman who at any moment may turn into the Mad Killer of Polperro.'

Chance of a Lifetime released April 1950 in which Patrick played Willie Kettle

On location in Stroud 1949 filming Chance of a Lifetime

Fellow actor fools around for the camera

Actors pose for Pat including Hattie Jacques

On location - Bernard Miles director discusses role with Pat

The film went on to be nominated for a BAFTA but failed to collect the acclaim it deserved. However, through working on this movie Patrick became a very close friend of Bernard Miles both socially and professionally. On the last night of filming both Margaret and Pat were invited to Stanley Mills, Stonehouse to hear a recital of songs and operatic arias by the world-renowned Norwegian opera singer Kirsten Flagstad.

The only other jobs Pat managed to get during late spring and into the summer were a number of 'spit and cough' parts as he called them or very minor roles in TV. These included *Someone at the Door*, *Trelawney of the Wells* and *Whitehall Wonders*. It was a very lean time for Patrick and his young family.

However, my father always lived life to the full regardless of what was thrown at him. He was an active person who could never just sit still. He always had to be doing something – a garden project, painting garden birds, photographing people, model building – the list was endless. In fact I sometimes wonder how he had time to work.

Fishing had been a great passion of his ever since he was a young lad and periods of unemployment would bring back the urge to dust off his old angling tackle box, grab a handful of spit cane rods and catch the bus over to Elstree reservoir. If he could afford it he would hire a wooden punt for the day and drift up and down the tree-lined banks waiting patiently for a bite.

Dad at Moat Mount pond in 1949 trying to lure the elusive carp with his angling skills

On the occasions he had no money, he would rise at dawn and walk from the house in Victoria Road to the local pond in Moat Mont and fish for the elusive carp that were supposed to grow well over twenty-five pounds. He told me,

'I enjoy the solitude, and you are forced to sit and concentrate for hours on end. It's a bit like meditation. It feeds the soul. Unfortunately it doesn't feed us because they are course fish and have to be returned unharmed. I do have a bit of a problem with cruelty question but my hunting instinct generally wins it every time.'

The other bonus of being out of work he always told me was that you could enjoy family life unlike most other dads who worked all the time. Margaret and Dad delighted in entertaining friends. Most of the summer 1949 was a long procession of impromptu parties with Pimms when they could afford it and cheap gin and lemonade if they could not. Their circle of friends was very separate from Pat's acting career and they hardly ever invited work colleagues to these boozy afternoons. They both had a circle of friends in Mill Hill and outside that had absolutely nothing to do with the profession. I am unsure whether this was deliberately engineered or just chance.

Patrick, Margaret and friends during the lean summer of 1949

In late July, Patrick's luck changed after a meeting with Walt Disney casting and director Byron Haskins. They were looking for actors with experience of sailing to become part of the crew of the *Hispaniola* in a major new production of *Treasure Island*. The actors needed to be at ease with rough weather during filming and able to climb and set sails under the guidance of the real crew. Dad's wartime experience impressed the company and he was initially cast as a 'bad pirate' to appear mostly in the background. This was to be the first entirely live-action feature film produced by the Disney Studio.

Filming began almost immediately with my father travelling away from home for the first time since Joanna was born. The location was centred around Falmouth in Cornwall aboard a spectacular sailing ship, which was originally known as the *Rylands* and had been used for just under a hundred years as a coal runner and carrier of other cargo.

My Dad explained,

'We would sail up and down the Carrack Roads on the estuary of the river Fal over and over again, climbing rigging, hauling ropes, shouting pirate like orders and generally performing sailor type acting - oh arh - it was bloody exhausting!'

After completing the filming aboard the ship they returned to Denham studios and began the interior shots. There was a full sized mockup of the *Hispaniola* deck and my father was involved in more background work. After around a week of working in the studio the director Byron Haskins picked my father for a featured role as the bad pirate Roach. The scene involved Pat's character getting into the blockade and attempting to kill Jim Hawkins but eventually being dispatched by 'the good doctor'.

There were two locations for this sequence that involved a pirate charge on the stockade and then an interior scene in the studio. My father's diary describes the days filming on location in Black Park, Iver Heath near Pinewood studios.

'Boyhood excitement today. Guns, charging pirates and acting wounded. What fun! Decided to rid myself of the hat - too comical and not evil

91

enough. Byron was very pleased with what I did especially when I was shot. At wrap, asked me to join him for a drink - I did. Perfect gentleman. Just have to wait now for interior blockade in studio.'

Patrick didn't have to wait too long to complete this sequence in the studio because his filming dates had to be brought forward. On September 27, 1949, a court in Beaconsfield, England declared that it was illegal for the twelve-year-old Bobby Driscoll who played Jim Hawkins to work in the country without a for foreign workers permit. The magistrates fined Walt Disney and Driscoll's father, ordering the boy to stop filming until an appeal was heard. However, the film continued production desperately trying to complete all Bobby's scenes before the deadline. It is thought that Disney Studio spent approximately $84,000 to rearrange the shooting schedule. Driscoll had to leave England after the appeal was rejected, but the production company had managed to complete all his filming in time.

The only other work that my father was able to get during this bleak year was a TV version of *Wind in the Willows*. The cast included Kenneth More as 'Badger,' James Hayter as 'Toad', Harry Secombe as the 'Judge', and David Askey as the rear of 'Alfred the Horse.' Askey would later go on to become a successful TV director and direct both my brother and myself in a sitcom called *Backs to the Land*.

This year had been a wake-up call for my father who had discovered that one month you could be sipping champagne at a film premiere and another waiting in the dole queue to collect unemployment benefit. He never forgot this cruel lesson and it would be a constant driving force behind all his work in the future.

On location in Black Park filming *Treasure Island* 1949 – continuity photograph

Chapter 4
The Real National Theatre

At the beginning of the fifties, a television was a luxury item - only 350,000 households had a set including my Grandma, but by 1959 almost three quarters of the population had televisions, and by the end of the sixties, nearly ninety-five percent. The growth over such a short period was phenomenal and drama production increased in sink with this expansion. My father was fortunate to be in the right place at the right time. His TV work during this decade was to become his main source of income and continued to be so, right up until his death in the eighties. He was to become so comfortable with the medium of TV studio performance by the end of the fifties that stage work he was offered would be turned down without a single thought. My mother told me Pat thought of TV as the real 'National Theatre.'

'I don't want to do all that shouting in the evening! With TV your audience is huge and comes from all walks of life. 'A sitting room auditorium' of millions of viewers. Not just a few privileged theatre-goers. Besides you only have to repeat your performance at most twice and then it's onto something new – marvelous.'

Although he would have to wait a while to evolve into an exclusive TV actor, he did begin 1950 with two TV drama productions. The first was a Russian comedy called *The Whole World Over* by Contantin Siminov and produced by Ian Atkin. It starred Miriam Karlin and John Slater and was a satire about the return to civilian life of soldiers sharing a Moscow apartment.

The second was a play that he had performed on stage already. BBC Sunday Night Theatre produced *Family Reunion* but this time although Eileen Thorndike played Violet, the same part as before;

David Markham took the part of Harry. Pat was cast instead as Harry's servant and chauffeur.

Photographed screen shots of Pat with Ronald Simpson
and Pat with Catherine Lacy in *Family Reunion*

By March 1950, work had dried up again and Pat feared another bad year. His diary entry for 4th March reveals his worries:

'God, another day goes by with no auditions or interviews. Electricity bill due soon. Still I'm not the only one. What do you expect with 2,000,000 out of work! Well there's more for today. I signed on at the exchange this afternoon. Smile on your face.'

After completing a number of radio plays including *Hugh the Drover* a romantic ballad opera, *Prince Igor* another opera and *On the Eve of the New Day* with Bernard Braden, Pat returned to the stage to make ends meet. On 9th May he opened at The Gateway Theatre Club, Westbourne Grove, London in a new play by Anthony Moore called *Heavenly Bodies*. The Stage newspaper wrote,

'In spite of the fact the author has chosen a worn theme and filled it with outworn characters, this is a comedy of distinction. The plot is of the slightest and concerns the efforts of a film magnate to persuade a film star to sign a new contract... the author has managed not only to provide his actors with an unfailing assortment of funny lines, but what is more to charm his audience quite early on in the play into a mood of pleasurable excitement in which to accept them.'

'Patrick Troughton's script writer was so well conceived as regards facial expressions that his excellent diction was almost unnecessary.'

He followed that with a second more successful play in the same theatre called *Eva Braun*. Patrick played the 'power drunk megalomaniac Hitler, sunk in a mystic speculation and belief in his Nordic destiny.'

'As Hitler, Patrick Troughton gives a very convincing performance. He is the complete egotist, with a lust for power, stamping and raving at times, clearly indicating his unbalanced mind.'

Margaret was very pregnant with her second baby while Patrick was working at The Gateway Theatre during that first week in June. A friend of Margaret's described how events unfolded,

'By the time of David's birth, I was working (entirely due to Pat) as an A.S.M. [Assistant Stage Manager] in a little theatre club in Westbourne Grove. The play was called 'Eva Braun' and Pat was playing Adolf Hitler! I can't remember much about the play, except that Pat looked exceptionally like Hitler.'

'There was great excitement at the Gateway when we heard about David – poor Susy (Deputy Stage Manager) glued herself to the book because Pat threatened to dry on every sentence. Of course he didn't, in fact I thought he gave his best performance of the week!'

'He and Sebastian Cabot (an enormous actor who played Goering) were brilliant together both on stage and off. David was born on 9th June 1950 and I remember Sebastian announcing to the assembled cast in the bar after the show that 'Pat's wife had given birth to a two-legged hermaphrodite' and proposed a toast to the new arrival.

Pat, Joanna and Margaret and baby David, June 1950

After the party that followed I 'poured' Patrick into a taxi and we went back to Mill Hill. Pat stumbled out as the taxi stopped and, spotting a total stranger walking his dog in Flower Lane, threw his arms around his neck, kissing him and shouting 'Michael, Michael! I've got a son!' (Michael being my brother and who was certainly not present at the time.) I got him back to the Dunlops or 'Mummy Dee's as Pat called his mother-in-law, to sleep it off. He was of course intensely thrilled and proud that day.'

The rest of the year echoed the previous with work difficult to come by and with another mouth to feed Pat doubled his efforts to scrape together as many jobs as possible.

After completing a few days filming in July on *The Franchise Affair* starring Dulcie Grey, Michael Denison and Kenneth More, Pat did a TV play by Terence Rattigan called *Adventure Story* with Michael Hordern, John Slater, Gladys Cooper and Andrew Osborn. The action of the story extended over a period of nine years, between 336B.C. to 323B.C. and took place in Greece and various parts of Asia. Pat played Ptolemy, a Macedonian officer.

A number of radio broadcasts including *The Duke of Darkness* and *A Study in Loyalty* filled the autumn followed by another TV play by John Galsworthy called *Strife* in which he played Simon Harness.

In *Gunpowder Guy* a children's play for TV he played Guy Fawkes with Barry Letts as a co-conspirator. Barry was later to become closely involved in Doctor Who.

The winter yet again forced Patrick's unwilling return to the stage first in *Celestial Fire* at the 'Q' Theatre and then at The New Boltons Theatre Club playing Horatio in a production of *Hamlet* directed by Peter Cole. After finishing both, his diary entry reveals the grave financial situation that loomed before him,

> *'Wrote to Robin and father for further loan of £70 in addition to recent £100 guarantee to cover six weeks out of work. God knows what March will bring but what else can I do. I need more TV! Perhaps it's time to call it a day and get a proper job. But what could I do? Smiles are thin on the ground. Margaret doesn't seem to worry. She tells me that things will be fine. Work will come and just to be patient. I don't know what I've done to deserve my Margot. Please God, I don't hurt her.'*

Work did come just before Easter 1951 when Patrick was offered a six-month contract with the Radio Repertory Company. After the Second World War, the 'Rep' as it was affectionately named, retained a 50-strong casting resource for the huge radio drama output of the BBC. For the first time in his life Pat would have a guaranteed regular income. The drawback to becoming a BBC Rep member was that he would not be able to take other work that was offered during the length of his contract but Pat was not in a position to object.

'The money wasn't a fortune but at least it was regular and I got time off. Family life and my career seemed to work together so well during my radio days.'

During those six months Pat worked on over a hundred drama broadcasts with many famous actors. Productions included *Adelaise* with Clare Bloom, *Watch the Wall my Darling* with Richard Hurndall, *The Dynasts* with Robert Harris, *1066 and all That* with Sid James, *Comedienne* with Dame Sybil Thorndike, *Measure for Measure* with Stephen Murray, *The Hawk and the Handsaw* with Paul Scofield, *Obligation* with Joan Miller, *Joseph Proctor's Money* with Moira Lister, *Uncle Vanya* with Margaret Leyton, *King Lear* with John Gielgud and *Lazarus* with his old friend Kenneth Connor.

March 1951. Official BBC Radio Repertory picture of Patrick   (BBC staff number 96211)

September 1st 1951 marked a turning point in Pat's career. A few weeks before he had been invited by Laurence Olivier to audition for two plays he was taking over to New York in December for a five month run. Diary entry 1st September 1951 read,

This day began a new era in my stage career. My audition to Larry and Michael (director) *was a success and if I want to go I can. I shall. I have talked to Archie* (agent) *about it over tea and he set my mind at rest. He*

thinks I should go. They might even guarantee my return. He will talk to Val. This is the end of the beginning. At last I am fulfilling my destiny. Olivier's kingdom is huge and his influence great. I will do the rest – just wait and see. Given peace and good health the beginning of the fulfillment is underway – America began it and has shown me what I should fulfill. Money must come somehow for my other life. It is my eternal sorrow that these two cannot be married and made one life. The Artist and The Family man.'

It is very clear from Pat's diary entry that nothing was going to stop him from 'fulfilling his destiny' as he described it. But Pat was torn between two irreconcilable problems – his burning ambition and his commitment to family life – The Artist and The Family man.

Patrick finished his contract with the BBC Rep on 20th October. At home he had convinced Margaret that five months away from the children would not be harmful and that he was 'investing in their future'. Only good would come from the short separation.

My sister told me she remembers being very upset as she waved Dad goodbye. My mother's friend Jill told me,

'Margaret was very brave. She had never been by herself for that long before, what with a young baby and Joanna to look after. I did some au pairing during that winter but Margaret found it very tough going. It was a particularly cold winter I remember. They were very short of money.'

Patrick performed two plays in New York at the Ziegfeld Theatre about Cleopatra - Shakespeare's *Anthony and Cleopatra* and George Bernard Shaw's *Caesar and Cleopatra*. They alternated the plays each night and won good reviews on the whole.

Olivier and Vivien Leigh played the titled leads with a strong supporting cast including Harry Andrews, Robert Helpmann, Niall MacGinnis, and a young Donald Pleasence.

While Dad was out in America he kept in touch with Margaret and Joanna through frequent letters and post cards. There was always a tinge of guilt in his communications especially to Joanna but as always Margaret set his mind at rest with reassuring replies.

A last photograph with daughter Joanna before Pat leaves for America

"I am dying, Egypt, dying; only I here importune death awhile." Laurence Olivier to Vivien Leigh in "Antony and Cleopatra" last night

Cleopatra (Vivien Leigh) to Caesar (Laurence Olivier): "I have not betrayed you Caesar, I swear it." Caesar: "I know that. I have not trusted you"

102

Patrick kept most of his letters from America, extracts of which describe his 'artist life' in New York and 'family life' at Mill Hill with vivid detail:

'Hotel Knickerbocker – 120, West 45ᵗʰ Street, New York February 2ⁿᵈ 1952

My dearest darling,

What a hell of a day you had! I think the last straw was the cats stealing the joint from next door. Troughton cats are very resourceful – but there are limits. I'm glad Jill was there to stand by. She's staying with you this week, isn't she?

Life here has been a bit grim. The weather has been lousy and skating which makes the day pass quickly has been out of the question. However, I did have a go this morning and feel all the better for it. Whoopee! Our holiday… It's easy only if I rejoin the Rep on my return. I can organize a four-week holiday so that there is a week free in June. Please try to pin mummy D down – It would be heaven to get away alone for a few days. Anyway I can assure you I'll think many, many times before going away again. I realize how close we are – that life apart is as you say an unpleasant dream existence. Cor blimey – only ten more weeks to go. I expect the last week will feel like a year.

I adore you Margaret, All my love Darling, Pat x

P.S. Tell Joanna that I will paint her bedroom blue with pink spots if she really wants.'

Hotel Knickerbocker – 120, West 45ᵗʰ Street, New York March 30th 1952

Margaret Darling,

Helen Hayes has invited the company to a big reception at the Waldorf Astoria. We'll get there about 12.30 and I suppose the dancing will go on until about four. It promises to be a magnificent 'Do' at the smartest Hotel in New York. Tuesday the cricket team hopes to get practice in the nets for our match. Wednesday it was Jean Claude's birthday and he gave us a cocktail party between shows. During the evening performance we were slightly squiffy – but not so that it noticed I'm glad to say! Friday after the show Larry invited a chosen few of us up to his apartment for drinks and nibbles. A bit formal I'm afraid. He can never relax. Sunday I got up at 2 o'clock after a superb sleep, having read until about 3am. Had a long walk in the sun and then saw a film. This evening I've planned a colossal wash of shirts, pajamas, underclothes and socks. When I am finished I am going to have my weekly bath and then read some more. And now sweetheart to a bath which I wish you could share.

See you very soon now Darling,

Pat xx

P.S. *Tell Jo Daddy sends his love and will be home again very soon now.*

Patrick's photograph of the skating rink in New York
where he spent a lot of his spare time.

March 30th 1952

Dearest Margaret,

Frances and Johnny (teachers from Leighton Rollins school) saw the show today. Loved Olivier and me because they could hear us amongst other things but hated (Vivien Leigh) 'Madame'! I knew Frances would hate her and could imagine the vitriolic way she'd direct her if she got the chance. She said she made her want to vomit, but she loved the production and the cast – when she could hear them. I have given rather good performances for the last 2 weeks. I don't know why. I suppose I've learnt a lot from L.O.

Hotel Knickerbocker – 120, West 45ᵗʰ Street, New York
April 6th 1952

Dear Darling,

Larry is developing a throat infection. He played Anthony twice on Saturday and I thought his voice was 'dickey' but shouted like a mad thing and didn't spare himself. So I am hoping he has done it some temporary damage. He always seems to have a Sunday to recover in, that's the trouble! But hitherto he has only always suffered from a tired throat. This time it's real live bugs. So maybe there will be a rehearsal call tomorrow. I hope so. I'd love to have a go at it. I know I could cope O.K.

All my fondest love Darling,
Pat xx

Hotel Knickerbocker – 120, West 45ᵗʰ Street, New York
April 12th 1952

My Darling Darling,

Today is the last day in New York. We played our last 'Caesar' yesterday evening – and in a few moments I'm off to the theatre, leaving the 'Knickerbocker' to play the last two 'Anthonys'. In twelve hours we will be on board the ship. I am sharing a cabin with Donald Pleasence. There will be about 25 of the company going home on the 'Franconia' with the remainder staying a few days and getting the 'Mauretania or 'Queen Mary'. The old man has arranged for a hot meal, a shower and free drinks on board.

Last night we had drinks with them on Viv's landing. They ought to have done this sort of thing more often – to get to know everyone better. The initiative has to come from them. This would have kept the company together better and ensured more teamwork and better acting. Larry and Viv know this now and feel they've rather failed us.

However the last night party made up for a lot. The old man said that he would meet me again in the future. So that's good!

11.50pm *Standing at the ships rail watching the city lights quietly pass us as we sail down the Hudson – passed the downtown sky scrapers, out past the Statue of Liberty and Staten Island. If sleep doesn't overcome me I shall stay on deck until the pilot leaves us. When you get this we will be two days out from Halifax. I will be docking early morning on Tuesday 22ⁿᵈ. Will send telegram when safe.*

Looking forward so much to holding you my love, Pat xx

On 22ⁿᵈ April 1952 Margaret received a telegram with the simple but wonderful words – 'HOME 3PM TODAY STOP LOVE PAT XX STOP.

Patrick's photograph of the Ziegfeld Theatre New York 1952

106

Dad feeding squirrels in Central Park

On top of the Empire State Building with a friend from the cast

A cold Sunday afternoon at Easthampton New York.
Pat accompanied by three other members of the cast.

Dad's diary read,

'Arrived Liverpool after waiting for tide to be right in Mersey. Misty England. Am I pleased to be home? I think so… felt free in America but missed Margaret and children so much. Will never go away for so long again. Wrong decision. Trip has changed me I think. I want more of the bright lights but feel guilty I have to sacrifice family. Instinct tells me one thing and brain tells me another. I am confused. Perhaps I should just give the whole thing up. My nerves are raw all the time. Sign on tomorrow. Smile on your face.'

It seems that when Pat returned from America he had changed. I'm unsure whether his friends and colleagues noticed it but Margaret must have done. Pat had a wider view of the world now. A world away from the cosy Mill Hill family man that he had so easily submitted too. In New York he had felt a free spirit and had enjoyed the independence and lack of responsibility. He would have had time to look back over his short life and seen how maybe he had married too soon. Margaret was only his second real girlfriend, after all.

Bad news greeted Pat on his return to Mill Hill. The BBC radio Rep had said yes to him doing another six months contract but not until August. This meant the planned holiday would have to wait as Patrick was desperately thrown back into the world of auditions and interviews. He was able to rely on his Rep connections and was cast in a number of radio plays including a version of *Tamburlaine the Great* with Donald Wolfit taking the starring role. Patrick played the King of Arabia. However, these did not pay very well and Pat sunk into a 'black mood' at home. Margaret described these melancholic moods,

'You just had to leave him alone. He would stare blankly into space for hours on end. He wouldn't get angry or shout or anything like that… I wished he had done sometimes! Nothing would bring him back, not even the children. The thing was… acting was so important to him he couldn't bear to be out of work for one minute. He always dressed it up as 'needing to support the family' but really it was something he needed to do or else he wasn't a complete person. No, you just had to leave him alone when he was in one of those moods.'

Finally in early May 1952 Pat secured a very well paid TV drama called *Lines of Communication*. It was a new play by Paul Scott adapted from his novel *Jonnie Sahib* based on his experiences in the Royal Indian Army Service Corps. They operated supply lifts in Bengal, Assam and Malay to the men of the self-titled 'Forgotten Army', the Fourteenth. It depicted a collage of life on the Bengal airstrips, the loading of ammunition and petrol, the turning propellers of the Dakotas, the monsoons, the communal life of soldiers whether Indian or British. Within this image is a story about Johnnie (Captain Brown) played by Pat who runs section three purely on his own personality and under the relaxed command of his happy Major. The idyllic life comes to an end when they are abruptly taken over by a larger organization entitled R.A.M.O. (Rear Airfield Maintenance Organisation) and Johnnie begins his fight to avoid becoming a cog in the machine.

Studio and film were combined including additional material released by the War Office and Air Ministry. A television film unit was sent out to India to obtain shots of the airfield but no actors were involved in any of the location work.

The Rebel of TV's "Lines Of Communication," Patrick Troughton, has only grim hatred for brass-hat control. "Star" picture.

'LINES OF COMMUNICATION'

A new play by Paul Scott
based on his novel 'Johnnie Sahib'

★

CAST IN ORDER OF APPEARANCE

Lieutenant Taylor, R.I.A.S.C. (Jim)	David Oxley
Havildar-clerk Nimu	Roger Snowdon
Jemadar Moti Ram Sahib	Abraham Sofaer
Sepoy Jan Mohammed	Charles Thomson
The Major	Edward Evans
Lieutenant-Colonel Baxter	Patrick Waddington
Captain Scott (Scottie)	John Boyd Brent
Captain Parrish (Bill)	Michael Rathborne
Lieutenant Ghosh (Ghoshey)	Hugh Munro
Havildar Dass	Peter Elliott
Captain Brown (Johnnie)	Patrick Troughton
Lieutenant Johns	Neil Gibson
Sepoy Kassa Ram	Y. Yunai
Major Shelley	Michael Kelly
Lieutenant Smith (Geoff)	Brian Kent

With the success of this programme under his belt and the impressive inclusion of Olivier's tour in his resume, TV work began to increase and Pat completed a number of children's educational TV dramas including *The Florentine Painting* about Benvenuto Cellini and the artists of Florence.

In July Patrick was cast as Alan Breck in Robert Louis Stevenson's *Kidnapped,* a story of treachery, betrayal, courage and political fervor in 18th century Scotland. This type of swash-buckling series was to become a staple diet of BBC TV in the 50s and my father would become a major contributor to many of them. John Frazer was cast as the young David Balfour whose birthright had been stolen by his scheming brother-in-law during the time of Bonnie Prince Charlie's bid to free Scotland from British rule. My father remembered really enjoying playing the happy-go-lucky Highland Scot who was in rebellion against the King. In fact, dad's character was based on a real person in the Jacobite rebellion nicknamed 'Breck' which means pockmarked face. There were six episodes in the series and it went out live every Monday at 8.15 pm and was repeated the next day. Patrick was contracted to do five of the six episodes ensuring his face would become a regular on BBC television.

One day after he had finished on *Kidnapped,* his BBC Rep contract began. Things were going well, as his diary records,

'Have survived since my return from across the pond with continuous work… unheard of! TV is the way forward. Money for old rope some say but I find it very rewarding. Pity I'm tied to the Rep for six months but all's good. Smile on your face. Holiday soon.'

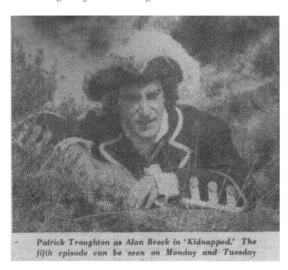

Patrick Troughton as Alan Breck in 'Kidnapped.' The fifth episode can be seen on Monday and Tuesday

Pat, Jo and David on the beach at Bexhill-on-Sea 1952

Patrick 'the family man' relaxes at home in the garden 1952

A week in Bexhill-on-Sea with the family during September allowed Patrick to renew his relationship with the children and to give precious time to Margaret who must have felt somewhat neglected ever since his departure for America. Patrick slipped comfortably back into his role as a family man during that week and returned refreshed and ready for a worry-free six months of radio broadcasts.

By March 1953, Pat had completed well over two hundred broadcasts including *The Silver Tassie* by Sean O'Casey, *To Clever for Love* with a young Nicholas Parsons, *The Whip, Back to Methuselah, The War of the Roses, Bomber's Moon* that depicted twenty-four hours in the life of an R.A.F. bomber squadron during 1943, *Journey to the Earth* with Flora Robson, and the dramatization of *Nicholas Nickleby*.

Patrick left the BBC radio repertory in March and was immediately contacted by Joy Harington who had directed him in *Kidnapped* the year before. Joy was looking for the new face of Robin Hood for a six part children's serial to be shot at Lime Grove studios. Patrick jumped at the opportunity and was cast as the leader of the 'merry band of outlaws'. The BBC made quite a fuss about the new series with my father being involved in a number of publicity promotions before the script was even complete. Pat noted in his diary a morning's photographic shoot in Regents Park, London,

8th March 1953

'Photos in the park today. Posed in full costume – forest green tights and all. Drew a crowd of lovely children. Hope I get some of the prints.'

My Dad remembered the live performances at Lime Grove studios well and how they often did not go according to rehearsals,

'We did that live. In one scene we had back projection, which of course everyone knows what that is – which is a sort of slide that comes in and it was

a picture of the forest, you see. And on this occasion we'd got a film crew to do the back projection and I don't think they quite realised that we were live on television. Anyway we started the scene... Leonard Sachs, I think it was, and myself... and there was a great crashing and banging behind us and we thought what's going on here...and there was a sort of shout of 'Right, it's your end', 'No, it's your end', and we turned around and the forest had come in sideways, and all the trees were that way round instead of that way round. And then there was more crashing and banging and the screen went blank, and then all the trees came up right and we had to go on playing.'

Sadly only one episode of this historic series survives because they were live with no recording facilities. But fortunately the BBC had starting to experiment with a specially adapted monitor that recorded televised material. As a result of this experimentation, an entire episode of Dad's *Robin Hood*, (Episode 2, *The Abbot of St Mary's*) survives in the BBC Archives.

APRIL

7 TUESDAY

1963

Patrick Troughton

as bold Robin Hood the merry outlaw of Sherwood Forest. He continues his adventures in Children's Television

Another children's TV series followed in June called *The Heir of Skipton* which was described by the Radio Times as 'A true story of the fifteenth century in four episodes.' Pat played Will Angram a young shepherd alongside Peter Sallis who would become famous for the British sitcom *Last of the Summer Wine* and also the voice of Wallace in Park's animation. The cast included Shaun Sutton who would later become a producer and be influential in persuading my father to take on the part of Doctor Who.

On September 3rd 1953 Patrick played The Sergeant in an adaptation of Conan Doyle's *Waterloo*. The play was about Corporal Geoffrey Brewster, a hero of Waterloo. When ammunition ran short at the farm of Hougemont, Corporal Brewster braved French gunfire and set out with two cartloads of supplies. The first cart was blown up, but he managed to get the other through to his beleaguered comrades. For this he was awarded a medal. Brewster lives in Woolwich, a very old retired soldier. Now sixty-six years later, a regiment in the barracks nearby learns of his identity and so the old soldier receives the tribute of his successors.

On a copy of Pat's old script of *Waterloo*, a hasty synopsis of the production is scribbled above the first few lines of the play,

'Nonagenarian soldier, 66 years after famous battle. Relives his memories of his heroic fight. Read for the part of Sergeant McDonald. Rehearsals two weeks end of August. Wonderful part! Quality of a theatre two-hander but on TV. What more could I ask for.'

The opening few lines read:

'**SERGEANT** (saluting). Beg your pardon, Miss, but does Corporal Gregory Brewster live here?
NORAH (timidly). Yes, sir.
SERGEANT The same who was in the Scots Guards?
NORAH Yes, sir.
SERGEANT And fought in the battle of Waterloo?
NORAH Yes, the same, sir.
SERGEANT Could I have a word with him, Miss?

115

NORAH He's not down yet.

SERGEANT Ah, then, maybe I'd best look in on my way back. I'm going down to the butts, and will pass again in an hour or two.

NORAH Very well, sir. (Going out). Who shall I say came for him? (**SERGEANT** returns and places carbine L. of sideboard L.)

SERGEANT McDonald's my name—Sergeant McDonald of the Artillery. But you'll excuse my mentioning it, Miss but there was some talk down at the Gunners' barracks that the old gentleman was not looked after quite as well as he might be. But I can see now that it's only foolish talk, for what more could he want than this?'

'Waterloo', with Patrick Troughton as Sergeant McDonald, Margaret Anderson as Norah Brewster, and Laidman Browne as Corporal Brewster

The forty-five minute live production received a warm reception from both the public and critics. It was one of the first TV plays to successfully utilize the unique intimate nature of television and began the idea of the single play format.

Late autumn 1953 Warwick Films contracted Pat to play King Mark in *The Black Knight* starring Alan Ladd, Peter Cushing, Harry Andrews and Patricia Medina. Patrick's scenes were mostly studio based but he did return to a location he had worked before during Treasure Island, Ivor Heath. Being able to ride well and fight convincingly with a sword were proving very useful skills and was one of the main reasons he had been cast by the director, Tay Garnett. My father's diary entry for October 14th 1953 records his thought about the film,

'Sneaked into screening room. Saw some rushes of the scene we did today. Must admit did look rather scheming and evil. I think it must be the moustache. Not my idea – makeups. Peter Cushing and myself are stealing the show! What a great man to work with. Such fun and he doesn't take it too seriously. A true professional though.'

Patrick as the scheming King Mark in 'The Black Knight'

117

Patrick's last job in 1953 was on Boxing Day at the newly built BBC Television Theatre. It was a production of *Toad of Toad Hall* by A.A. Milne before an invited audience of children. Gerald Campion, better known for his role as 'Billy Bunter', took the role of Toad and my father played Badger. The radio times notes that 'Alfred the Carthorse will be played by Miles Brown ably supported by the back legs played by John Barker'.'

The costumes Dad remembered were rather 'make do and mend' in their style. They looked as if someone had rummaged around in a dressing up box and not quite found what they were looking for. Judging from the photograph in the Radio Times clipping stuck into my father's scrapbook, he was right! Joy Harington directed the show; she had used Dad in past productions and would continue to do so as TV drama output increased in pace during the late fifties.

TELEVISION

BOXING DAY

5.0-6.30 Children's Television
'TOAD OF TOAD HALL'
by A. A. Milne
From Kenneth Grahame's book
'The Wind in the Willows'
Produced by Joy Harington
Before an invited audience of children
at the Television Theatre
Cast in order of appearance:
Marigold...Gillian Gale
Nurse..Hilda Barry
Mole..Jack Newmark
Water Rat...Andrew Osborn
Mr. Badger..Patrick Troughton
Toad..Gerald Campion
Alfred..Miles Brown
The back-legs of Alfred........................John Baker
Chief Ferret..Dennis Edwards
Chief Weasel..Don Tasker
Chief Stoat..Derek Tansley
Policeman..Leslie Kyle
Gaoler...Dennis Edwards
Usher..Derek Tansley
Judge...Erik Chitty
Phoebe..Gillian Gale
Washerwoman..Violet Gould
Bargewoman..Hilda Barry
Other parts played by
Rowena Bragg, Sharon Duke, June Harley
Sally Keogh, Gail Mackenzie, Jean Minett
Judy Nash, Brenda Oliver, Sally Pearce
Jacqueline Smith, Susannah White
Music by H. Fraser-Simson
Orchestra conducted by Eric Robinson
Settings by Richard Wilmot
Assistant producer, Stephen Wade
Second performance: December 31
★   ★   ★

Mole, Badger, and Rat try to urge a sense of caution on the flamboyant Toad. The adventures of 'Toad of Toad Hall' are told again at 5.0

After the New Year, Patrick was out of work for the first time since the spring. It must have been at the start of 1954 that his relationship with Margaret began to breakdown. What the reason was for this happening is lost in the mist of time. None of my family has any idea as to why such a loving couple that had been so devoted to one another should have started to drift apart. Mum once told me,

'Ever since Pat's return from America he was different. Nothing you could put your finger on but there was a change in his affections towards me. It was slight but it was defiantly there.'

In all likelihood he probably had a fling with one of the female actresses on that tour – a momentary need for comfort brought on by the distance from home and the stark loneliness of being away from his family. My father was a very tactile man, especially when it came to women. He adored them and enjoyed their company far more than men. They of course adored him. In fact, many mature actresses who I have worked with in the past have often shuffled up to me in rehearsals with a wicked twinkle in the eye and quietly whispered 'I knew your father very well, an adorable creature!' The trip to America I think was the beginning of an addiction that would cause all sorts of personal problems throughout his life.

January saw no work but at the beginning of February, Joy Harington cast him in yet another swash buckling adventure series for the BBC playing the lead role this time. *Clementina* was a romantic cloak and dagger story set in the first quarter of the 18th century. Patrick took on the role of Charles Wogan who had been given the task of rescuing Clementina, bride to be of James Stuart, The Old Pretender. C.A.Lejeune adapted the novel by A.E.Mason into six thirty-five minute adventures. I wonder how many viewers at the time, knew from the title of Clementina what sort of serial they should expect to see? Not very many I imagine. Mason's novel was fairly unknown and to the best of my knowledge had never been filmed up to that time, although there had been plans for making it a vehicle for Robert Donat. The story contained spy, plot and counterplot but at the heart of the story was romance. Lejeune described his adaptation to my father in a letter and later in a Radio Times article,

'I am not going to give away the plot of Clementina, but a few notes may help to set the background of the story. The period is first quarter of the eighteenth century. The House of Hanover has succeeded to the throne of England. James Stuart is living in exile in Italy after the failure of the first Jacobite rebellion. He has not given up hope of a successful return to the land of his fathers, but these expeditions cost money. His counselors have advised him to take a rich wife, and the choice has fallen upon Princess Clementina Sobieski, daughter to the Prince of Poland, and reckoned one of the greatest fortunes in Europe. Naturally, such a match would be opposed by the House of Hanover, so the notion is to bring Clementina quietly south to Bologna, for a private, very hush-hush marriage. But the secret leaks out and by the time the story of Clementina opens the Princess and her mother have been stopped and imprisoned in Innsbruck on the orders of the Emperor of Austria who has his own reasons for wanting to keep on good terms with the British throne.'

Patrick prepares for a shot on location as director Joy Harington adjusts his cloak.
Photo by Carl Sutton

At this point in the story a loyal Jacobite and veteran campaigner Charles Wogan (played by Pat) suggests a plan for rescuing the Princess, and bringing her to Bologna under the very noses of the enemy. Lejeune continued,

> 'What happens now is part fact and part fiction. It does not do to divide the one too sharply from the other. Joy (Harington) and I found that out when we were working together on the adaptation. Some of the more astonishing incidents at which we jibbed turned out to be as authentic as a railway timetable. We came to the conclusion that the best thing to do was to let the story run almost exactly how Mason wrote it: cutting trick endings, retaining original names, following the picturesque road along which signposts lead us, and keeping as much of the original, courtly duologue as possible.'

My father became very close to both Harington and Lejeune during the filming and live studio telecasts. Joy was by now an experienced producer of children's television programmes for the BBC. She had started as an actress appearing in various British repertory companies followed by a period working at Paramount Studios as a script editor and dialogue director. After the war, Harington joined the BBC as a stage manager when the television service re-opened in 1946 at exactly the same time my father began to discover the new medium of TV. She became producer of BBC Children's Television in 1950 and for the next ten years excelled in productions of children's classics often casting my father in various character roles.

After the completion of *'Clementina'*, C.A.Lejeune wrote a 'fan letter' to my father,

> *'Dear Mr Troughton,*
> *I said I would write you a fan letter, and here it is. You must know that I shaped 'Clementina' and wrote my bits of it, with you in mind from the first. Often the planned thing doesn't come off. This time it did. It was*

a delight to see and hear my 'Wogan' come to life, week after week. It must have been a hard and breathless sort of task, and I do most warmly thank you.

I tried to get Michael Barry [Head of Television Drama] *on the telephone to ask him about a possible 'Jane Eyre', but he is rehearsing all this week. I have had another idea, too. What about 'A Tale of Two Cities'? It hasn't been done for a long time. I was wondering too – could you be in it? I think this would be right up your street.*

However, if not, and if they let me keep on writing I will turn up something else for you. It such a fascinating job writing words. I have learnt so much from 'Clementina'.

Yours sincerely, C A Lejeune

Patrick playing swashbuckling Charles Wogan in the BBC 1954 production of *Clementina*.

122

Pat went on to appear in many productions written by C.A. Lejeune and a firm professional relationship developed between them during the late fifties. The letter that L.A. Lejeune sent to Pat highlights the intimate nature of this fledgling TV industry and the rather incestuous way it operated at that time. Everyone was new; everyone was trying to find his or her feet, actors, directors and writers alike. A sense of security seemed to focus on professional friendship networks that producers could rely on to deliver the product without too many mistakes. Patrick understood this well and he did everything in his power to become one of the chosen few by writing regular casting enquiry letters, banging on office doors, forming professional friendships and generally keeping his name and face at the top of the programme makers list.

Dennis Vance was another producer that was aware of Pat's talents for TV acting and also happened to be a close friend of Joy Harington. Dennis had begun his career the same way Joy had by acting until the late forties. In the early fifties he had switched jobs and after taking a BBC course had become a producer of drama. He would oversee many successful productions such as *The Scarlet Pimpernel* before leaving to become Head of Drama at ABC (Associated British Corporation) and developing the highly acclaimed *Armchair Theatre* format for ITV.

Vance had seen Patrick in *Clementina* and asked to see him for the part of the Marquise of Montrose in an adaptation of *Witch Wood* by John Buchan. This was quite a controversial play to perform since it dealt with an apparently god-fearing Christian community who were involved in a secretive devil-worshiping cult. It was a very risqué subject for the BBC to take on in those days. Patrick completed the live telecast on 30th May with a second performance three days later with surprisingly little complaint from the viewing public.

He followed this with another TV play called *Misalliance* by Bernard Shaw in which he played Gunner. It was a production to mark the playwright's birthday and examined rather ironically the mating instincts of a group of people who gather together on a Saturday afternoon at a wealthy man's country house. The cast included a 28 year old actor called Kenneth Williams, Patricia Laffan, and Maurice Colborne. Peter Black of the Daily Mail wrote in his Teleview article that 'Patrick Troughton's memorable performance on B.B.C. TV was outrageously amusing and harrowing at the same time…'

The producer Douglas Allen would become another close college of Dad's and provide him with work throughout the late fifties and early sixties.

Patrick's entry in his diary for 3rd August 1954 reads,

'Larry has come good as he said he would. He wants me to play Tyrell in his film of Richard the Third. A real baddy – murders the two princes in the tower I think. So many good actors in it – all British cast with four 'sirs'. Already feeling nervous about appearing with such greats! More – I am to understudy him in rehearsals. Don't know what this will involve?'

Filming started in September with three weeks out in La Mancha, Spain where the Battle of Bosworth opening sequence was shot. Patrick later explained his under study role in the location work and later at Shepperton studios.

'I not only had a great part in the film but I was Olivier's acting understudy. I was dressed in identical costume, identical makeup. I had to watch him rehearse a scene and then do it for him – exactly as he had done it. I had to learn all his lines each evening ready for the following days shooting. This was so he could compose the picture as a director. Then he would do the scene with the cameras rolling. It was a marvellous experience and I learnt so much from him. He was quite a fierce personality to work with and a lot of people found him difficult, but he was charming and very patient with me. I think if he liked you and respected your acting then you were fine. He never shouted at me even if I mucked up, which I rarely did because I was so frightened!'

'Out in Spain we were filming at a bull farm in Castilla-La Mancha. I remember it being very dangerous at times with wooden arrows raining down and horses bolting from fright. I think Larry got struck by one of the arrows in a particular sequence and had to be taken to the local doctor to have it bandaged up. Quite a few people had minor cuts and bruises after that three

weeks but everyone was so dedicated to what they were doing it seemed a small price to pay. It would never happen that way nowadays!'

'Many of the long shots in the movie are me as Richard the Third and not Larry because such sequences required him to be in the director's chair rather than the actual shot. When he was acting during the takes the assistant director Gerry O'Hara would take over control of the scene, reporting back to Olivier after it was complete. Each time they finished a shot there would be a short whispered chat between the two of them and we would either go again or move on. Larry must have trusted Gerry one hundred percent.'

'I have to say this was the first film I did where I felt as if I had been there from start to finish. So many times you would just go in and do a week here and a day there. Bit like with 'Hamlet', which only took a week. I didn't feel part of the whole piece. It was different on Richard because I had been there every day for seventeen weeks.'

'I got to act with some really big actors and actresses all be it only during rehearsal when Larry would be framing up the shots. Sir Ralph Richardson as the Duke of Buckingham was a lovely man, so gentle and easy. Sir John Gielgud played the Duke of Clarence with a young Clare Bloom as The Lady Anne. John Laurie, Stanley Baker, Andrew Cruickshank and Michael Gough were also in it.'

Just before Dad had begun filming *Richard II,* Margaret had been told the good news that she was pregnant for the third time. It is probable they had made the decision to have another baby during their summer holiday in August. It is also likely that this was an attempt to re-cement and prop up there failing marriage that by now was causing both of them to feel desperately isolated from each other. Patrick wrote in his diary,

'Holiday time — going down to see Margaret and John Wyberg in Ferring. Jill and Ken will be there. Good time to relax and sort out problems. John still having nightmares about Japanese war camp — I am lucky to have survived the war so unscathed. Jill and Ken seem so happy — new love is so fresh. My life is grey, never black and white. I am so unsure of myself at the moment. Can I stay with the same partner for the rest of my life?

125

Acting allows for too many temptations. Family life inevitably suffers. God, I hate myself sometimes. Must sign on when I return. Smile on your face.'

My father seemed increasingly troubled about his personal life at this time and as the winter turned towards the spring, things only began to worsen. Patrick seemed to be torn between the contentment that family life brought him and the wilder and more exciting 'other life' of acting.

Chapter 5
A Double Life

My sister told me,

'I have very few memories of Dad leaving Mum. When we moved to the new house in Uphill Road, Mill Hill, the story was that Dad had to stay elsewhere as he was working too far away - a useful excuse that I'm sure countless male actors have used down the ages! Dad's absence was *never* talked about - it was a taboo subject. I have a memory of telling this porky pie to one of my teachers while walking to Mill Hill swimming baths from Goodwyn School. I'm sure she twigged the reality of the situation!'

My mum told me,

'The day he left home, the one thing that I will never forget was the screaming chants of 'no don't go' from David and having to prise him from Pat's legs. It was quite traumatic. That's all I really want to tell you. It was a long time ago.'

Mum's friend Jill told me,

'I am really vague about the order of events during 1955 as I was so wrapped up in my own affairs, and constantly turning to Margaret for advice and help, never realizing at the time that she was probably dealing with troubles of her own. Michael was born in March 1955 and I remember they moved to a new house in Uphill Road, Mill Hill at the end of December. I know that the arrival of Michael caused great rejoicing and the move to the new house appeared on the surface to be normal and relaxed. I imagine it was just after the move that their marriage finally came to an end, though it was done so unobtrusively that it was some time before I realized what had happened. Pat was still around a lot, and as it was an accepted fact that he was often away working as he had such a busy career, I don't think anyone would have questioned it at all.'

'Naturally, through people who worked with Pat and my husband the writer Ken Taylor, we learnt quite a lot about Pat's new double life, but by silent mutual agreement the subject was never touched upon by us. Many years later, Margaret explained that her one desire was to protect her family's right to privacy, and that this had meant total secrecy (with the exception of her own mother). This strategy worked extremely well but probably today it would have been absolutely impossible to maintain.'

I can't remember when Dad left the family home because I was just 10 months old but it seems it was not a complete separation. Patrick still continued to spend time with Margaret and the children all through the early stages of his affair. It became a bizarre slightly surreal time where Patrick became a divided soul who rushed from one world to another, taking on the role of family man on the one hand and young free lover on the other.

I think Patrick had met his new girlfriend Ethel Nuens at a party during the mid-fifties. She was a children's nanny working for an American family in London.

When Patrick was trying to decide whether to leave Margaret he sought the advice of a local Mill Hill priest who told him in no uncertain terms that 'marriage was sacred and that he would be going against God's will if he were to leave the marriage.' It seems that Pat was riddled with guilt and remorse for what had happened to him but the urge to change and renew his life was very strong and of course it won out in the end.

During the spring of 1955, Patrick worked on a number of children's plays for TV including *The Bargain* directed by his friend Joy Harington, *The Olive Jar* produced by Rex Tucker and set in Italy and a series in six parts called *Benbow and the Angels* adapted from the book by Margaret J. Barker.

By May, work was becoming difficult to find and Patrick wrote in his diary,

> 'Have got one TV in April – Midsummer Fire *is a Mexican Love story and I am playing the schoolmaster. My old friend Wolfe Morris is in it with me. Money is not good at the moment and home life tense. Will have to sign on after. Not looking forward to summer. Joy has told me there's not a lot around at the moment. Plan – write letters and contact Harold at BBC. Smile on your face.'*

In fact, Patrick wouldn't get work for another six months, the longest period he was ever unemployed during his whole career. It is probable that Margaret and Pat's relationship became more and more difficult because of the lack of money as Dad slipped further and further into debt. If it hadn't been for his brother Robin lending him funds to cover this period I feel sure he would have had to call it a day and go and get a 'proper job.' A letter from the bank manager refusing an increase in his overdraft is pinned to the inside of his diary for 1955. It reads,

> 'Assets and liabilities – he owns his house in which he lives with his three children. It was purchased for £2,750 in 1947 and is charged by way of the first mortgage to the Westbourne Park Building Society for £2100. Household furniture and items of little value apart from a Hoover washing machine and 14' table model television subject to H.P. As a freelance actor his income naturally comes in spasmodically, but it has not fluctuated greatly above or below his average figures during the last few years until now. Major outgoings arc mortgage interest and a life endowment policy that amounts to £16 per month. His daughter aged eight attends a private school. On the whole Mr Troughton has done well professionally since January 1953 and a part in the film 'Black Knight' has improved his financial position somewhat, and enabled him to avoid excessive overdrafts up until now. However it is felt that due to the

unpredictable nature of his work and lack of any substantial assets that a further advance should be refused.'

Underneath this, Pat has scrawled across the bank manager's signature *'Bugger!'*

In November with one radio play completed called *The Great Desire I Had* starring Marius Goring and Irene Worth, Patrick decided to sell the family house in Victoria Road, Mill Hill and to look for a larger but cheaper house that he would be able to do up.

This was not the only reason for the sale. Dad had come to a decision by this time – he was going to leave Margaret and his family and live with his mistress Ethel. My sister has suggested that the purchase of the larger house in Uphill Road, Mill Hill was his way of reconciling his guilt for leaving the family. Whatever the reason, we all moved in to the new house in January 1956, with financial and legal help from his brother Robin.

The large ramshackle old house in Uphill Road,
and the young author poses with friend in huge wild garden

The house in Uphill Road was in a state of some disrepair when we arrived, but my father had grand plans to do all the improvement work himself. I remember at the back of the house rickety patio doors opening out onto a raised porch of broken quarry tiles which then gave way to uneven red brick steps down to an ant infested crazy paved patio area. The garden was huge and mostly overgrown with brambles and stinging nettles, which seemed to be the native species. It must have been over 300 metres in length and had a strangely pungent smelling pond at the bottom filled with newts and frogs. My sister recalls,

'My bedroom had metal double doors that opened out onto a balcony which overlooked the huge uncared for garden. The wooden rails and support posts were pretty rotten and the whole structure seemed to be supported by an ancient Wisteria that had crazily wound itself around every rail and plank.'

She also remembers the house was very cold and damp. Condensation would form on all the walls in late evening and run down in dribbling rivulets, staining the overly ornate and peeling wallpaper. There was no fridge but a huge larder almost as big as the kitchen scullery that contained a 'fly-box food safe'. The front room that had probably been a dining room became the children's nursery and I can remember spending hours playing with toy cars and trains with my brother David on the odd smelling yellow carpet.

While all this change was taking place in our lives, Patrick had returned to the stage and was playing the part of Cobb the Cobbler in a Christmas production of *Puss in Boots* at the Lyric Theatre, Hammersmith that later transferred to the Fortune Theatre in the West End. The stage newspaper wrote,

'This play, a straight forward telling of the fairy story, treated soberly and uncondescending, yet with humour at times reminiscent of 'Alice in Wonderland', is as superior to the conventional type of variety show pantomime as the cat is here shown to be superior to the common mortal... Patrick

Troughton is the embodiment of accommodating mildness as the cobbler who makes the magic boots.'

My sister recalls going to see Dad in *Puss in Boots* and talking after the show to Nicholas Stuart Gray who played Puss,

'It was the first real theatre production I had been allowed to see. I remember that I felt so proud when the curtain went up to reveal Dad on stage. I suppose this experience cemented my love of the theatre for life.'

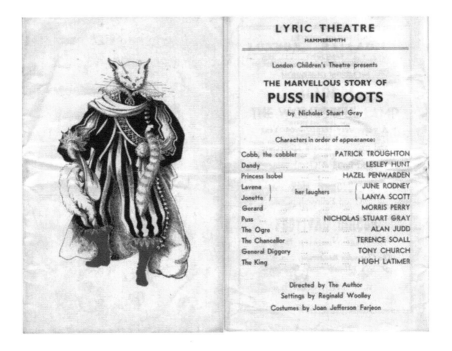

LYRIC THEATRE
HAMMERSMITH

London Children's Theatre presents

THE MARVELLOUS STORY OF
PUSS IN BOOTS
by Nicholas Stuart Gray

Characters in order of appearance:

Cobb, the cobbler		PATRICK TROUGHTON
Dandy		LESLEY HUNT
Princess Isobel		HAZEL PENWARDEN
Lavena	her laughers	JUNE RODNEY
Jonetta		LANYA SCOTT
Gerard		MORRIS PERRY
Puss		NICHOLAS STUART GRAY
The Ogre		ALAN JUDD
The Chancellor		TERENCE SOALL
General Diggory		TONY CHURCH
The King		HUGH LATIMER

Directed by The Author
Settings by Reginald Woolley
Costumes by Joan Jefferson Farjeon

After Christmas, TV work became more prolific and Patrick was cast in *The White Falcon*. This was perhaps a typical example of the period TV dramas that was becoming popular in the late fifties. Rudolf Cartier, who would later go on to create and direct the *Quatermass Experiment* series produced this Sunday Night Theatre with Jeannette Sterke, Marius Goring, Margaretta Scott and Paul

Rogers starring. The cutting in my father's scrapbook written by the Austrian producer reads,

'Many plays have been written on Anne Boleyn and her tragic love, but this new version deals with it in an up-to-date, one could almost say, cinematic manner. First of all, the dialogue is fluent and modern prose. All the characters speak a language everybody can understand; no one uses 'Methinks' or 'F'sooth', or similar archaic words, and together with a romantic, lighthearted treatment, the well-known story is divested of all the heaviness of a 'historical costume drama'. The White Falcon is essentially a love story, charming, but rather sad in parts, as we know already the bitter ending. It begins with the first meeting of the King and Anne and ends in the hour of her execution. And in between there is a colourful cavalcade of scenes ranging from Bridewell Palace, via Greenwich and Hampton Court to the Tower. I had seen Paul Rogers and Jeannette Sterke two years ago at the Old Vic playing the same characters in Henry VIII, and as Shakespeare's play give the King and Anne very little opportunity to develop their love story, these two artists jumped at the chance to play the leading parts in The White Falcon. And I was also very fortunate to get Marius Goring and Rupert Davies again who were so successful in The Devil's General.'

Pat played Cardinal Wolsey alongside his friend Roger Delgado who had been cast as Mark Smeaton, the Queen's dancing master. Delgado later went on to play The Master in *Doctor Who*.

By now Pat had worked with Marius Goring on a number of occasions and they had become close friends. After completing *The White Falcon*, Marius had been asked by producer Harry Alan Towers to play the Scarlet Pimpernel in an ITV production. This was the first attempt at costume drama adventure that the new independent broadcasters had done, and the production company based at Highbury Studios wanted to make sure that they employed experienced TV actors who would turn in a good performance.

133

With this in mind, Marius suggested Patrick for the part of Sir Andrew Ffoulkes, one of the Pimpernel's regular confederates. Pat's diary on 5ᵗʰ March 1956 reads,

'I can't believe it. At last some luck goes my way. Thanks to Marius I got the part and start at middle of March. Money very good - guaranteed 11 episodes. Work until the end of June. Bank manager will be pleased. Smile on your face!'

Photographed television screen shots from live performance of Patrick and Marius in 'The Scarlet Pimpernel 1956

Throughout the rest of that year, Pat continued to be cast in adventure period drama TV that had become a mainstay for both the BBC and ITV. *The Count of Monte Cristo*, *The Adventures of Robin Hood* with Richard Greene and a shorter remake of *Kidnapped* were just a few. In addition to these Pat was still contributing to children's television and performing single TV plays such as *The Man from the Sea* in which he played the title role opposite a young Bernard Bresslaw and Peter Wyngarde.

By the summer of 1956, Pat's partner Ethel had become pregnant with their first child Jane. I think the moment that Dad told my mother the news was quite a turning point in their relationship. Up until that point I think Margaret had been clinging to the hope that his relationship with Ethel was just a momentary affair and that he

134

would come back. This changed everything. Not only was it a shock that this had happened so soon after the birth of Margaret's third baby but the fact that Dad had decided to set up a new home and family only confirmed what my mother had probably feared all along - there was no going back. This was not just a simple affair – Ethel had become more than that.

I am sure my mother considered divorce but in those days you had to prove adultery, which involved a huge amount of legal manoeuvring, cost and even photographic evidence. This was out of the question. Margaret and Pat decided to avoid divorce and continued to keep the whole thing secret. My mother said,

'I didn't want anyone to know about our separation – not even my closest friends. My mother was the only one I told and she was sworn to secrecy. In those days it was a terrible thing to have happen. I kept quiet for the children. I didn't want them to know about us breaking up. We told everyone that Pat was away a lot, working. It worked well for a few years but later rumours began and I had to explain what had happened.'

I think my father was fortunate Margaret did not want a divorce. He did nothing to change her decision and probably realized that he was better off financially and socially living the white lie. Patrick continued to pay the mortgage on Uphill Road and send as much maintenance as he could afford, but the promised renovation of our ram shackled house never materialized. From that point on our family struggled to make ends meet and to this day I will never know how mum managed to bring three children up independently and with so little money.

The 14th January 1957 began a run of parts for Patrick in *The Adventures of Robin Hood* produced by Yeoman Films of Great Britain. Throughout the spring he would play five different roles in the series showing his versatility and skill at characterization.

The first was in an episode called *The Dream* where Sir William Fitzwalter, Maid Marion's city dwelling cousin played by Pat, comes to visit her for the first time since they were children. However, Sir

William intends to hand Robin over to Prince John played by his old friend Donald Pleasence in return for a large parcel of land. Sir William kidnaps Robin aboard his ship, but his band of merry men rescues him.

Patrick as Sir William Fitzwalter in *The Adventures of Robin Hood* opposite Richard Greene

The following week on 21st January, Dad played a completely different character called Seneschal in *The Blackbird*. This would be unheard of nowadays but it seems that the fifties TV audience just took it in their stride and accepted the fact that the same actor was now playing a different part. I suppose that they were more used to the repertory theatre system where the same cast played different parts each week. There is no doubt that in 2011 it would have thoroughly confused such a sophisticated TV audience!

Pat in *The Blackbird*   Pat as Raoul in *The Bandit of Brittany*

The week after that he played another completely different character called The Traveler in an episode entitled *The Shell Game*. On the 18th February he took yet another role in *The Bandits of Brittany*, playing the bearded Raoul only to return in April as Seneschal in *Food for Thought*.

Patrick remembered,

'Those Robin Hood weeks in 1957 were marvelous. We did it all on film so no live studios, and proper food! Richard was so more in control than me as Robin. I did mention the fact that I had played the part before and he said he had watched it through a snowy haze on his friend's television. I think getting the part – both financially and professionally saved Richard. A lovely man but a bit serious at times. I had a number of mates in that show – Donald Pleasence was in it playing King John I think and the debonair Alan Wheatley as the Sheriff.'

Later in the year Patrick took on yet another TV adventure drama called *Sword of Freedom* which was a 'doublet and hose' series set in Renaissance Florence.

This used the well-tried formula of historical figures, swashbuckling adventure and elegant costumes but the result was poor. It lacked the pace and tension of previous series forcing one critic to complain, 'We have seen this all before!'

Despite the critics, the TV viewing public couldn't get enough of these historical adventure stories and Patrick continued to be cast in them all though the late fifties. *William Tell*, *The Rebel Heiress*, *Ivanhoe*, *The Moonstone*, *The Adventures of Robin Hood*, and *Assignment Foreign Legion*.

By 1959 Patrick's partner Ethel had given birth to a second child. Pat and 'Bunny', as her family knew her, lived in a bungalow in North Road, Kew with their two children. Dad continued to make the journey over from South to North London by bus quite regularly in order to spend time with us in Mill Hill and keep up the marriage pretence with Margaret.

My first memory of those days was waiting with my big brother David at the 113 bus stop to meet Dad. I had an old red three-wheeler bicycle and I remember Dad chasing me, pretending to be a monster, jumper pulled tight over his head and growling like a wild dog! He was a wonderful father - that is, when I saw him. He would take the time to play with all his children and give them as much attention as he could. When he was older he told me,

'If I hadn't have been caught by the acting bug, I would have become a teacher. I love children. They keep you young.'

The one thing I did miss was Dad being around at school events such as sports day or a carol concert. I was always very jealous of my friends who were able to boast that both their parents were going to be present at the cricket match or the prize giving. I'm sure he could have found the time but the threat of people finding out about his double life must have made him stay away.

As the fifties came to a close, TV work for Patrick had become his exclusive means of earning money through acting. He was to return to the stage just once during the rest of his career. In 1959 productions included, *Three Golden Nobles, The History of Mr Polly, Interpol Calling, The Moonstone, The Naked Lady, The Scarf,* and *The Cabin in the Clearing.* He also played Vickers in an episode of *The Invisible Man* with a future *Doctor Who* companion – a young Deborah Watling.

Patrick's personal life during the fifties had been regenerated with his separation from Margaret and his newfound friendship with Ethel. However, he now had the responsibly of caring for two families, both financially and emotionally. The double life that he had begun in 1955 would prove difficult to maintain.

Patrick as Vickers in *The Invisible Man*, 1959

Chapter 6
Donkeys, Dickens and Harpies

A close friend of Patrick's told me,

'I'm amazed now when I think of it… at the huge amount of energy Patrick needed and had, just to keep things going. The early sixties were a very busy time for him career wise and it is incredible looking back at how he kept all the balls in the air! There must have been very little time for himself between caring for two families and working as much as he did.'

It wasn't quite like that. Work and his young second family always came first – in that order. David, Joanna and I hardly saw anything of him during the early sixties. Our father had become a distant and mysterious figure who communicated by hastily composed postcards or short rushed phone calls. It was a lonely and confusing time for me when I began to become aware of the situation and the difficulties of being part of a single parent family. One of those postcards I have kept reads,

'Dear Margaret, Here is a picture of me riding my friend 'Messara' a rather stubborn horse. Have got two more weeks in the sweltering sun of Aghios. One or two dramas here between cameraman and overeager Joy! Kenneth Mackintosh and I had two days off and went exploring. Working at Ealing when I get back, so hope to see you all then.

The date on the card was July 1960 and Dad was on the Island of Crete filming the series called *Paul of Tarsus*. Yet again, Joy Harington had cast Patrick in one of her productions. She was not only directing and producing this biblical drama but she had written the screenplay as well.

The Stage newspaper clipping in my father's scrapbook reads,

'Joy Harington deserves the fullest possible credit for 'Paul of Tarsus'. Not only has she written the script but she produced it. *The Feast of Pentecost* was the title of the first episode in this ten-part cycle telling the story of the Acts of Christ's Apostles. It was both moving and dramatic and held the attention from beginning to end. Joy Harington's script is both tasteful and modern. An example is the beggar who is cured of being crippled. He speaks in a broad cockney accent yet this doesn't jar because the whole conception is perfectly based. Patrick Troughton as Saul (Paul) was notable in a role that towers above most of the other characters.'

'This series, with all the advance publicity and the serialization in some papers should more than live up to its advanced reputation.'

Patrick's postcard featuring him filming *Paul of Tarsus,* riding his stubborn mule Messara on location in Crete 1960

142

The public absolutely loved the series and my father was inundated by fan letters. This production proved a real turning point for Patrick who was highly acclaimed by his fellow professionals for such a 'moving and sympathetic performance.' His reputation as a first class actor within the world of TV drama was firmly established by this outstanding performance. Sadly, no known copy of the production remains. Even today people still remember the series with affection – an anonymous comment on a blog about Patrick Troughton reminisces,

> 'It used to be broadcast on BBC on Sunday evenings at 5.30pm, and I remember it clearly because I always went to choir practice afterwards, and was usually late because I had waited until the credits had finished. Even now, after so much time has passed, I can remember the effect of Patrick Troughton's portrayal of Paul. It was electric, and I was riveted each week. I think that is why he has remained my favourite Doctor Who - his acting was superb.'

It is perhaps a little ironic that Dad made such a success out of a religious drama series and would later become famously associated with the part of a priest in the 'Omen'. His opinion on formal Christianity was pretty clear – he detested it!

I remember on many occasions watching Dad slam the door on religious doorstep visitors like Jehovah's Witnesses or Christian Aid. He would always retort,

'It should be Christian Aid week every week not just this week!'

He set out his rather confused ideas on religion while writing to a fan in 1972,

'I'm interested that you are studying theology. I don't think I could ever have done that – in a conventional church. There seem too many stumbling blocks to me – though I know the private views of churchmen are sometimes different to the 39 articles etc. But only if those great difficulties had not been there, I might well have been a professional churchman myself,

143

though not in the Church of England. It does seem to me that so much is just watered down Mediaeval Christianity with no real attempt made to solve the problem, 'Love or be damned'. To me, love can never reject, only fail to draw, and then only temporarily. I cannot get around the issue that Jesus seemed to believe in and advocate eternal torment – and that for no remedial reason. Either he is not the full embodiment of the spirit of Christ of the Cosmos – or the record is sadly wrong. I think it is the latter; I think men may well get into torment and Jesus's reaction is always to get them out of it, but not, I'm afraid, in so many places in the Gospel. I wish I had been a vegetarian too – not that I am – but Buddha was and I think that is more loving.'

His youngest son Mark told me that when he had decided to become a priest he was unsure of how Dad was going to take it,

'When I broke the awful news to him that I had become a Christian, I thought it would be a bit of a bombshell. Now, even though Dad was very open-minded about stuff and had read theologians and philosophers like J.A.T. Robinson and the Huxleys (as a discovered box of wartime reading matter of his demonstrated), in his tolerance of other beliefs he was intolerant of Christian ones.

"What, you believe in Adam and Eve and all that?"

"Er, yes I do."

Despite our differences on that score, I owe him my unwillingness to believe unless it can be argued rationally. Shades of *Doctor Who* inquisitiveness and Star Trek 'Spockian logicality' (Dad loved *Star Trek* - sorry, am I allowed to say that?).'

He even refused to attend my brother's wedding church service because he felt so strongly about 'formal Christian religious ceremonies'. A friend of the family recalled,

'I remember seeing him briefly at David's wedding reception, he having refused to come to the church service because he disapproved of formalized religion! This illustrates Pat's combative side very well, something that caused many arguments with us down the ages.'

I don't know where this intolerance of Christian beliefs stemmed from but probably his public school upbringing had something to do with it. My mother's friend Jill puts it down to his mischievous character and recalled the infuriating way he would always take the opposite side of an argument just to wind you up,

'Politics and religion were a frequent challenging ground, but in the right mood Pat would challenge ones views on practically anything. He could be absolutely infuriating, and I can remember complaining that he was about to cause me to have a miscarriage if he didn't stop insisting on some idiotic theory – something to do with Archbishop Makarious and Cyprus I think. Ever afterwards referred in our house as 'Archbishop 'Macarrycot'! I'm pretty sure a lot of this was just pure devilment and a desire to wind people up. It is testament to the strength of his character that he was so good at this.'

Whether 'pure devilment' was the reason he took on this 'anti-Christian opinion' it is a fact that throughout his life, Dad seemed to be searching for something to believe in but was never quite able to find what he was looking for. He experimented with Hinduism, Buddhism, humanism and many other ideas but always, as his youngest son said, would reject them because he believed the proof was not there.

Paul of Tarsus was released as a book by Hodder publications soon after the series was complete with my father on the cover looking suitable biblical. It was probably one of the first spin-off publications of a TV series. The critics said,

'A splendid piece of writing, simple and vivid… it is evident that much research has gone into the creation of the historical background.' And 'How fortunate are those children who will have a copy of this wonderful book to keep for their very own.'

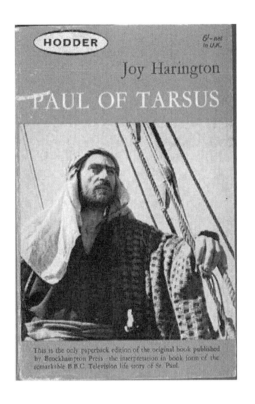

The month before Patrick had completed an ambitious TV production of *The Insect Play* by the same playwright who wrote R.U.R. – Karel Capek. *The Insect Play* was a satirical take on the failure to improve the follies and evils of Mankind. It was directed by Hal Burton and required two studios, a cast of over one hundred characters, Kirby flying equipment for a butterfly sequence and elaborate costume designs. My father took the role of a worker ant and wrote about his costume in his 1960 diary,

> *'Although my costume is beautifully made – felt head mask, padded thorax and flipper hands – I think the audience is going to have real trouble distinguishing between the characters. I suggested to Hal at lunch that it was far too naturalistic for the piece, which is essentially an expressionistic piece. He was not very impressed! I still think costume*

would do much better to just suggest the insect like qualities and allowed the actors to create the illusion.'

After filming *Danger Man* in which he played Brenner, the leader of a criminal group who had kidnapped the daughter of a wealthy industrialist and appearing in yet another episode of *Robin Hood* as Sir Fulke Devereaux, Pat was offered a movie. Morningside productions had contacted him about meeting Don Chaffy the director to read for the part of Phineous in a fantasy adventure entitled *Jason and the Argonauts*. This was a high budget movie ($1million) that was to include special effects that had never been seen before. Dad recalled,

'I read for the part and afterwards Don immediately told me I had it if I wanted it. I think he must have seen a lot of my TV work and knew I was right for the part of poor old blind Phineous. He had wanted someone who the audience would really sympathize with but come over as real. He also wanted someone who could play older than their age because it was quite a physical part – lots of rolling around on the floor and waving at imaginary flying creatures.'

Dad's appearance as Phineas, a blind man who has been banished to an island and is forever tormented by the harpies, is quite brief but took around three to four weeks to film. His character has displeased the god Zeus, and as a punishment, he is doomed to have his food taken by flying devils called harpies every mealtime. Jason and his crew arrive on the Island and agree to capture the harpies in return for directions to the fabled Fleece.

The filming of my father's sequence took place in Italy near Sorrento. A postcard to the family describes the location,

'Dear Troughton Family, boiling hot, glorious blue sky and breathtaking scenery. Filming all week amongst incredible Greek temples near Sorrento. Amazing preservation, almost like new! The props chaps have just added a stone table made out of foam. Very convincing. They told me not to lean on it or it would break. Very odd - acting to nothing most of the time. Don just calls out where the 'Harpies' are and I react accordingly. Doing sequence today with wire attached to me. Hope I survive!'

147

The 'wire' sequence my father described in the postcard was used to make his character's belt sash appear to be pulled off by one of the flying devils. He recalled,

'A wire was attached to my sash in one shot and as the cameras rolled Don shouted 'Harpies pull' and three technicians pulled the wire which made me roll on the ground over and over until the sash came right off. In the shot it looks really good. We did it a few times before they got it right. I had quite a number bruises after that sequence.'

'I never met Harryhausen but those 'Harpies' were very frightening. I remember thinking twice before allowing my kids to see it when it came out in sixty-three. It didn't do too well at the American box office I remember, but I think my bit the critics applauded.'

The New York Times wrote, 'This absurd, unwieldy adventure – if that's the word – is no worse, but certainly no better, than most of its kind...' The New York Herald Tribune commented, 'In Jason and the Argonauts, a rehash of how Jason got the golden fleece, our hero suffers such a plethora of trials by the special effects department (about twice as many as in the legend) that one's visual appreciativeness is dulled long before the fleece sparkles into view.' During the autumn of 1961 my father completed another movie that was to introduce him to Hammer Studios and the beginning of a long association with the low budget company. Unfortunately this movie was also a bit of a flop but again my Dad seemed to come out unscathed. *Phantom of the Opera* was directed by Terence Fisher and starred Herbert Lom, Heather Sears, Thorney Walters and Michael Gough. Pat played the cockney Rat Catcher who sounded as if he had a very heavy cold all the time. It was a short but impressive cameo with Edward de Souza who would later become a very close colleague. Patrick recalled in a letter to a fan,

'...been working with Edward de Souza who has that dreadful twinkle in his eye. There are some actors that you know will make you laugh and he is one of them. Had real difficulty with the line about the rats in my bag - 'I could let you have them for tuppence. They'd make a lovely pie' to which Edward replied 'We're vegetarians'. I nearly 'corpsed' every time on that line!'

Dad plays the rat catcher in *The Phantom of the Opera*

The New Year brought more TV. *Sir Francis Drake* was a 30-minute filmed children's drama. It was set in the late 14th century, and told the swashbuckling adventures of the captain of the Golden Hind. The series starred Terence Morgan as Francis Drake, Jean Kent as

Queen Elizabeth I and a young Michael Crawford who would go on to become associated with the musical version of *The Phantom of the Opera* and more. Roger Delgado had a semi-regular role as Count Bernadino de Mendoza, the Spanish Ambassador to the court of Elizabeth. The series was produced by ITC and broadcast on ITV. Patrick played two episodes in quick succession during the spring of 1962. First in an episode called *Doctor Dee* as Gazio and directed by Clive Donner and then in *Drake on Trial* playing the same character.

One of my first real memories of watching Dad on TV was *Sir Francis Drake*. I was aged 7 and I remember being really proud going into school the next day when all my classmates came up to me to ask if that was my Dad on the telly. It was the first taste of having a famous Dad and it felt special.

Dad managed to visit on occasions but I missed him dreadfully. I suppose my brother and sister felt it more than I did because they had known him as a proper father. I had never really known what it was like to have him there all the time so it didn't affect me as much, but I was always very overexcited whenever he announced a visit. One such occasion happened in the summer of 1962 when for some strange reason my mother and sister had decided we were going to have a garden fete. It was in aid of the R.S.P.C.A charity and was quite a big affair all set up in our back garden with mostly friends and relations attending. My Dad had a huge megaphone, which he used with real enthusiasm announcing different stalls and activities throughout the day.

Each of the family had control of a stall and mine was a Hornby railway roulette track. Dad had set it up my train set with varies flags positions at different locations around the oval track. On each flag there was written a prize – mostly small amounts of money. The customers would buy a flag for a couple of pennies and position it where they thought the train would stop. The train would be wound up and released and the winner would be the one whose flag was closest to the train after it had run out of steam.

Dad making an announcement at our fete in 1962,
and my sister showing off her dog training skills to the crowd

During that rather damp summer of 1962 my mother was finding it more and more difficult to manage financially. In order to top up her rather meager maintenance from Pat, she secured a job with Anglia TV as their script reader sifting through the hundreds of manuscripts, ideas and synopsis sent in by the public to the company. I don't know about his second family but his first still struggled to make ends meet even with this extra money coming in. For Patrick, work continued to stream in to his agent and by the autumn he had completed a TV play called *The Sword of Vengeance*, a thriller series entitled *Man of the World*, *Dr. Finley's Case Book* and *Sword of the Web*.

On the 25th November 1962 one of Patrick's most masterful creations, Mr. Quilp was aired for the first time in episode one of *The Old Curiosity Shop*. Director Joan Craft had seen Dad in *The Phantom of the Opera* as The Rat Catcher and had immediately drawn comparisons with the old money lender Quilp. He was cast without even reading and began rehearsals for the BBC drama series at the beginning of November.

On Pat's original *Curiosity* scripts is written Dickens's description of the character and a short collection of ideas as to how he thought the character should be played,

'An elderly man of remarkably hard features and forbidding aspect, and so low in stature as to be quite a dwarf, though his head and face were large enough for the body of a giant. His black eyes were restless, sly, and cunning; his mouth and chin, bristly with the stubble of a coarse hard beard; and his complexion was one of that kind which never looks clean or wholesome. But what added most to the grotesque expression of his face was a ghastly smile, which, appearing to be the mere result of habit and to have no connection with any mirthful or complacent feeling, constantly revealed the few discolored fangs that were yet scattered in his mouth, and gave him the aspect of a panting dog. His dress consisted of a large high-crowned hat, a worn dark suit, a pair of capacious shoes, and a dirty white neckerchief sufficiently limp and crumpled to disclose the greater portion of his wiry throat. Such hair as he had was of a grizzled black, cut short and straight upon his temples, and hanging in a frowzy fringe about his ears. His hands, which were of a rough, coarse grain, were very dirty; his fingernails were crooked, long, and yellow.'

Playing ideas
Hunchback – bend to make myself as small as possible. Almost deformed.
Hair – shoulder length, spiky and greasy. Wig. Grow stubbly beard and 'tache.
Snake-like eyes with rapid movements.
Blackened teeth – bad and decayed. False perhaps… ask Betty.
Face stuck in sickly smile even when discontent.
Fagin like character.'

Dad worked for a long time with Bettie Blattner, the make-up supervisor, getting his facial characteristic just right. The unkempt straw-like wiry wig, the thick and out of control eye brows, the yellow stained and blackened false teeth and the dark stubble growth around his chin and under his nose. I think the thing I remember most was the incredibly awkward position he was able to adopt to convince the viewers he was a dwarf. How he accomplished this feat of contortionism I don't know, but the effect was astonishing.

My sister recalls a school friend approaching her and asking how he lost so much height. Jo replied that he just took dwarf pills from the chemist. The girl went off quite satisfied with the answer!

Patrick later told me that he had really done his back in during the series,

'I had to take on a stoop and then added to that I bent my knees in a sort of crouch. This meant my head was naturally facing the floor. I had to bend it sideways or upwards to be seen or talk to characters. It was bloody uncomfortable and after each rehearsal I felt pretty stiff. I suffered for my art on that one!'

Despite the painful physical demands of the part, it was undoubtedly one of Patrick's favourite roles. The picture of Quilp took pride of place on his toilet wall amongst an assortment of other notable character creations – his 'Rogue's Gallery' as he called it. In later years whenever I visited him I would always linger a while in his loo just admiring the sheer number of different faces on that wall.

'The name is Quilp, sir'—Patrick Troughton as the dwarf

During the first week, the Radio Times boasted,

'In the next three months you will meet a whole gallery of wonderful Dickensian characters. Among those making their first appearance this afternoon are Little Nell herself, played by fifteen year old Michelle Dotrice: Dick Swiveller – Anton Rodgers: Kit Nubbles – Ronald Cunliffe; and the villainous Quilp – Patrick Troughton. Oliver Johnson is cast as the grandfather who, when Nell asks him where he goes on his mysterious nightly outings, replies "The day will come when you are rich."'

This series was undoubtedly the beginning of a long love affair the BBC was to have with Dickens and Joan Craft would be the director most associated with their production. In fact one of my first ever TV roles was as a 'bottleboy' in *David Copperfield* 1972 directed by Joan Craft and starring Arthur Lowe as Mr Micawber. It is a real shame that no known copy of the original 1963 series exists and even photographs are hard to find.

The previous year Dad had played a small part in the popular TV soap opera *Compact*, which told the everyday story of a glossy women's magazine and its staff.

This was not particularly career enhancing but importantly it did introduce him to one of the actresses who would become a very close lifelong friend. Annie Morrish who played Clancy in the series and Patrick hit it off right from the start. Annie had moved over to England from Canada after the breakup of her marriage and forged a very successful career based in London. After Pat's death in 1987, she told me about her friendship with Patrick,

'He was immensely kind to me and supportive too and as I had fairly recently left my husband in Canada I really appreciated it. I was of course, astonished at his family arrangements and was introduced to 'Bunny' fairly early on. Whether she knew that we were lovers or not I don't know. I went to their house in Richmond sometimes when she wasn't there and Pat wanted to show me something he was doing in the garden or making in the house. He talked a lot about all the children and obviously loved you all. How he found time for me and mine I just can't think - as

154

well as working almost non-stop. But he didn't talk about his feelings much though - I think it was a great relief to him that he could talk freely about both families to me. It was ages before I was allowed to meet your mother and Jo and you and David.'

'We were very fond of each other and at one time it might have come to more but I knew he'd always be dashing off to see all the other families and I don't think either of us could have coped with that. I used to get a bit fed up with looking at all the lovely photographs of his camping holidays with family number 2 knowing we would never be able to do the same (and you must have felt the lack of holiday time with him as well.) In 1966 just as he got *Doctor Who* and he was thinking about getting back with Margaret, I got rather involved with someone else down at the Bristol Old Vic and so the affair with Patrick ended. I felt it was time and maybe he did too but you never quite knew what his deepest and difficult feelings were because he was always trying to be so positive and make things 'work'.'

'I did meet wife number 3 but didn't really like her and I felt it was not a happy arrangement though as usual when we occasionally met for coffee or something, he would make it sound as if all was well while I knew underneath he was pretty sad.'

Both families at Swanage during the holiday, 1964,
and Annie's photograph signed for Joanna

Annie had three children, one boy called Nick, and two girls, Sian and Sara who are successful actresses in their own right now. I recall that my family and hers became very close during the early sixties with holiday visits and a number of outings together. Sian Thomas her eldest daughter recalls,

'…coming round for fireworks on November 5th to your place. You and David and Jo were there too - and of course your Dad. I recall feeling very grown up and excited as all of you were that much older than us lot and I felt I'd been allowed in to a new and rather glamourous world! I remember going to Corfe Castle with you. Patrick was amazing - we kids adored him - I don't really know how he managed it given the fact that he had not one but two proper families - but he was always popping in to see us and I'd often come home from school and there he'd be with Mum, both of them looking so sweet and happy… I think we loved him partly because he was such good fun and always ready to play with us or show us how to put up a new tent in the garden or have a game of football or something - but also because we knew how happy he made our mum. We were still a bit dazed and forlorn with moving back over here from Canada and leaving our Dad behind - and Patrick would instantly cheer us up and make us all feel better about life. I remember his warmth always and sense of fun; he turned up in Dorset for a few days when we were staying on holiday near Swanage - maybe it was the same time that we all went Corfe Castle - but he came with us to have lunch one day and this mad Irish waitress recognized Mum from the soap Compact in which she played Clancy, an artist and recognized your Dad (this was pre-*Doctor Who*) but was convinced that he was Anthony Quinn - and wouldn't take no for an answer - and then told the whole cafe that Clancy and Anthony Quinn were over there by the window and we got besieged by mad autograph hunters. I can't remember whether he signed his own name or stayed as Anthony Quinn. It was on 'Compact' that they actually met - he was playing her boyfriend in it - Eddie - I think was his name.

Towards the end of their affair - it lasted quite a long time 3 or 4 years I think- I do remember them having a few quite serious rows, when we were supposed to be in bed asleep, but I could hear them shouting in the other room, one was about religion I seem to remember, but I don't know who was arguing for what!

Anyway it remains a special time in my memory, when Patrick was seeing Mum, he was a bringer of life that's for sure.'

At the end of 1963, I recall returning from my primary school, at about four o'clock, to my Mill Hill home in Uphill Road to be met with the sight of Dad, Mum and Roger Moore having tea together. I was dumbstruck by the occasion and when introduced just murmured a weak 'hello'. To actually have The Saint - Simon Templar - in your kitchen was amazing but to have him shake your hand was crazy! It turns out that Dad had been filming an episode called *Romantic Matron* up at Elstree studios and had invited Roger back for a cup of tea during a break in filming. He stayed for around an hour I remember and I was reluctantly persuaded to show him my railway set that he thoroughly enjoyed playing with.

On another occasion early the following year I spent a day watching rehearsals of the police soap drama *Z-Cars*. I met James Ellis who played P.C. Burt Lynch, Colin Welland who played P.C. Graham and a rather frightening Stratford Johns who played the tough Detective Chief Inspector. In those days they recorded the show in a very primitive way, which consisted of a film camera photographing the television monitor feed from the studio floor. My Dad always said,

Thank goodness that live TV had finally come to an end by the mid-sixties. I don't think my nerves could have stood anymore.'

The second Hammer production followed this TV work and saw my father take on a rather different role to the Rat Catcher in *The Phantom of the Opera*. Inspector Kanof, Chief of police, was a much neater and controlled character. My father sported a Poirot-type moustache and had cut his hair short for the part. *The Gorgon* was set in the German village of Vandorf at the beginning of the 20th century. A number of foul murders had been committed over a period of five years and the victims all had one thing in common –

they had been petrified into a stone figure. Rather than my father's character admitting to the truth of a local legend where a snake-haired Gorgon was to supposed to turn victims to stone during the full moon, he dismisses the idea with terrible consequences.

The film was not a great success even though Peter Cushing and Christopher Lee headed the cast.

Pat in *The Gorgon*

Original photographs from the stars of *Z-Cars* given to me at the studio

The next few years continued to bring Patrick plenty of work, including a film called *The Black Torment*, TV work including *The Third Man, Detective, The Midnight Men, Crane,* another *Dr Finlay's Casebook, Artist Notebook, HMS Paradise,* and *No Hiding Place* with Raymond Francis. In 1964 Pat worked with Margaret Tyzack in a series entitled *The Indian Tales of Rudyard Kipling.* In the episode *The Bronckhorst Divorce Case* my Dad played Bronckhorst, a thoroughly unpleasant man who treats his wife very badly. He decides that he wants to divorce her and falsely accuses a close friend Biel of being her lover. Strickland a friend of Biel's disguises himself as an Indian and discovers exactly what has been going on, and frightens the 'witnesses' into withdrawing their stories. The case collapses, Biel horse-whips Bronckhorst, Strickland acquires a splendid new horse, and Bronckhorst's wife takes him back.

Some of the scenes of this drama must have been fairly violent for TV and I am unsure how much of it was screened. My father notes in his diary the violent manner of the character he is about to play,

'Bronckhorst was not nice in any way. He had no respect for the pretty public and private lies that make life a little less nasty than it is. His manner towards his wife was coarse. There are many things including actual assault with the clenched fist that a wife will endure; but seldom a wife can bear as Mrs. Bronckhorst bore with a long course of brutal, hard chaff, making light of her weaknesses, her headaches, her small fits of gaiety, her dresses, her queer little attempts to make herself attractive to her husband when she knows that she is not what she has been, and worst of all the love that she spends on her children.'

A further entry notes,

'Biel came out of the Court, and Strickland dropped a gut trainer's-whip in the veranda. Ten minutes later, Biel was cutting Bronckhorst into ribbons behind the old Court cells, quietly and without scandal. What was left of Bronckhorst was sent home in a carriage; and his wife wept over it and nursed it into a man again.'

159

I could find no record of how this part was received by the viewing public and press but it does seem a very brave character to have taken on and performed in rather different times than today. A final note taken from the short story is copied into my father's diary which is clearly meant as a reminder to himself about this foul man,

'In the daytime, when she moved about me,
In the night, when she was sleeping at my side,
I was wearied; I was wearied of her presence.
Day by day and night by night I grew to hate her
Would to God that she or I had died!'

Patrick and Margaret Tyzack in *The Bronckhorst Divorce Case*

By the summer of 1965, Dad was earning enough to start taking summer holidays in France with his second family. His son Mark fondly recalls those vacations spent together,

'One of my earliest memories of Dad is on holiday in Norfolk at Bacton 1965, not too far from where he was stationed off the coast in the war years on motor launches. I recall a black and white photo of us out for a sunny walk - Dad must have been in his 40s, strong, healthy and always cheerful. He never talked about the war years to me. We were too young to ask and when we were older he'd already left home by the time I was 16. But I found out later through an article written by Michael, 'What Doctor Who did in the War' that he had distinguished himself on a particular night when they were told to go and search for an American Airman who had ditched in the North Sea. It was a stormy night with very poor visibility, but Dad never gave up until he found the man. There was also the day when they struck a German mine which blew a hole in the side of the boat. Thankfully, Dad was on the other side of the not too large motor launch.

But nothing compared with the South of France where we would go every year camping once we (Jane, Peter and me) were in our secondary school years. Dad and mum loved camping and were proud of the 'Tentomatic', which assembled while still on the roof rack in a matter of minutes; you then drove the car away and brailed down the canvas. Easy-peasy. Useful for those rainy Nord Pas de Calais camping sites. But the piece de resistance was the Cote d'Azur and Cagnes-sur-Mer. We'd spend two glorious weeks there, lazing on the beach, enjoying ordering ice-cream in French and then having the treat of our lives - a meal out in a restaurant in Vieux Cagnes where the menu reached the dizzy heights of 13 (old) francs a head! Don't ask me how much that was, but suffice to say it was as cheap as frites but seemed like a king's ransom then. My love of France and French started on those holidays as is partly responsible for my becoming a Modern Languages teacher and for my family spending 9 years in Switzerland working in a French-speaking Baptist Church in Martigny. Dad's French was passable, Mum's better. He never tired of sending up his own ignorance and often said of the arrogant that they had ideas au-dessus de leur gare ('above their station?' Groan!). I blame him for my dreadful habit of saying "Ton Oncle, c'est Robert!"

Only once was the summer holiday interrupted, when we were in Italy on Lake Idro near Como; Dad had to – shock-horror- work in the holidays - some episode of some BBC series called *The Six Wives of Henry*. He dutifully came back once it had been 'canned' and we continued our wonderful foreign escapade. My own family still tries to get over the channel each year.'

I was rather jealous of the other family and their holidays at the time. I know we were able to go to Cornwall every year but abroad seemed so much more exotic. I only ever spent a few holidays with dad, the last when I was in my twenties. He had bought a cabin on the Norfolk Broads and we spent time together fishing and sailing his dingy. I asked him then, why had he left us, why had he gone off to start a new family? He replied,

'I needed change. Things have to change all the time for me I'm afraid, that's the way I am made. I am sorry if I hurt you.'

It was a simple answer.

Patrick in *Sword of Vengeance* 1962

Chapter 7
An Astonishing and Preposterous Proposal

The BBC's decision to cast my father as Doctor Who in 1966 was both prudent and risky at the same time. The corporation obviously felt very secure offering the part to such an experienced actor, especially one who was so comfortable with the relatively young medium of TV. After all, he must have been one of the first actors to make a good living exclusively from television drama. In fact, if his agent ever suggested a theatre role he would always retort the well-worn phrase, *'God... I don't want to do all that shouting in the evening!'* However, I have always thought that the risk of casting someone so different to William Hartnell showed great faith on behalf of Sydney Newman (Head of Drama), Shaun Sutton (Head of Serials) and Innes Lloyd (Series producer). Sutton was later to confirm this absolute commitment to Pat during an interview he did in 1992.

'The producer and I were absolutely determined to have Patrick Troughton, because we knew Patrick Troughton and I had actually been a drama student with Patrick Troughton many years ago, before the war. And even back then, Patrick had those deep lines on his face, he had the look of a thousand-year-old leprechaun, and I remember saying to him once, before the war, 'Pat, you have the secret of eternal age', and I thought that was a very good quality for *Doctor Who*.

'Anyway, we both knew he was a good actor, I'd done many television plays with him, and I wanted him, I thought he had a magical quality about him, a wizard quality, and so did Innes Lloyd. Any good actor, like Patrick Troughton, can go and get work anywhere. And the fear with a part like Doctor Who is that you'll not only get typed as that part, you simply won't get work anywhere because people will say "Oh, no, everyone will think of him as Doctor Who", so we did have to persuade him...'

Spring 1966 was a troubled and turbulent time in Pat's private life. He had just begun a tentative reconciliation with my mother Margaret who he had been separated from for almost ten years, but never divorced. Home life with his partner 'Bunny' was proving difficult and strained because she had become very close to a writer friend of theirs.

Pat confided in Margaret, seeking advice on what he should do - after all he had a very young vulnerable second family and was experiencing exactly what my mother had endured when he left us. He must have been guilt ridden through and through to have the same situation repeating itself. It is odd that my mother should have been so understanding, but I think she never really stopped loving him and as a consequence never found another soul mate to replace him.

Obviously during this period they must have begun to get closer together. I remember how his regular weekly visits became longer and more frequent. My sister recalls coming home from Hornsey Art College early one afternoon during that spring to find them both hurriedly coming down stairs from my mother's bedroom, looking flushed, flustered and a bit embarrassed. Later that week we were told by both of them in a rather uncomfortable and formal way, that they were going to get back together again and we were to become a family once more.

My brother remembers how happy he felt at the prospect of regaining a father. We were all going to move to a house on the banks of the Black Water estuary in Essex. Dad had promised David a canoe and I was going to learn how to sail. I can't remember what he promised my sister but her reaction was to tell my mother that if he came home she was going to move out and live with a student friend of hers. I think Joanna was very suspicious of the reconciliation and did not really forgive my father for walking out on her at the age of nine.

In late spring of 1966 my father sort of moved back to Mill Hill and even invested in some central heating and decorations for our by now very damp, cold and crumbling house. This was a strange feeling for me because I had never experienced what having a father was like. I found it very odd and a bit claustrophobic to see Dad every time I got back from school. I had been used to seeing him once a week for a couple of hours in the evening before he would hurriedly disappear back to south London and his other family. I even felt a little jealous that my mother was being taken away from me. After all she was my only security apart from my big brother and sister.

By early summer, Pat had been offered the part of an Iceni warrior named Tristam, in a B movie Hammer production called *The Viking Queen*. So in the first week of July, Pat and my mother packed their bags and went to Ireland for two weeks filming and - as he put it 'to rekindle their relationship'. My mother was so happy. I remember how she looked as my sister and I waved them goodbye at Mill Hill station. She seemed so relaxed - relieved and content. Radiant in a blue spotted dress and thick cherry red lipstick.

My father had rented a beautiful flat in an elegant Regency terrace overlooking Dublin bay. Filming took place in the Wicklow mountains, surrounding countryside and interiors were completed at Ardmore Studios in Bray. When my father wasn't needed on location he took my mother on a lightening tour of the Irish coast, staying in local pubs and getting as far south as Skibbereen.

Hammer was better known for its horror movies, but this film was a departure from the usual kind of gore and a rather unsuccessful experiment in pseudo-historical drama. I remember Dad saying that the script had little resemblance to history, as we know it, but was just a bit of fun fantasy.

Set in Roman-occupied Britain, it stared Carita as Salina, a very large-breasted Finnish Raquel Welch look-alike, who became head of the Iceni tribe of Celts after the death of her father, King Priam. His dying wish was for Queen Salina to rule the Iceni jointly with a Roman general, Justinian, played by Don Murray.

On her last day, Tuesday 12th July 1966 my mother joined Pat on location at Loch Tay, near Glendalough in the Wicklow National Park. She watched a scene in which my father rather nervously took control of a chariot pulled by a very lively horse. The more dangerous shots were completed by his stunt double Eddie Evans. They were filming a day-for-night sequence that involved a column on route to Anglesey. My mother recalls that the day was filled with screaming scantily dressed woman, blood spurting battles and charging chariots.

It is against this background that Patrick was first contacted about playing Doctor Who. On their last night they had decided to stay at the location hotel Montrose near Bray with fellow actors Donald Houston, Nicola Pagett, Sean Caffrey, Wilfred Lawson and Don Chaffey the director. When they arrived at the hotel that evening there was a message waiting at reception to contact his agent Maurice. He was told to wait for a phone call from Shaun Sutton, Head of Serials at the BBC who wanted to talk to him about a casting for a major TV series. My mother Margaret recalls that Pat immediately thought it was a practical joke and that he wasn't even going to bother staying in the hotel to take the call. Dad enjoyed practical jokes – very often on set at the expense of his colleagues, so was always suspicious of unexpected offers.

169

My mother managed to persuade him to stay and they both sat down in the hotel bar to wait. Even when Shaun called ten minutes later and a message went out for Dad to go to reception, he still was reluctant insisting that it was probably just a wind up.

He returned to the bar with the news he had just had the strangest offer from Shaun and Newman – to take over from Billy Hartnell as Doctor Who.

'Quite preposterous', was Pat's comment. *'Quickest way to make it die a death! casting me in the part. They must be mad. They must be absolutely stark raving mad!'*

They both laugh it off, and thought nothing more about it.

My mother returned to England the following morning in order that she could take us on our regular holiday to Cornwall. Every year we would have a fantastic summer break in St. Ives Bay with our very close friends the Taylors. I recall sitting with my nose pressed up against the cold carriage window of the Cornish Riviera train watching the city melt into countryside and being told about Dad's offer of *Doctor Who*. But my mother told me not to get too excited as my father felt 'he was the wrong type for the part' and that 'they must be mad to consider such a young actor for the role'. I remember feeling incredibly disappointed.

As each day past during that week, Shaun kept phoning Pat's agent with better and better financial offers until on the Friday just before he was to return to England he finally agreed to meet up with Newman, Lloyd and Sutton in London.

The night before he went to that meeting at Television Centre my father called us in Cornwall. The cottage where we were staying had no phone so my mother had to wait outside the village telephone box politely asking any locals not to use the phone until she had taken her call. Opinion in the cottage was divided as to whether he should take the part. Those against including my brother David and my sister Jo who felt it was the wrong career move. They thought he would be forever labelled and not taken seriously as an actor again. At that time he had just received brilliant reviews for his highly revered television reincarnation of Paul of Tarsus.

It is clear his worries must have centred round the undeniable fear he felt of being typecast. He had worked very hard during the 1950's and early 60's to establish himself as a highly respected and successful TV character actor. He felt that accepting a role like Doctor Who would almost definitely destroy this reputation and everything he had set out to do. He revelled in the freedom of being able to create such individual and different characterizations each time he was offered a TV role. This could all be taken away from him as the public and profession labelled him Doctor Who 2. He seemed so set in a decision to turn the role down that night.

I can only guess at what changed his mind – the thought that the series would only last six weeks or the financial package and security that the BBC offered. Certainly educating me at an independent school in Harrow was quite expensive and I believe all his other children were being educated privately. Perhaps he was considering the financial burden that breaking up with Bunny was going have on his pocket. Or more likely he wanted the huge exhilarating challenge it presented, the buzz of being able to test his acting ability – a life changing experience that he just could not turn away from.

In one of the rare interviews he did later Dad told us,

'They kept on offering more pennies for it. So I'd got a young family and I thought I don't know… I could get them educated on this. And in the end after about a week … I sort of kept it going for a bit… I thought now I could educate the kids. I thought I'd do the part. And that's why I really took it.'

On August 2nd, Bill Hartnell's imminent departure was announced to the press. That same day, Patrick signed a contract to appear in twenty-two episodes as the new Doctor, covering five serials. I remember the expression on his face when he arrived at our house soon after that meeting with Newman and Lloyd. A grin from ear to ear – like a cat that had not only got the cream but bought shares in it as well! However, with this enthusiasm came a stark reality of what had actually happened to him. He was about to

171

become a very well-known personality – someone who could not step outside his front door without being recognized.

Even before he had seen a script, my father began to agonize over how to portray the new time traveler. Billy Hartnell had been such a success during his stint that Dad thought the public would be unlikely to stay with the series longer than six weeks if a new Doctor appeared as a simple copy of the amiable white haired professor.

During the ensuing weeks, Pat found the process of creating character ideas contradictory and frustrating. A number of wildly varying characterizations formed from personal rehearsal sessions at home including appearing as the Victorian Prime Minister Gladstone complete with mutton-chop side burns, a mad scientist with spiky black hair and a ridiculously high voice, and a turban headed character out of the *Arabian Nights*.

He confided in my brother David and I, wanting to know what we thought of his ideas and if we could suggest anything else. He showed us a number of sketches completed in a black A4 sized notebook with annotated scribbles. One was a picture of a Mississippi paddle steam captain who wore a dark uniform and naval cap. I think it was supposed to look like a character that W. C. Fields had once played in a movie. Another was a pirate with an eye-patch similar to the part he had played in the Disney film version of *Treasure Island*. On the last page was a tramp with tattered clothes and a tall felt hat, pushing an old pram full of his belongings and playing an old tin whistle. I remember David asking him why so many of his ideas involved such elaborate disguises to which he replied, 'I don't want anyone to know who is playing Who!'

Still full of uncertainty Patrick attended a preliminary costume session at Burnham and Nathans in London. As he explained in a later interview,

'We went to Berman's, I think it was Berman's, and we looked through all the old rubbish, really. We just got things out of hampers and had a look.'

The series producer Innes Lloyd and Sandra Reid the costume designer who had been charged with the task of engineering the look of the Second Doctor, helped select a number of outfits that day. They spent the afternoon trying to rank them in order of preference. I think the final list included, Mississippi captain, Harpo Marx, a tramp, Sherlock Holmes, a pirate and an *Arabian Nights* character - but not necessarily in that order. Innes Lloyd preferred the tramp outfit that was a sort of ragged imitation of Billy Hartnell but a bit more way out. I think Sandra Reid encouraged Dad to choose the Harpo Marx outfit but Innes said it was too over the top. My dad's choice was the costume that gave him the best disguise from the public,

'Well, I thought we had to do something a bit different. My original idea was to black up and wear a big turban and brass earrings and a big grey beard and do it like the Arabian Knights. I thought that would be a wonderful idea, but when I'd finished, I could shave off, take the black off, take the turban off and nobody would know who I was and I wouldn't be typecast. But they didn't think that was a very good idea.'

The following week my father met up with Innes Lloyd and Shaun Sutton in a small dressing room in Green Area basement, BBC Television Centre. They had arranged a small costume parade for Sydney Newman who had asked to see the progress that was being made on Dad's version of Doctor Who and to give Pat the first draft of the script.

My father had decided to try on the W.C. Fields inspired Mississippi captain style costume first. Newman arrived and took one look – *'you could tell he hated it. In fact I thought I was going to be sacked on the spot!'* Sydney Newman did hate it and took Shaun off for a talk that took them all the way round the whole circle of TV Centre and back to the dressing room. Shaun Sutton described the moment vividly in an interview filmed by Reeltime Pictures production,

'Of course, we had to sell him to Sydney Newman, so we prepared a sort of parade, as it were, and we were down in the dressing room in the basement of Television Centre. And he was dressed in his first costume, which for some reason was the captain of an American Mississippi showboat. I don't know why that was

173

his costume. And we called Sydney down, Sydney took one look and said 'Shaun, let's take a walk', and I said to Innes 'Out of the costume'.

Dad didn't know what they had said during that 'long walk' but Shaun revealed in the same interview that Newman had been less than impressed with the look and he had been having second thoughts about the casting.

'And Sydney and I walked around the entire basement of Television Centre, and believe you me that is a long way when you're getting your fortune told by Sydney Newman. By the time we got back, Innes had Patrick in the costume he would eventually wear for *Doctor Who*, that funny little suit and odd tie and the hat and the penny whistle. And I think it was here that Sydney actually proved himself to be a great boss, because he looked and he said 'I still don't see it, but if you and Innes say it's okay, okay, go ahead' and he stamped out and on the way he said 'You'd better be good!'

During that 'long walk' Shaun had taken with Newman, Innes Lloyd had persuaded my father that he should not get dressed in the Arabian Nights outfit as this might confuse Newman who was so used to the Billy Hartnell's look. They had argued about this but finally he had gone with Innes Lloyd's first choice that he had made at Burman and Nathans, the rather disheveled tramp.

An initial read through of the first script idea with a working title *The Destiny of Doctor Who* took place in an office at Television Centre with Innes Lloyd, Shaun Sutton, Gerry Davis and others. By all accounts it was a chaotic and heated occasion with everyone present putting in his or her own ideas of how the new Doctor should look and act. As the morning went on Pat could sense that if he did not act quickly to take control of the situation his opinions on the character were going to be ignored and marginalized.

The first story was to have the new doctor pitted against his old enemy and public favourite – the Daleks. My father knew that Innes Lloyd was still concerned about the way an audience would react to a change of lead actor and agreed with him that a popular monster such as the Daleks would provide security during this change over.

The problem was that the draft script had been written with Billy Hartnell in mind and obviously the new Doctor Who image that my father was trying to created did not fit the same remit. My father complained it was meant for,

'…a very long winded and complicated autocratic Sherlock Holmes type who never stopped talking. Well that was no good to me!'

In fact, much to my father's annoyance, a profile of the new Doctor had already been circulated to a number of BBC staff by the production office. It outlined a rather different character to the one my father was trying to develop,

'**Appearance** – Facially as strong, eyes of the explorer or Sea Captain. His hair is wild and his clothes look rather the worse for wear (this is a legacy from the metaphysical change which took place in the TARDIS.) Obviously spares very little time and bother on his appearance. In the first serial, he wears a flyblown version of the clothes associated with his character.

Manner – Vital and forceful – his actions are controlled by his superior intellect and experience. Whereas at times he is a positive man of action, at other times he deals with the situation like a skilled chess player, reasoning and cunningly planning his moves. He has humour and wit and also an overwhelmingly thunderous rage which frightens his companions and others.'

'A feature of the new doctor will be the humour on the lines of sardonic humour of Sherlock Holmes. He enjoys disconcerting his companions with unconventional and unexpected repartee.'

'After the first serial – Daleks- (when the character has been established) we will enjoy a love of disguise which will help and sometimes disconcert his companions. To keep faith with the essential doctor character, he is always suspicious of new places, things or other people – he is the eternal fugitive with a horrifying fear of the past horrors he has endured, horrors were experience during the galactic war and account for his flight from his own planet.'

'The metaphysical change which takes place over 500 or so years is a horrifying experience - an experience in which he relives some of the most un-endurable moments of his long life, including the galactic war. It is as if he has had the L.S.D. drug and instead of experiencing the kicks, he has the hell and dank horror which can be its effect.'

Dad said he didn't see the part like this at all. He saw it as a listener. Sydney Newman came in at this point to see how things were progressing and Pat basically said he wasn't happy with the way the script had been adapted from Bill's era. After a long discussion Sydney suggested that what Pat was getting at was that the Doctor wasn't an intellectual type – more of an eccentric child-like character that would listen to people and act upon what they had said. He also concluded that the tramp outfit my father had been wearing the day of the costume parade would be a perfect expression of this character. Pat knew from this point on he had Sydney Newman on board and from that moment was able to feel a little more secure about what he was doing.

Gerry Davis and Pat continued to thrash out this new idea after everyone else had left the meeting. As Davis later confessed,

'I ejected everyone else from the meeting and just Patrick and I worked out the character. Really it came out of Troughton's own personality.'

Davis was inspired by Pat's approach and encouraged as many aspects as possible that would contrast the positive and dogmatic character of Hartnell. He took these ideas to David Whitaker who began to draft a fresh set of scripts with the new version of the Doctor. In preparing his storylines, David Whitaker consulted with Terry Nation (the creator of the Daleks) as to how they might best be utilised. Whitaker submitted draft scripts to Gerry Davis, the

177

story editor, in late September, around which time the title became *The Power of the Daleks.*

My father read the scripts and liked the initial draft. Episode one included ideas that showed the Doctor had been renewed several times, was 750 years old and had vivid memories of the destruction of his home planet by the Daleks. During the transformation scene, the Doctor would refer vaguely to relics from his previous incarnations, including an earring and a metal bracelet and to his granddaughter. However my father still thought, 'the character was saying too much.' He insisted to Gerry Davis that he wanted to be a re-actor. Someone who watched listened and then acted upon the situation. Davis later described how he responded to my father's request,

'I thought it would be very interesting to have a character who never quite says what he means, who, really, uses the intelligence of the people he is with. He knows the answer all the time; if he suggests something he knows the outcome. He is watching, he's really directing, but he doesn't want to show he's directing like the old Doctor'.

The pressure on my father to come up with a new Doctor must have been extremely high. One newspaper clipping my mother has kept reported,

'William Hartnell as Doctor Who was very human and warmly appealing. With him lay the series peculiar character. The new Doctor Who is Patrick Troughton and with the change the very substance of the series lies in the melting pot.'

Filming for *The Power of the Daleks* at the Ealing Television Film Studios began on 26th September 1966 without the final version of the script complete. Luckily, my father was not involved in this material that was mainly concerned with scenes set in the Dalek capsule. When Whitaker did submit his new scripts Newman met with my father and they both agreed that they were still unhappy with the portrayal of the Doctor, and requested further rewrites. However, Whitaker was now unable to fulfill their request due to other commitments. Dennis Spooner, later to become *Doctor Who*'s story editor, was brought in to finish the job of paring down the overly long drafts to satisfy both Newman and my father.

On the 8th October 1966 my father began telerecording his transformation scene at the Riverside Studio 1, Hammersmith, London. Director, Derek Martinus knew although the sequence was just a simple mix from one face to another, it was going to be critical that both actors remained very still for an agonizingly long time. My father later told me that he came away from that days recording with a frozen face,

'I felt as if someone had injected local anesthetic into both my cheeks!'

Derek Martinus remembered the day well,

'Doing the regeneration was interesting, we were trying to get a slow transformation, which wasn't really possible with roll back and mix. We were trying out new techniques using inlay and overlay. I can picture now the gasp of joy as that changeover actually worked – it was most important because it had to be good for the future of the show's sake, which was far from certain then.'

I worked on a TV play during the 80s with the vision mixer Shirley Coward who had recorded the sequence that day. She recalls that both Bill and Pat had to be very patient with the floor that day. They had both 'spent hours being told to stay perfectly still as we tweaked and re-angled shots.' Shirley had discovered an excellent use for a faulty fader unit in Studio 1 that day. It turned out that whenever she tried to cross fade the shot from Bill to Pat they managed to get a flared and broken image on the screen – just right for the transformation. 'It may have taken two or three takes only, but hours to set up each'. It is odd to think that the transformation sequence of *Doctor Who* was due to a faulty fader rather than any technical wizardry on behalf of the special effects department.

By the end of that weekend the scripts for *The Power of the Daleks* were still not completed and my father received a phone call to say that rehearsals for the first episode were to be put back a week to 17th October. Dad had mixed feelings – on the one hand he was delighted about being paid a retainer fee for not working that week but on the other he was very worried about the lack of script to work on and the length of time he would have to study.

In fact, that week off work turned out to be far more stressful for my father than he had ever thought. Around this time 'Bunny' his partner and mother of his second family had ended a relationship with her close writer friend. The day after my mother Margaret had returned from Ireland, Pat had invited Bunny out to stay for a week. She had discussed the possibility of getting back together again and resolving their differences. This must have been a gut wrenching decision to have thrust upon him during an already anxious time in his life. After all he had promised so much to my mother and family during the summer. However the decision was made to forgive Bunny and to return to the bungalow in Kew. He had done this by the end of the weekend. My mother was devastated at the news but I don't think this took her by surprise. She knew my father too well. All my sister would say was, 'I told you so.'

Monday morning, 17th October 1966 saw my emotionally drained father traveling not from Mill Hill to the rehearsal rooms just off Shepherd's Bush but from Kew. He had now skimmed through the final draft of episode one by Dennis Spooner who had managed to reduce Whitaker's word heavy original down to eight scenes. The post transformation scene in the TARDIS had been lengthened and now took up a quarter of the episode. Pat and Newman had insisted that the new Doctor's appearance should make sense and feel plausible before launching off into fresh adventures.

Dad explained later that he had real difficulty working on the vital explanation of regenerating the Doctor. It seems that Pat and Spooner changed a chunk of the original scripted dialogue during those first few tentative steps in rehearsal. The outcome however was a much slicker scene that seemed to flow with real truth and credibility. Just a few poignant lines replaced the overly complicated and clumsy scripted explanation of why Doctor Who had changed faces.

BEN : Now look, the Doctor always wore this. So if you're him, it should fit now, shouldn't it? (Ben grabs the Doctor's hand, and slips the ring on. However, the ring is far too big for the Doctor's finger.)
BEN : There - that settles it.
DOCTOR : I'd like to see a butterfly fit into a chrysalis case after its spread its wings.
POLLY : Then you did change!
DOCTOR : Life depends on change - and renewal.
BEN : (sarcastically) Oh so that's it, you've been renewed have ya?
DOCTOR : (taking Ben's remark seriously) I've been renewed have I? That's it, I've been renewed! It's part of the TARDIS - without it, I couldn't survive. (The Doctor rushes back to the storage chest, and begins to search through the vast array of items.)
DOCTOR : Come here! (softly) Come here. The Doctor kept a diary, didn't he?
POLLY : Yes.
DOCTOR : I thought so. I wonder where. I wonder where.

The chrysalis analogy probably came from a genuine knowledge and love of butterflies. He used to collect them as a boy when it was a legal pastime! My mother tells me he had a huge net and scores of jars to keep the many specimens he managed to capture. I have this vivid memory of him lounging on a deckchair in our garden during the summer stripped to the waist tanning himself in the afternoon sun and bellowing out the names of species that fluttered around our huge Buddleia bush.

Although I am unsure how much of that first scene was influenced by my father, I like to think that the 'Life depends on renewal' section was his idea. Michael Craze, who played Ben, described how my father struggled with those early rehearsals at Shepherd's Bush,

'I remember him struggling to start with, with the character, because in the very beginning he had this imagined character of the cosmic hobo and he was struggling to find the level for it. When he started, he had the big tall hat and the whistle, and I could see him working within himself to see how far he could go, and how far his mannerisms… internally I could see him working at it, which was the mark of a very good actor, the Stanislavski thing of working the character out. And he was doing this in rehearsals. Once he got over the initial trauma of creating the character, I think he settled in very well.'

The director Chris Barry had worked with my father before on the series *Smuggler's Bay* in 1964 and had been an admirer of his work for a long time. He had been very enthusiastic about the choice of actor for the role and in a later interview described that early rehearsal period,

'For *The Power of the Daleks,* we discussed a lot of different approaches that Patrick Troughton could have taken in rehearsal. He ended up doing it totally different from the first ideas, and of course totally different from William Hartnell's portrayal. He couldn't have done an imitation of Hartnell because as those dreadful Peter Cushing movies had shown, there was just no substitute for the real thing. Patrick was truly wonderful to work with on that first one – and it could have been a very difficult time for the show. I must admit I was surprised that it had gone on after Hartnell's departure, but that's television for you.'

On Friday 21st October at 10.00 am they commenced a technical run in the rehearsal room with all the technicians and crew from the studio followed quickly by a producer's run-through with Sydney Newman present. In order to release the tension of that occasion Michael Craze and Anneke Wills had arranged that everyone present should be wearing t-shirts with the slogan, 'Come back Bill Hartnell, all is forgiven.'

My father always told me he never forgot what a marvellous release of tension that was, to see everyone's smiling laughing faces and to know that they were all on his side rooting for a successful first episode.

'I felt so at home with both of them after that – they completely understood the situation that day and how much pressure I was under to deliver the goods, especially with Sydney's powerful presence.'

However, in later years he revealed to me that the infamous t-shirt story wasn't strictly accurate. He had gone along with all the publicity around the incident at the time and had been, *'a little economical with the truth'*. The fact was he had been very upset by the joke that had actually happened while preparing to record the first episode of *The Highlanders*. Michael and Anneke had hidden in the TARDIS at the end of a dress rehearsal and appeared suddenly in front of him and the crew wearing the t-shirts that had been made and bought in Soho. My Dad told me that he laughed along with the others but underneath took that slogan as hint from his two companions that they weren't happy with his new character. He told me,

'Deep down I was a bit upset. I hurried off to my dressing room, closed the door and went into a bit of a selfish sulk. I think Michael and Anneke had realized what was going on and arrived in my dressing room after the recording looking rather sheepish carrying three glasses and a bottle of Teachers. I told them I was just being too sensitive and to ignore me. They seemed very concerned that the practical joke had backfired. Serves me right. I just got a bit of my own medicine and felt what it was like to be on the receiving end.'

The following day, 22nd Oct 1966, my father arrived early in the morning at Riverside Studio R1 and got his first real look at the interior of the TARDIS. He remembered that moment well,

'I just stood by myself in the dimly lit studio playing with the TARDIS control leavers thinking about all that had happened to me in the past few weeks and wondering how long the series would last.'

There were five sets for episode one of *The Power of the Daleks* constructed on the spacious 6000 square feet of grey smooth camera-friendly floor. Lesterson's laboratory containing the intimidating space capsule that opened out through a metal sliding door into a further interior set containing the two Daleks.

There was a stretch of short corridor, some small guest quarters and the bleak rock strewn surface of the planet. The exterior of Vulcan spread out across almost a quarter of the space complete with rock cliff edge that was used to frame some of the camera shots. Styrofoam boulders were strewn randomly around the vapour spewing mercury swamp that had been constructed from a garden fishpond liner. This would be filled with dry ice to create a mysterious mist-covered surface. The Police Box sat rather precariously right on the edge of the swamp. Dad's original copy of episode one reads,

'The TARDIS has landed in a rough, mist-covered landscape. The ground is littered with rock formations and small bubbling pools of liquid. At regular intervals, a small spray of liquid is emitted from one of the pools, causing the rocks to be covered by a small silver filament.'

Underneath this description my father had scribbled a note – *'watch out, don't slip over or crawl below level of mist. Can suffocate!'*

The whole morning and most of the afternoon was taken up with blocking camera shots and rehearsing the technical aspects of the episode. Camera and boom positions were worked out by Chris Barry (director) for each scene so that the cables did not have to cross each other when moving between sets and get tangled up. Lens choices were plotted and noted by the vision mixer in the control room. In 1966 the black and white cameras were equipped with a turret of fixed lenses that were changed from one to the other by pressing a switch or, on earlier models, by turning a handle. This studio probably had four pedestal cameras and a two man operated mole crane camera. Manoevring such unwieldy machines between sets called for an almost military plan of operation. My father described it as *'like watching a herd of elephants doing Swan Lake.'* Studio drama at that time was recorded in sequence without breaks between scenes as if it were live, in order to reduce the cost of the very expensive recording time. Shaun Sutton described vividly what a TV actor had to endure during such technical rehearsals and underlines why he and Innes Lloyd had cast such an experienced TV actor as my father,

'The inexperienced television actor, thrust overnight into the hubbub of his first studio, might feel some dismay that the director who has been so sympathetic in rehearsals has now abandoned him. Now the attention has moved to the cameramen peering into their viewfinders, the sound operators swinging their booms over the actor's heads and occasionally making contact; the electricians staring discontentedly up at lamps; with property men hanging last minute curtains. The actor might feel his importance to the play, so evident in rehearsal, is now secondary to the costume designer darting into the set to tweak a collar, or the beautiful make-up girl peering impersonally at his wig. The scenes, so flowing in rehearsal, now limp through, constantly interrupted to accommodate the director's visual dreams. When the moment finally comes to run the scene, the actor's sonorous tones are drowned out by a band of carpenters correcting the wobble on a banister rail. His friendly director is largely invisible, glimpsed briefly as he flits down from the control gallery to set up a shot, or discuss an obstinate shadow on a leading lady's face. He is clearly too busy to spare the actor more than an abstracted glance before darting back to more important things in the gallery. This abrupt shift in concentration is inevitable. It is therefore essential that the actor enters the studio with his performance so solid, that nothing can chip its quality.'

By 6.00 pm the studio was gearing up to record the first ever episode of Pat's Doctor Who. Most of the cast and crew would have been on supper break but my father sat alone in his dressing room. He told me he would never eat before a show. He had this theory that all the blood needed to keep the brain working well would be diverted to your stomach for digestion. I don't know how scientifically accurate that is but I have always followed his advice. It does make a difference. You feel clearer in the head and able to concentrate much better.

Even at this late stage everyone apart from Pat was unsure about his makeup and hair. He had already convinced Gillian James during rehearsal (makeup designer) that he should be wearing a Harpo Marx type wig, which she had duly supplied.

'It was a wonderful mass of wild black curls that cascaded down… a bit like wearing a massive mop head on your bonce. I thought it was just the job. It fitted the rather eccentric tramp like character that I had created and would allow me to hide my identity enough so perhaps people wouldn't know who was playing the new Who!'

It was left to Anneke and Michael to convince him otherwise. As he was having it fitted in the makeup room beneath R1 control room, Anneke took one look at him and said she wasn't acting with that! My father used to tell me this story over and over again uncontrollably barking with laughter,

'They were responsible for that absurd Beatle cut… just before we went on I got down to makeup and I'd had a lovely wig fitted which had loads of mad thick curls. I put it on and took a look in the mirror and I thought that looks lovely. They both stared straight at me and said, you look just like Harpo Marx and we are not going on with you if you wear that wig. I said don't be ridiculous but they insisted! So Gillian took it off and started hastily 'doing things' with my hair. This was about five minutes before transmission. The next time I looked in the mirror I saw a Beatle! I looked like Ringo Starr! But it was too late to do anything about it. I was stuck with it and I stayed the same through the whole series.'

How much of this version of the story is accurate is subject to debate. Innes Lloyd suggested to me that the decision to cut the wig was actually a production judgment from the control box and that Anneke and Michael had merely been the messengers of that news. However, Pat would not lose the stove hat for his first appearance even though they hated it as much as the wig! 'I hung on to that hat to hide my horrible hair!'

Michael explained how he teased Pat about it until he finally gave in after the first couple of stories had been completed.

'Anneke and I used to tease him, and say "Oh take that bloody hat off, for God's sake." Once he got over the initial trauma of creating the character, I think he settled in very well.'

The transmission light above the studio R1 entrance door glowed red and began to flash at 7.00pm. The recording would take around two hours to complete and by all accounts it went fairly smoothly. According to Innes, the only hiccup was a set of lenses on one of the cameras. The switch that operated the selector had jammed and just continued to revolve endlessly. They took it out of commission and completed the nights recording with hastily adapted shots. Frazer Hines described vividly what that studio recording must have been like,

'It was hard work, because we shot it almost as live … and when that red light went on at night you could shoot maybe three scenes in one go. Whereas now they'd shoot all the interior scenes of the TARDIS in one go, all the baddies in one go, we would shoot it as live from page one, right through to the end in story order, which they don't do now. And they didn't have the wonderful tape editing facilities they have now, and so if something went wrong in scene three they couldn't cut it and say 'We'll go from there' so we'd have to go back to the first scene, and so the pressure to do that, and luckily we're all theatre-trained, but the pressure to do that was enormous.'

At about 9.30pm the phone rang at my home in Mill Hill and I answered it. It was Dad. I hadn't expected him to phone after all that had happened. He sounded exhausted but very relieved that he had got the first one over – bit like a first night in the theatre.

Hello matey, I've just finished. They seem very pleased.'
A thousand and one questions flooded into my mind – 'what was it like in the TARDIS set, how were the Daleks, did you get to sit in one, when can I come to see you film an episode, can I meet Polly and Ben…', but I couldn't speak. Then I blurted,

'When are you coming home so we can all be a family again like you promised.' He didn't answer me. He wanted to speak to my sister but she motioned 'no' with a fake cut across her throat and walked out of the room. I told him she was out with friends. I don't think he believed me. I was the only one to speak with him that night. My mother was too upset and I don't know where my brother was - out with his mates. It was a difficult time for all of us. I felt such a confusing mix of excitement and sadness at the same time. No one heard me cry myself to sleep that night. But I wasn't crying for myself – I was crying because I felt so sorry for my mum.

By the second week, my father was beginning to think more deeply about the character he was playing. The first episode had 'shot by in a haze of panic and adrenaline.' He admitted later that he felt like a rabbit caught in the lights of an oncoming car during that first week.

To begin with I found myself playing it over the top, mostly because Sydney Newman kept urging me too… but Shaun Sutton… was a little wiser than Sydney Newman. In fact considerably wiser in many ways! He said "No, no, just do it in your head old chap; you don't need all those stunts and so on." So I toned it down more and more each week after that and it became warmer and a bit more successful.'

However, right at the beginning of his first season such a radical change was bound to upset some of the regular 'Who' audience. Dad's reaction to 'crits' of his performances had always been very healthy. After the first episode of *The Power of the Daleks* had been transmitted he had been prepared for harsh words. That first episode transmitted on 5th November 1966 received remarkable little press coverage. The Daily Sketch was the only paper to advertise the return of *Doctor Who* with a small article in their TV guide,

'If you believe the programme overlords, most viewers have a compelling urge to be frightened out of their wits. And that explains the strange affair of The Changing Face of Doctor Who. The time travelling Doctor is back as usual on BBC1 this afternoon - and advance reports say that his return will be an explosive event to woo the kids away from Guy Fawkes bonfires. But something is very much out of the ordinary - instead of being played by William Hartnell, the Doctor is spooky character actor Patrick Troughton. When veteran Bill Hartnell decided to drop out it could have meant the end for *Doctor Who*. Scriptwriters have been turning mental somersaults to explain why a new hero is appearing, without warning, to young fans. Full details of his debut are being kept a secret, until today...'

Another clipping my mother still has in her scrapbook was part of the 'Post page' in the Radio Times. There were two letters with very contrasting opinions:

'I would like to send my heartiest congratulations to the production team of the BBC1's *Doctor Who*. Patrick Troughton and the superb character he has created have dragged the programme out of the unfortunate mess it had degenerated into. Given sensible scripts the series could possibly immerge as one of the real successes of television science-fiction.'
G.Howard, Leeds 2

'What have you done to BBC1's *Doctor Who*? Of all the stupid nonsense! Why turn a wonderful series into what looks like Coco the Clown? I think you will find thousands of children will not be watching *Doctor Who*, which up till now has been the tops. *(Mrs.) Estelle Hawkens.*

My father's reaction was simple and seemed to be full of confidence:
'Mrs Hawkens is wrong. Anyway the Radio Times will be fish and chip paper tomorrow but I'll still be Doctor Who!'

I think the initial criticism to his performance did cut him deep but he never showed it. This was only compounded when he was given a copy of the audience research report that had been undertaken during the transmission of episode three on Saturday 19th November 1966. This information certainly must have affected the way he developed the character, especially the toning down of his performance. He later confessed to me that Sydney Newman was not at all happy with the report and hoped that Patrick could do something to rescue the show. Out of an audience sample of 217 the show scored a B/C overall. Viewers in the sample were mostly indifferent about the episode. Most of the criticism centered on the new Doctor.

'I don't care for the new style doctor. He didn't seem right somehow.'

'Once a brilliant and eccentric scientist, he now comes over as a half-witted clown.'

'The family has really gone off *Doctor Who* since the change. They do not understand the new one at all, and his character is peculiar in an unappealing way.'

'Patrick Troughton seemed to be struggling manfully with the idiotic new character that Doctor Who has taken on since his change.'

'I'm not sure I really like his portrayal. I feel the part is over-exaggerated – whimsical even- I keep expecting him to take out a great watch out of his pocket and mutter about being late like Alice's White Rabbit.'

'Frankly I prefer William Hartnell!'

This barrage of criticism greatly outnumbered by the positive comments:

'He made a refreshing change and brought a new dimension to the character.'

'It was immensely exciting and interesting and Patrick Troughton is a brilliant actor who has improved the programme greatly.'

This less than positive reception at the time was probably due to his somewhat daring and extremely unusual initial characterization. As Anthony Clark says in DWB No. 117 dated September 1993:

'What is most remarkable about this story is just how little Patrick Troughton does. Okay, so he's on screen for quite a lot of the time, but right up until the end he does little more than half allude to his suspicions whilst getting in the way. In fact, this early manifestation of the hands-off approach established itself as one of the new Doctor's main characteristics...'

Innes Lloyd disclosed to me in the late seventies that these first few episodes of *The Power of the Daleks* were almost the death of *Doctor Who*. He explained to me that they had been very close to pulling the series after reviewing the first few episodes. My father had been called to an impromptu emergency meeting with Shaun and Innes where they all discussed the 'unenthusiastic reception to the new Doctor'. Audience research was taken extremely seriously as it is today and Sydney Newman was not a man to nurse a failing patient.

If it had not been for my father's quick reaction to public opinion, his strength as an adaptable character actor, and a confident cool nerve, the show would never have recovered - his prediction that the series would not last longer than 6 weeks could have undoubtedly come true. Michael Craze recognized how important it had been for Pat to hone and adapt his performance in response to criticism,

'You could have put all sorts of other people in the role and I think it would've sunk like a lead balloon. I think it was the devotion and the real integrity and the insight that Pat brought to the character that allowed it to carry on.'

Dad's final characterization of the Doctor that secured a continuation of the series has been described as a clown or a 'cosmic hobo' – whatever that is? It was neither of these. Pat's portrayal was brave, complex and departed absolutely from his predecessor. Only on the surface did he appeared to be a clown, tramp, hobo, drawing on child-like qualities, dressing in scruffy clothes, playing his recorder when all around him was in chaos, delving excitedly into a bag of jelly babies and acting the fool to confuse his dangerous enemies.

This was just a veneer. Concealed within and plain to see was a powerful intellect, a great thinker, a solver of puzzles, a doer of good, a wild wizard who could calmly play a hand of cards when faced with danger. Even as he delved into his seemly bottomless pockets and withdrew with a mad flourish such useless items as gobstoppers, conkers, string, half-eaten apples or a bag of marbles, one always knew that each of these ludicrous objects would have purpose and meaning and eventually save the day. The fact that he would always leave everything until the last moment and then have to make a snap decision simply showed us the workings of an eccentric genius – this was Dad's Doctor.

Consequently, whenever I watched my father as Doctor Who I was never really sure that he was going to be able to 'beat that monster' or 'save the planet from destruction.' This in a way was more frightening than having a Doctor who was in total control of the situation like Bill Hartnell's wise white-haired version. It was this ineffectual and indecisive characterization of my Dad's The Doctor that left me with a feeling of doubt and worry whenever he came up against a problem. I felt the need almost to shout out advice in order to help him, yell at him to run because there was a monster behind him or calmly explain a problem that confused him. This ability to draw the audience in and involve them totally within the story was a wonderful strength of my Dad's Doctor.
Michael Craze summed up Patrick's unique qualities brilliantly,

'By the same token that it wouldn't have been anything without William Hartnell starting, I don't think it could have carried on with anyone but Patrick Troughton. He was one of those actors where you knew his name, and then you thought "Of course I know Patrick Troughton, who did he play?" Pat always played characters, you'd never recognise him in the street from his roles before *Doctor Who*. He was well known in the business, and then when people said "Don't you remember he was in so and so?" you went "Oh, of course he was"'.

'He wasn't just saying the lines, the emotion came with it. He might suddenly change the position of an object if he was fiddling, and you'd respond, which is good acting because it's instantaneous and you've got to be able to do that.'

'It was hard work because although it was fun, it was very serious because it had to be right. He was very professional in that he insisted everything was right, the props were right, but it was light-hearted because he wasn't strict like William Hartnell.'

Innes Lloyd told me that Dad had been so nervous about his first appearance as the Doctor that he refused to watch the first episode of *The Power of the Daleks*. While the crew and cast, who were about to tape episode three, crowded around a television set in the green room of the Riverside studios, my father had sat all by himself in the canteen. He later admitted that he had felt physically sick with the pressure of it all.

'Everyone expected so much,' he confessed. 'The whole thing had got out of control in my mind.'

However, when he had returned from the canteen to begin recording episode three, the entire studio crew and all the actors had stood up and cheered him. I recall him explaining,

'This really made me feel great although I went red as a beetroot and started getting very embarrassed. You see up until that point I just didn't know how my fellow actors and the production team were going to react… their opinions really mattered to me.'

Sidney Newman's faith in my Dad had paid off and by the end of episode six of *The Power of the Daleks* viewing figures had jumped from around 5 million to 8 million. My father's continuation as the Doctor was assured.

194

Chapter 8
The Happiest Time of My Life

There was a real hope for the long-term continuation of *Doctor Who* at the beginning of December 1966 when the rehearsals for *The Highlanders* began. This was a time of renewal and regeneration for the programme. The whole production team had a feeling of wanting to free itself from the restraints imposed by the William Hartnell era. As my father said at the time,

'This is going to last longer than I thought!'

My father had initially read the first draft of *The Highlanders* at the beginning of December under the title *Culloden*. It was to be set in 1746 Scotland against the background of the failed Jacobite uprising and would be the last time the TARDIS materialized in the historic past. My father warmed to the swash buckling style of the story that was loosely based on Robert Louis Stevenson's *Kidnapped*. Pat had appeared in a good number of historical TV dramas during the fifties and early sixties. But he liked the script above all because it was written exclusively for his new version of the Doctor. It contained comic and dramatic scenes, disguises, subplot and believable historic characters.

Dad met Frazer Hines while pre-filming sequences for *The Highlander*s at Frensham Ponds in Surrey. The young actor had been cast in the role of Jamie McCrimmon, a piper boy who had survived the Battle of Culloden. Both my father and Innes Lloyd were impressed by Frazer's professionalism and acting skills. Dad had previously acted with Hines on the BBC series *Smugglers Bay* in 1964. I recall Dad's comments about 'the young Scot' being warm and very complimentary,

'Some actors just have that something and some don't. Frazer has got more than just that something.'

I am unsure whether Dad had any influence in the decision to include Jamie as one of his companions but it is clear that Innes Lloyd and the director Hugh David recognized great potential in him. It was for this reason that Frazer's contract included an option for a further twelve episodes which were taken up straight after his pre-filming at Frensham Ponds. This meant changing the end sequence of *The Highlanders* to include a scene showing Jamie leaving with the Doctor and hurriedly altering scripts for the next few series. I remember Dad telling me how excited he was to have Frazer joining the team.

Frazer Hines and Patrick (Photo © Bill Chesnau)

By the beginning of December 1966 my father had realised he was not going to be able to visit Jo, David and myself in Mill Hill as regularly as he would like. The rehearsal, filming and transmission schedule just did not allow him that luxury. It was agreed that he would either telephone every week or send an update by postcard or letter. We were to do the same. My father had always enjoyed

196

writing letters and postcards and was rather good at it, and he continued to so throughout his life. I think he must have enjoyed the distraction during times he was waiting to rehearse a scene or while waiting to record in the studio. Although at the time I felt disappointed by this development and rather jealous of the other family who had him all the time, it did mean that I was able to create a good weekly dairy of the *Doctor Who* years, part of which I still have and treasure. The first postcard I received was a picture of a space rocket – a mockup of the Saturn 5 rocket sitting on its transporter. My Dad and I shared a fascination in space and followed news about it avidly. The message on the other side was rather short and hurried but included some information about the first rehearsals of *The Highlanders*.

'Dear Troughton family... have started rehearsing Highlander at Shepherd's Bush. This is a very funny script and some of the disguises I have to use are wonderful. Dressing up as a washer-woman like Toad and doing a pirate oh arrr! Hope it's not too over the top. You must tell me what you think when it's broadcast. Michael and Anneke keep hiding my hat. They hate it! I think it's alright isn't it? Having such fun with Donald who I've work with before. Can't remember what it was? Hope school is still OK Mike and the journey is not too much for you. Sorry I couldn't get to the carol concert at Rayners Lane but mummy tells me you were brilliant reading. Try to phone soon. Love Dad xx'

When episode four of *The Highlanders* went to studio on Christmas Eve 1966 Shaun Sutton the producer threw a party afterwards to celebrate. My father just couldn't believe the mood of excitement and anticipation during that evening. Everyone associated with the new look *Doctor Who* seemed so confident and sure that the future could only bring success. He admitted to feeling rather overawed by it all because so much depended on him. He had never dreamt that an acting role could take on such huge proportions as Doctor Who had done. Later that evening when he returned home to Kew this feeling of overwhelming responsibility was only compounded by an enormous pile of cards from fans wishing the Doctor a

Happy Christmas and successful New Year. This was the first break he had had since October and that Christmas week must have seemed long overdue.

On Christmas day 1966 Dad arrived at our home in Mill Hill like an over excited St. Nicholas, bearing armfuls of presents and a wicker hamper filled with festive fare. I recall that he seemed the happiest I had ever seen him. I think for the first time in his life he wasn't worrying about money or finding work. A deep dread of being unemployed and unable to financially support his families had always burdened him, especially since the breakup and the addition of three extra children. But that Christmas day those worries seemed to slip away. He appeared happily lost in a world of carefree over indulgence and I for one was not going to question it.

He had bought me the most fantastic electronic experiment laboratory and a new bicycle. I was not used to such expensive gifts and was so overwhelmed I remember couldn't say very much. I just ran off and proceeded to construct a crystal diode radio, which began to blare out music from the Home Service by the time we had to leave to visit my Gran.

On the way to Amersham where Pat's mother and sister Molly now lived, he reminded us with quite a serious tone that Gran still knew nothing of the other family and he wanted to keep it that way. It was a ritual that he repeated every Easter and Christmas, just to make sure he knew that we were all playing the same game. I recall my mother's sarcastic comment about the situation – 'beware the tangled web you weave, when first you practice to deceive!'

To this day I still do not understand why he wanted to keep Jane, Mark and Peter a secret from his mother. Perhaps he thought she wouldn't have been able to cope with his adultery being from such a 'proper' generation. In fact, she would always 'tut' rather loudly if ever anyone mentioned the swinging sixties. The word 'sex' to her was more like a swear word and the very mention of anything to do with separation and illegitimate children would have filled her with horror. If anyone had mentioned the word 'vagina' or 'penis' in a conversation I'm pretty sure she would have dropped dead on the spot!

I still think that Dad was a coward for not facing up to this responsibility. She had a right to know whatever the outcome and his three other children had a right to get to know their Gran. I'm pretty sure Pat's mother would have forgiven him – after all he was the blue-eyed favourite, which makes his self-imposed position even more of a mystery. I never discovered what his brother Robin or sister Molly thought, but they must have all played the same ridiculous game as we had too.

Christmas lunch at Gran's was a fidgety, excruciatingly uncomfortable dreary two hours where all I wanted to do was run off and play with my presents, but I never did of course. It was a bit like a surreal combination of having a meal at 'Miss Havisham's wedding table but with Mr Scrooge supplying the catering. Of course there were no cobwebs or dust and the heavy velvet curtains were not drawn but the turkey portion, sprouts and chestnut stuffing were defiantly consumed in one mouthful with no invitation for seconds. Flat lemonade probably past its sell-by date, and sparkling sweet white wine was served by Aunt Molly in cut crystal glasses that hadn't been used since last Christmas. A half melted candle with berryless holly centred the table and one lonely Fortnum and Masons cracker perched sadly to the side of each silver plate cutlery setting. The most exciting moment of the meal was when my father poured rather too much blue flamed brandy over the stodgy pudding and announced that we should all be grateful for having full stomachs unlike the poor starving of the world. I don't know about them, but I was always starving after that bloody meal.

At about four o clock after a bone china cup of over perfumed tea and a slice of marzipan-topped fruitcake the ordeal was over and we were free, speeding back to our house in Mill Hill. My father didn't stay long at the house. Just enough time to inspect everyone's presents and then swiftly out of the front door whistling a Carol, into his car and heading towards the North Circular to rejoin 'Bunny' and his secret life in Kew. The Christmas performance was over for yet another year.

Although *The Highlanders* was a catalyst for a new style of *Doctor Who* it was the last historical story to be used for another fifteen years. Innes Lloyd and Sidney Newman had discussed with Dad that they thought a more science fiction styled series would prove a greater success with audience and writers alike. My father had enthusiastically encouraged this direction not only because it divorced him further from the William Hartnell era, but because he was genuinely interested in exploring 'real science in drama'.

It was therefore unfortunate that this new direction in storylines kicked-off with such a weak series - *The Underwater Menace*. My father began rehearsals for episode one on 2nd January 1967 but it was not until he had completed the first studio that he expressed his concerns to Julia Smith the director. Dad had thought the idea of monsters in the shape of Fish People who had been created by medical experiment to serve as slaves was a very sound science-based story. His complaint was that there was clearly not enough budget to make the set and costumes convincing enough. He was particularly concerned about the underwater sequence done in Ealing studios with uncomfortable looking actors on very visible wires set against pantomime style backcloths.

'They had obviously taken on something far too big to handle on a 'Who' budget'

The director, Julia Smith and Patrick came to blows over the first few episodes with Dad complaining bitterly about the ridiculous costumes and makeup of the Fish People. In fact one director had turned down the story because they knew the money to make it look real was not available.

As Lloyd later confessed,

'It did look like something from a fifties American B movie!'

Not surprisingly the viewing figures plummeted alarmingly from 8.3 million to 7 million. I believe it was Michael Craze that calmed my father's increasing worries about *The Underwater Menace*.

Both Michael and Anneke had become very close friends with Dad during the early part of the first season. Most days on the way home after rehearsals they would all stop off at Finches Wine

Lodge on the Fulham Road for what my father described as *'a little drinkies… just one to lay the dust.'*

My father was very shocked when in early February 1967 he heard the bad news that a decision had been made to write Ben and Polly out of the series. I think Dad blamed Innes Lloyd for this sudden and regrettable move although who was responsible is unclear. I believe it was felt that the large number of companions in the TARDIS was proving a difficult obstacle to planning good plots and also that the characters were left over from Bill Hartnell's era and were past their sell by date.

Despite this setback my Dad was still happy playing the Doctor. His characterisation was beginning to evolve and blossom as confidence grew. Newman and Lloyd showed how pleased they were with their new Doctor by extending his contract for a further seventeen episodes until the end of the fourth season.

Studio recording for *The Moonbase* began on February 4th 1967 and the first episode was transmitted a week later. Although he never admitted it, Dad must have been feeling the grueling weekly schedule, which involved five days rehearsal, one studio-recording day, and then filming inserts every other Sunday. He told me,

'During those early days of Who I didn't have time to do anything but work and then go home and sleep… then get up again and go to work.'

Increasing the time between studio and transmission from one to two weeks was seriously considered during this period. However, it was never taken up although the threat of actors being struck down by illness or accidental injury must have been a constant worry. There were no understudies or plans for such occasions – the show had to go on.

In fact my father narrowly escaped being injured by a falling section of the 'Gravitron' weather machine that had been built for *The Moonbase*. While inspecting the studio layout before recording, he was nearly squashed flat by metal and wooden pieces that had previously been suspended from the studio roof. I remember the shock in his voice as he describe to the family what had happened,

'I was inspecting the weather thingy machine that moved up and down on cables… you know having a good look to familiarize myself with it so I knew

where to stand when it was flown in and out of the scene. As I turned to go out of the studio for a cup of tea, there was the most awful crash behind me and the whole Gravitron prop had smashed to the ground. My instinct made me dive forward and I hit the ground really hard...'

He then proceeded to proudly lower his trousers to show us a huge purple bruise on his left buttock!

'When I told Morris Barry [director] and Innes what had happened they both turned pale and suggested politely that my inspection of the studio should be done with a member of the crew in future.'

By the end of transmission for *The Moonbase* Dad was relieved to see that the viewing figures had recovered back to an average of 8.3 million. This seemed to confirm that good story lines and frightening but believable monsters were very popular with the audience. This was a trend that would continue to be developed with great success in season six.

In the next story, *The Macra Terror*, which began rehearsals on 4th March 1967, the production team made sure that they did not make the same mistakes as in *The Underwater Menace*. Although the budget was similarly modest, they were able to achieve a very scary crab-like alien through a combination of clever model construction, increased location filming and subtle lighting. I remember being really terrified of the two evil Macra that chased Jamie in the mines beneath the futuristic colony.

When I told my father he just laughed and explained when he had first seen the creature, *'it looked like one of those plastic crabs you see hanging on the walls of a fish and chip shop... only bigger!'*

Later, when he caught some of the transmissions of *The Macra Terror* he had to admit that it was a very effective and startling image the production team had created.

'It did look very frightening on the TV.'

I have always been impressed by the special effects created during my father's years as Doctor Who. One has to remember during the sixties all they had to work with was either the real thing or specially designed models. The simplest computers capable of graphics and overlays were yet developed or used by TV companies until the mid-seventies. Even the credits at the end of *Doctor Who* were not produced by an electronic machine. They were actually printed in white on rolls of black paper and moved past the camera at the correct speed.

My father showed great interest in the models that were built for various stories. He was himself a keen model maker and constructed highly skilled replicas of sailing ships, an MTB and many model gliders. I shared this interest and he often helped me make radio controlled boats which we sailed together on Hampstead pond.

He used to talk enthusiastically about various miniature sets constructed in Ealing film studios by the BBC special effects department. One in particular I remember him describing was a model of a melting glacier that was achieved by using bicarbonate of soda and lots of smoke. Others included a detailed lunar landscape covered with icing sugar, an erupting volcano that used coloured porridge, Dalek city, which was literally blown up in front of slow motion cameras, and an incredibly detailed Tibetan monastery.

The Cybermats were a big favourite of his and he often threatened to kidnap one for me so I could 'keep it as a pet'. He always joked with me that they *'drank Guinness, ate pickled onions and needed to be stroked at least once a day.'*

Some of those Guinness drinking beetle-like robots were built around single channel radio control units and often ran wild across the studio floor when their receivers picked up interference from studio equipment. My Dad remembered that the most reliable type were the ones pulled along the studio floor by clear fishing line.

On April 8th 1967 the recording of episode two of *The Faceless Ones* was completed and with it a long *Who* partnership finally came to an end.

My father was very sad to see Anneke and Mike leave the series since they had shared such good times together. He described them later,

'They wet-nursed me through the initial terror of Doctor Who. *They encouraged me to be brave with my character. But best of all they became my good friends.'*

The remaining four studios of *The Faceless Ones* seemed rather empty without Polly and Ben. Dad especially missed Anneke's trusted opinions and comments on his performance each week,

'She had always kept an eye on my character... you know, made sure it was not too over the top. I missed that support from her... I really did.'

I'm unsure whether Dad kept in contact with them both but I am sure he followed their careers with interest. Michael continued as an actor until the beginning of the eighties when he took over the running of a pub until his tragic death in December 1998. Anneke went onto star in the series *Strange Report*. In the Seventies, she left acting to travel the world, in the process taking up residence in India, the United States and Canada over the next quarter-century before finally returning to the UK.

Anneke Wills, Patrick and Michael Craze

During late April 1967 Dad's sense of loss was replaced by excitement on hearing the news that Debbie Watling had been chosen for as a new member of the TARDIS crew. She had been chosen after long and extensive auditions conducted by Innes Lloyd who originally had offered the part to Pauline Collins. Jack Watling (Debbie's father) and Dad had known each other for a very long time and had often worked together in the fifties and sixties on stage, screen and TV. It was for this reason that Dad felt more confident about the coming new season. With Frazer and Debbie on board he felt sure that a good working relationship would develop.

'When I heard Jack's lovely daughter had got the part I knew next year was going to be fine… Frazer and I had already got something good going but with Debbie joining things must only get better.'

Six months had now passed. While Dad had travelled to historical Scotland in *The Highlanders* and recruited Frazer Hines, landed the TARDIS in the lost City of Atlantis, fought his old enemy the Cybermen on the moon, defeated giant crabs in a holiday camp and taken on faceless aliens in Gatwick Airport, I had waited patiently for that first visit to the studio.

It wasn't until 24th June 1967 that I got my first chance to go to Lime Grove Studio D. The seventh episode of *The Evil of the Daleks* was being recorded. Dad had managed to take a holiday in France with his second family a couple of weeks earlier. This was long overdue. I remember how progressively more and more tired and grey he looked as the fourth season had drawn to an end. He had been working a six-day week which covered some 35 episodes from November 1966 to June 23rd 1967. Most episodes had been recorded the week before transmission, which had put him under an enormous additional amount of pressure. I think we were all concerned about him at this time but all he would say was,

'Don't worry…it's just like doing weekly rep. and I survived that. Besides, it's a lot better paid.'

My day at Lime Grove began at seven o'clock with a loud honk from the road outside our house in Mill Hill. Dad had bought a new car – a Renault 16, green with a large roof rack for his camping

205

holidays in France. This was quite a change from the old rusty Morris Traveller that I was used to. After a short journey down the North Circular we swept through the studio gates with a nod from the BBC security man, parked and raced up to the canteen where we devoured a huge cooked breakfast. Dad was obviously stocking up energy for the day. I was then ushered into studio D, given a dusty canvas seat and told to be very quiet by the young floor assistant David. Most of the set was Dalek control room on Skaro. Constructed from a maze of white tubular scaffolding, sheets of silver covered ply and a painted black shiny floor, it took up nearly all of the surprisingly small studio space. Set to one side was the huge Emperor Dalek connected to an unseen power supply by what looked like vacuum tubing and probably was!

I still have part of the original script written by David Whitaker, which Dad had pinched for me on that day. My favourite scene will always be watching the 'dizzy Daleks' questioning commands from their black couloured superior.

My clearest memory of that visit was talking to John Scott Martin, one of the Dalek operators. During rehearsals the Daleks would move around topless – without revolving head and eye-stalk. This was so that they could hear instructions and notes given to them by Derek Martinus the director and also for their own comfort. The inside of a Dalek was extremely sweaty and cramped! John said that driving a Dalek was, 'like being in a fairground dodgem car' and 'quite disorientating sometimes'.

I was allowed to climb into the Black Dalek during the lunch break. When its head was on you could see very little. The only view of the outside world came through a piece of metal gauze. No wonder they bumped into the sets and cameras all the time.

John and Dad gave me some tuition in Dalek movement which involved shuffling your feet in small steps – a bit like those children's pedal cars without peddles. There were hand controls to operate the exterminating gun, revolving head and a piece of string which when pulled flashed the lights in sync with the Dalek voice.

Peter Hawkins and Roy Skelton created those metallic voices with the help of a primitive synthesizer. They both sat at a wooden trestle table in a lonely corner of the studio with sports commentator microphones pushed close to their lips, peering at a black and white monitor and reading from scripts. I remember being really shocked that the Daleks didn't really talk.

I also recall that Frazer Hines and Marius Goring, who played Theodore Maxtible, and teased me about the Dalek operators. They told me at night John and Robert turn back into a horrible green slime and slither down the Uxbridge Road exterminating passers-by. I was too old to be taken in - after all everybody knew that the Dalek's innards were just wallpaper paste, rubber chippings and green powder paint, weren't they?

Chapter 9
The Year of My Monsters

'What's happening? Has it gone yet?' Tell me when it's safe to look!' my sister Jo would always scream hysterically, cushion held firmly to her face and hands clenched in terror.

The emotionless silvery faces of the Cybermen, the huge lumbering menace of the Yeti, the evil electronic voices of the Daleks or the cold towering threat from a sonic gun wielding Ice Warrior. These were some of the clever nightmare creations of the BBC special effects and costume departments that terrorized my sister every Saturday teatime during the late sixties. My Dad called season five 'the year of my monsters' and I believe for him it was the most productive and fulfilling period as the Doctor.

For me, teatime 5.30 pm just after *Tom and Jerry* had become a regular Saturday focal point. Out had gone our old Cosser television on which I had watched all Dad's first year, half squatting at a flickering out of focus image. In had come a modern rented Rediffusion set with a crisp black and white picture and clear undistorted sound.

I recall watching the first episode of *The Tomb of the Cybermen* in early September 1967 from a completely different perspective. The clarity of image produced a story, which seemed far more menacing and real than others that had preceded it. I had been introduced to the evil Cybermen before in *Moonbase* but this time these emotionless, non-humanoid, purely logical beings from the planet Mondas seemed to me no longer just monsters but plausible sinister cybernetic creatures.

Dad had always thought the Cybermen were the most believable of all his enemies, although they weren't his favourite. He was convinced that the intricate legend behind the Cybermen was their strength. As one of his letters enthusiastically explains to me,

'It is entirely credible for a race of human type aliens to have developed rapidly to the point where they had the ability to replace entire body parts by cybermatic equivalents. Given time and natural survival instincts their whole bodies would become cybernetic and eventually non-human. This blind struggle for survival at any cost underpinned the true success of these creatures and their brilliant story. Here is something that could really happen on earth in the not too distant future. Gerry has injected real science into science fiction drama.'

My father was passionate about including real science into his performance as the Doctor and suggested to Gerry Davis and others that they should approach prominent scientist like Patrick Moore and Arthur C Clarke for inspiration. When my father first met Kit Pedler who had become the unofficial scientific adviser to the *Doctor Who* production team he said, *'this man is a real scientist... not just a writer of science fiction but a doctor and surgeon at London University. He's the real McCoy... an expert.'*

Kit Pedler, who became a good close friend of my father's, was brought on board by Innes Lloyd to inject more hard science into the stories. Pedler formed a particular writing partnership with Gerry Davis, who was story editor on the programme. Their interest in the problems of science changing and endangering human life had led them to create the Cybermen.

Both Dad and I shared a mutual love of science, especially space travel and astronomy. We used to talk for hours about what we thought the future would bring – especially the Apollo missions. How men would colonize the moon and eventually travel out to the stars. Whether time travel would be possible and what use it would be put too. How humankind might conquer the extremities of space by the mind rather than by the use of slow rockets.

I am sure that it was my father's enthusiasm for space and science that overflowed into the character of Doctor Who. He believed totally in the possibilities presented by the Who stories. I think he instinctively knew that it was this germ of reality that kept people watching and maintained such healthy viewing figures, especially in season five.

Throughout his time as the Doctor he always made sure through discussions with Innes Lloyd or the relevant director that the story lines and monsters remained believable and had an element of truth to them. This seemed to be important to him with respect to the process of continuing to produce an effective and genuine characterization of the Doctor.

The previous year mum and Dad had clubbed together to buy me a small refracting telescope for my 12th birthday. Dad enjoyed teaching me how to use it correctly. Where his busy schedule allowed, cold clear nights would be spent together in our back garden in Mill Hill staring in awe at the Orion Nebular or counting the moons of Jupiter. Secretly though, I was really looking for UFOs full of Cybermen and Daleks or some signs of intelligent alien life or maybe even a planet called Skaro.

Filming for *Tomb of the Cybermen* had begun in early summer 1967 with new girl Debbie Watling joining the TARDIS crew. On a postcard dated 12th June my father wrote,

'Dear Troughton family, filming at Wapsey Woods quarry today not far from Don's place off the A40. Scrambling up and down mountains of loose rocks all day. My hands are cut to ribbons. Debbie is being great. Frazer and I have started to tease her already! Sorry I can't get to see you sooner but filming at Ealing next week. Never mind - soon be the hols!! Can't wait. Fishing Elstree reservoir Mike before I go camping in France with Bunny and the children. Hope mum got the money last week. Will write again soon. Love Dad'

During the rehearsals for 'The Tomb of the Cybermen', which began in late June '67, I remember my father describing the difficulties he had while acting with the 'Tinmen' as he affectionately called them.

'Outside rehearsals during the week at the church hall off Shepherd's Bush would always go swimmingly right up to the producer's run. But as soon as the monster actors donned their silver boiler suits, handle bar masks and metallic sprayed army boots ... that was when all the trouble would start! I could never tell which bloody Tinman was talking! I felt like Mr Magoo mistaking a hat stand for a person.'

During the morning technical stagger-through in the studio all the Cybermen would be costumed up for the first time. This meant that my father had no idea which actor was in which suit. To make things even more complicated, like the Daleks, the voices were added on live by actors off-set using sports microphones – the ones with a mouth piece. Unlike the Daleks, the Cybermen had no flashing light or quivering head stalk to identify which one was speaking. All they possessed was a small mouth flap that could open and close very slowly.

'I would constantly hear hissed advice from the Cybermen actors such as – "you're looking at the wrong one Pat!" or "it's not me speaking!"'

The identification problem was finally solved not by any technical wizardry but by my Dad simply asking the Cybermen actors to secretly signal him before it was their turn to speak or rather mime. They would lean forward slightly or twitch their arm so that my father had time to turn in the right direction. Having re-watched some episodes of *The Tomb of the Cybermen* I can just make out the secret code in operation.

The Tomb of The Cybermen was taped on successive Saturdays at Lime Grove Studio D, beginning on July 1st and concluding on July 22nd, bringing to an end *Doctor Who*'s fourth recording block. At this point, Lloyd returned to the producer's chair, Bryant shifted back to story editing and the cast went on a well-earned holiday for four weeks.

Dad had arranged a camping holiday in France with Bunny and his children. However as he had promised in his postcard, Dad and I went fishing at Elstree reservoir. My father had been a keen angler since the war and it provided a focus that bonded us father and son. I remember him buying me a copy of *Mr Crabtree Goes Fishing*. For the uninitiated this was the book to have in the sixties if you were going to take fishing for fresh water species seriously. I think we both empathized with the Daily Mail characters of Mr Crabtree and his son Peter and saw in them a similarity of spirit. This would transfer to golf in later life when my father became increasingly guilty about enjoying the process of hunting wild animals.

He returned from France and the very next day, August 23rd, started filming *The Abominable Snowman* at the Ealing Television Film Studios. The scenes involved my father in the Yeti caves and also a shot of Padmasambhava's wizened head melting, which was due to be incorporated into part six. This was considered too horrific, though, and went unused.

At the end of that month Dad suggested that my brother and I should go with him on location to Snowdonia where he was to film the exterior scenes for a new story entitled *The Abominable Snowman*. This was going to be the longest location shoot ever allocated to *Doctor Who*. It would be six days, beginning on September 4th, and was to take place at Nant Ffracon Pass and Ogwen Lake in the Snowdonia Mountains at Gwynedd, Wales.

This would have been my second visit to the *Doctor Who* set and David's first. The plan was to travel up with dad, stay a couple of days in the unit hotel and then return back to Mill Hill by train. Unfortunately on September 2nd, just two days before we were due to go my brother came down with a high temperature and flu. The trip had to be cancelled and I still haven't forgiven David to this day!

As it turned out the filming week was a nightmare anyway with persistent driving rain for three days and freezing cold howling northerly winds. The only warm people on those Welsh mountains were the actors who wore the Yeti costumes. Everyone else froze solid. I recall Innes Lloyd telling me a few years later about his memories of that location work in Snowdonia.

'It had seemed such a great idea using the Welsh mountains to suggest Tibetan landscape. Of course we hoped for snow but that wasn't really necessary. The weather was filthy! Fifty mile an hour winds, driving rain and freezing temperatures. I still have this image of your father crouching under a BBC umbrella in his camel coloured duffle coat, eyes raised to the sky and rain drops running down that roman nose of his. He was a real trooper. We all were that week. What's amazing is we got it all done on the last two days.'

When Innes Lloyd was looking for the location he stopped in a small village to ask if anyone knew of suitable sites. He was directed to a Mr Jones the local mechanic who apart from having a very thick Welsh accent which was almost impossible to interpret, he proved overly eager to help. After trekking for what seemed miles across moorland full of bleating sheep and up steep mountain tracks they finally reached a vantage point, which perched high above the valley. Pointing to various areas spread out below them, Mr Jones announced,

'This is where they filmed *The Inn of the Sixth Happiness*, just over there is booked for *Carry On Up the Kyber*, and over there they did a B movie about landing on Mars. Now let me see… Tibet could be filmed over there… couldn't it?'

Innes couldn't answer, but just nodded in amazement. The area that Mr Jones had pointed too looked absolutely perfect.

215

Of all the stories transmitted during season five it was The *Enemy of the World* that would test my father's acting skills, emotional stamina and physical fitness to the limit. Dad had been very excited with the first draft of an idea presented by David Whittaker in early 1967, involving an evil scientist called Salamander who would closely resemble the Doctor. Up until this point most of the second Doctor's stories had involved a predictable (all be it) monster based format which Dad always described as, 'Doc arrives, problem to solve, monster attack, almost knobbled, Doc destroys monsters just in time, Doc lives to fight another day.'

The Salamander story, based around political intrigue and dictator style world domination, would buck this trend. It would be very different and prove to be quite a brave attempt to produce an exciting monster free dialogue based script similar to *The Highlander*s. It was for this reason that my father was so attracted to the story. Not only would it give him the chance to show his

217

diverse acting ability by playing two completely opposite types of character, but also it would provide a change of direction to the regular format that he believed was becoming a bit stale.

Before location work began in early November, I recall a conversation my family had with him over supper at Mill Hill. He expressed concern that the scripts for *The Enemy of the World* were delayed and would not be complete until rehearsals began for the studio work. This had unsettled him because filming was just about to begin on November 5th but he had been unable to pencil out a rough character for Salamander.

He talked to me at length about how he thought he should play the part. The real problem was that he could not hide behind heavy make-up or disguise himself in anyway because the story relied on Salamander being the Doctor's doppelganger. Almost everything had to be achieved by his characterization.

He had already decided to use a foreign accent, restyle his hair and darken the colour of his skin slightly. I suggested it might be helpful to look through some of his old theatre photo albums from the fifties for a picture of himself in younger days. After flicking through many pages of dusty albums we eventually came to a picture of him in *Hamlet*. I think this was a great help to him. The character seemed to fall into place a little easier after that evening.

The following week, Dad went on location filming in Littlehampton and Redhill still with an unfinished script and feeling that he was not really prepared enough. Added to this worry was the inexperience of the new and untested director Barry Letts who had only just recently completed the BBC director's course.

Actor turned director – his only credits were a few episodes of *Z-Cars* and a soap opera called *The Newcomers*. Dad and Barry were very wary of each other at the beginning of filming. Although they had been colleagues and friends since the fifties the relationship started out very professionally with each very careful not to tread on each other's toes. I am certain that because Barry had been an actor in the past he was well aware of the demands of playing two roles in one story. Likewise, Dad was aware of the unbelievable pressure involved in preparing shooting scripts and editing over such a short six-day turnover. I also think Barry recognized that Dad was such an experienced professional that it was best not to offer any advice unless asked too! Dad admitted that,

'It must have been a very daunting task for Barry Letts coming in cold like that! I hope we weren't too rough on him.'

Towards the end of the filming period Dad went into Ealing studios to shoot all the Salamander/Doctor confrontation scenes. This was very tiring work as it required him to change costume, makeup and character quite frequently. I think the process included split-screen techniques where the Doctor was actually seen to be talking to Salamander.

However, much to my father's dismay all the doppelganger work was ruined by a technical failure in printing the film. I remember him being very upset by this dreadful setback when he visited Mill Hill after rehearsals.

A lot has been written about my father's style of acting – mostly complimentary. In fact, numerous actors and directors who worked with him often commented to me in later years about his extraordinary ability to be able to snap in and out of character at the click of a finger. This was undoubtedly true but no one could realize the depth of preparation that had to go into such effortless performances. As Dad always reminded me about acting,

'You've got to be like a swan… all beauty and grace up top but underneath thrashing and paddling like mad.'

My father's style of working during *Doctor Who* sometimes surprised fellow actors and directors. I am sure they expected a disciplined professional type of rehearsal period but what they got was often what appeared to be completely the opposite. As my brother David always observed,

'It always appeared he was having far too good a time for any serious work to happen.'

Although Dad was not a method actor who would feel the need to 'become the part', he believed that in order to present a truthful character you must first understand the emotions that drive that person. I often talked to him in my early days as a struggling actor about technique and how to achieve a truthful character. He was absolutely wonderful at explaining the secrets of his working methods and apart from David, I don't think he ever talked this frankly about his instinctive approach to anyone else during his life.

'I always work from the inside out. By that I mean I first try to get a feel for the characters emotions during a scene. It's a bit like playing some music. There are highs and lows within the piece and everything must balance. The lines are superficial at that point. I try to improvise the story before learning any lines.'

'A lot of actors work from the outside in, developing facial expressions or physical movements first and from that, projects the characters emotions.'

Dad always called these actors 'mirror actors'. He suggested that they were far too worried about how they looked and not enough about how they felt.

'They are the sorts of actors I dread. They never listen to what you are saying but just wait for their turn to speak. You have to listen and react to create the truth of a scene.'

'If my character needs to cry in a scene… I don't think about how I should cry physically. All I do is think of a past experience in my life that was sad and hey presto I get tears. It's so simple and uncomplicated, but requires real bravery and above all a relaxed atmosphere in rehearsals.'

I don't think my father realised but what he was describing was the Stanislavski method of acting, which had been, ingrained him in during his six weeks in America in 1939.

Frazer Hines described my father's sense of truth in his acting really well,

'Whatever he did, if he put his hand in his pocket and said "Jamie, I have a rope ladder here", you could believe, "Yes, that Doctor would have a rope ladder". His character was whacko, but believable, you never went "Oh no, he wouldn't have that in his pocket", you actually believed, and I think it was Colin Baker who said "If it wasn't for Patrick, the rest of us wouldn't have got the part", because if Patrick, when he got the part, when he took over, if he'd made a dog's breakfast of it, it would have gone another series and then folded.'

It was interesting to observe that if anyone other than his close family asked him about his working methods such as friends, fellow actors, directors or interviewers he would always dismiss the question as unimportant and retort rather flippantly,

'I just say the lines, never bump into the furniture, and take the money and run!'

It was to his credit that even under the punishing schedule of *Doctor Who* he still managed to work his relaxed method of rehearsals and was not lulled into the easy option of just 'learning the lines.'

I recall the actor Bill Kerr who played Giles Kent in *The Enemy of the World* asking the producer Innes Lloyd from where he thought my father got his enthusiasm and energy. Innes raised his eyes to the heavens and said,

'God knows but I wish I had some of it!'

Bill Kerr became quite close to Dad during the six weeks together. I think he enjoyed the way my father worked. There was a lot of corpsing and uncontrollable laughter between them during rehearsals. On one occasion my father had to hide from the 'baddies' in a large wooden box while Bill Kerr tried to convince some guards that he was alone. But each time they tried to complete the scene strange farting noises would be heard coming from the closed box followed by the whispered words,

'Speak quicker I'm suffocating!' This of course brought the scene to a grinding halt every time they attempted it. I believe even in the studio they had problems which were only compounded by my father adding the line 'I hope I have enough air in here', before he got into the box. The whole studio just exploded with laughter. This defused the corpsing problem they had both experienced in rehearsals and the scene was completed without further disruption.

The last episode of *'Enemy of the World'* transmitted on the 27th January 1968 and had very high viewing figures of 8.3 million. It is such a shame that only episode three remains to be enjoyed. I am convinced that this was one of Dad's best performances in *Doctor Who* but most of it has been lost. Not only did he succeed in convincing the audience that Salamander and the Doctor were two different characters (most of my class mates later asked me where they found an actor so similar to my Dad!) but he was also successful portrayed the Doctor disguised as Salamander.

The last episode of *Enemy of the World* completed studio during the first week of the New Year 1968. The Doctor / Salamander story had drained my Dad more than he realized, but still the relentless seven-day-week *Who* schedule ground on with the read-through for *Web of Fear* beginning immediately. They certainly got their money's worth in those days.

It was about this time he was approached by The BBC to do yet another season, which would bring his total to three years. Barry Letts talked about how Pat confided in him and asked his advice on whether he should do it.

'While we were making *Enemy of the World*, Patrick Troughton said 'They've asked me to sign up for another year of *Doctor Who* and I don't know what to do. This once a week pace is really killing me'. We were so pushed for time, I had to use doubles for the long shots of Patrick, Frazer and Debbie on film because they were in London recording while we were down on the south cost. It was a ludicrous situation. So I said to Patrick, 'Why don't you say you'll do another year, but then suggest that everybody would produce much better shows if they cut down the number of them and had gaps between each story to do the filming. I think he went back and suggested this, but of course by this time the next season was already down on the schedules and it was too late. Nevertheless, the planners decided it was a good idea and set it up for the following season, with the connivance of Peter Bryant and Derrick Sherwin, with the idea of the Doctor being confined to Earth so they could make use of ordinary locations.'

The discussion of whether he should do another year was not just confined to his colleagues. I recall a conversation between my mother, father and sister in the Orange Tree pub at Totteridge. I am sure Frazer and Debbie were there too. It was early evening but quite a few drinks had been consumed which had relaxed my Dad and allowed him to talk more openly than usual. My father was renowned for keeping all his worries bottled up.

The group was having a debate about how Dad had been offered another season but he didn't know whether to take it. Dad had explained he had asked Barry Letts for advice as to what he should do. Barry had diplomatically suggested that Dad ought to agree to another season but with a stipulation that it should be shorter – around six months. Debbie had already decided to leave at the end of March and I know this concerned my Dad because the three of them had become very close and worked so well together.

At the end of that evening Dad had decided to continue for another season. The truth was he couldn't afford not to do another series. He had two families to support, three children attending expensive private schools and a huge tax bill. His worries over type-casting, the exhausting nature of the part and the loss of companion paled into insignificance. He needed at least another year of financial stability to even consider leaving *Doctor Who* for the all too insecure world of freelance television acting.

At the end of January 1968 Pat took a week off during episode two of *The Web of Fear* because he was not involved in studio work and his filming had already been completed. It was a cold crisp week with a biting easterly wind but despite the dreadful weather, Dad and I went fishing on Elstree Reservoir.

We didn't catch many fish that day but I remember so clearly him helping me decide on what costume to where to a fancy dress party I was going to at school.

'Well, you have to go as the Doctor! I'll try and pinch some stuff from wardrobe next studio. And what about using my recorder?'

I didn't want to hurt his feelings but explained I was worried that going as him might look a bit big-headed to my friends. I suggested that I thought it would be more diplomatic to go as one of the *Doctor Who* monsters, maybe a Dalek or Cyberman. The last hour of that day's fishing was ignored as we scribbled out rough drawings and plans for a Cyberman outfit. In between ideas my father kept reciting the most filthy limericks and telling the corniest jokes ever, some of which have remained with me.

'How do Daleks climb the stairs?
One sink plunger at a time.'

'How do Yeti go to the loo?
They have to get their balls out first!'

By the time the sun began to sink below the reservoir and we had pulled in our mud anchor and rowed to shore, not only had we designed the winning costume but we had shared a very close and special day.

Three weeks later I found myself standing on the dusty platform of Piccadilly Circus underground station in London with Douglas Camfield, Nicholas Courtney, Jack Watling and two huge vicious looking Yeti. This was my long awaited second visit to studio D Lime Grove and I was making the most of being shown around the set for episode six of *The Web of Fear.*

'Watch out for trains as you jump down from the platform', said a muffled voice from one of the Yeti skins. 'Don't tread on the live rail!'

Although I laughed and shared the joke with the monster actor John Lord, I recall that I did quickly glance down the dark tunnel for any signs of a speeding tube train.

Douglas Camfield and my Dad continually praised the efforts of the set designer that day. The whole scene looked and felt so authentic. Dad said he even thought he could feel 'that familiar warm dry flow of musty air that continually blows in the real underground.' In fact, during the transmission of episode four on 24th February the BBC received a complaint from London Transport who had assumed that filming had taken place in the real underground without their permission. Douglas Camfield later described what happened,

'Originally we planned to film *The Web of Fear* in the Underground itself, and approached London Transport for their permission. They wanted the ridiculous sum of two hundred pounds an hour! So, with a lot of hard work, we built our own Underground in the studios, copying from the originals. After the serial had been broadcast, we received a letter from the Transport authorities saying that they were going to sue us for using their tunnels after all, and we hadn't been anywhere near them!'

The small studio was crammed full with set, far more than on my first visit during the recording of *The Evil of the Daleks*. Along one whole studio wall the design team had built a length of tube tunnel cut in half so that the cameras could have easy access. On the floor of the tunnel ran what looked like rail track mounted on white mushroom insulators and set on a false concrete base. The tunnel wall arched upwards supported by grey steel girders made from ply with false grey dust covered power cables running neatly along its full length.

On the other side of the studio was the platform set of Piccadilly Circus station that had been built with the use of wooden scaffolding supports and included its own short length of track that disappeared into a painted backcloth tunnel entrance. It was so complete right down to the peeling advertising hoardings and varnished wooden seats. Squashed at one end of the studio was a ticket hall on grounds level.

During the morning I was able to watch a technical rehearsal, which included a scene on the station platform where the Doctor, Jamie and Colonel Lethbridge Stewart and two other characters were being held captive by three Yeti.

The Yeti of the London underground were very different to the friendly looking bears of Tibet. They were slimmer and seemed to have spiky course hair. I remember John Lord showing me the evil battery operated red glowing eyes. He had taped his wires to the inside of the head-piece to stop them poking him in the face and the battery sat in a specially made pocket in his trouser section. The Yeti looked very comical when they walked around without their headpieces on during rehearsal. The fur trouser section was padded out with cane and held up with a pair of braces. They seemed to waddle like ducks and had great difficulty climbing even the smallest of steps because of their rubber clawed feet.

'It was a bit like walking around with flippers on…' John Levene told me. But when those evil headpieces were put on they became very fierce looking monsters. I know my father was a bit worried about how much they had changed from *The Abominable Snowman*. I am sure he had something to do with the warning for younger viewers that was broadcast at the beginning of transmission of *Web of Fear*.

After lunch I watched Debbie and her father, Jack, doing a scene in the ticket office set. Two Yeti had captured them and brought them to meet their controller called 'Intelligence'. In the middle of the set was a frosted perspex pyramid, which glowed with light. Inside could be seen a seat and some controls.

Towards the end of the scene I remember nearly jumping out of my skin as the voice of 'The Great Intelligence' boomed out over the studio speakers. It was a chilling, echoing, emotionless voice, which seemed to come from everywhere. I still recall some of those eerie final words from the rasping disembodied voice,

'You will cooperate, Professor… I advise you not to interfere. My Yeti can destroy you so easily. Soon the Doctor's mind will be absorbed by the Great Intelligence.'

I ended my second visit by watching the actual studio recording of episode six in the control gallery. I sat quietly behind Douglas Camfield and his P.A. who shouted out shot numbers like she was drilling troops on a parade.

'Doing a *Doctor Who* studio is a bit like running for a bus. Lots of adrenalin, always the possibility you tripping up but great when you make it.'

Dad had needed plenty of adrenaline during the filming of *Fury from the Deep* which took place on an old disused sea fort in the Thames estuary. My father was terrified of heights and suffered severely from vertigo. Just standing on a chair would make all the blood drain from his face. He was very embarrassed by this problem and so kept it a secret with only a few of his close friends and family knowing the truth. So when he was asked to get into a helicopter and be flown around by a stunt pilot, director Hugh David was surprised at Pat's reaction,

'No Hugh, not on your nelly! I've climbed up and down ladders on this bloody fort all day, stood looking out over a fifty foot drop to the sea without flinching and now you want me to go up in that contraption and do my own stunts? No way!'

I remember watching the helicopter sequence when it was transmitted during March. It had been very well edited so you couldn't tell that Dad's bits had been shot firmly on the ground with the poor cameraman being pushed around in an old pram.

'Fury from the Deep' was one of my favorites. I remember Dad's reaction on seeing the seaweed monster for the first time,

'I found it difficult not to laugh. There was this man dressed in a skin diver's outfit on which had been stuck what looked like spaghetti. Hugh [director] *was smiling too!'*

Dad later found out that Hugh David intended to flood the creature with white foam to make it look more frightening. He wrote to me explaining the childish excitement Frazer and he had experienced when the foam machine was used for the first time at Ealing studios stage 3.

'The mind grabbing seaweed entity is supposed to live in a foam to protect itself – like cuckoo spit...'

'They have got this fireman hose connected to a machine that pumps out white bubbles. It's brilliant. You would love it. I must admit Frazer and I got a bit carried away when they turned it on for the first time!'

'When we started the scene things got worse... nobody could see a thing inside the dam stuff. It was like having snow blindness. Added to that, everybody kept slipping over all the time and disappearing beneath the foam in fits of giggles.'

Despite these problems, when *Fury from the Deep* was broadcast at the beginning of March the weed creatures came across with a terrifying reality. Hugh David's idea of allowing only the smallest glimpse of the monster thrashing around in the foam combined with a throbbing heart beat sound effect created a superb air of menace. But the real strength of this story was in the writing.

Victor Pemberton knew that possession by an alien inside a human body was a frightening idea. He had previously written a similar seven-part radio series called *The Slide*, in which an intelligent mud life form threatened to engulf a town. My father especially like the idea of possessed humans who were capable of breathing poison gas from their mouths.

I remember a truly chilling scene involving two possessed workers called Mr Oak and Mr Qill spewing out gas breath over a poor innocent woman. I still don't understand how this scene escaped the censor's scissors as it must have been one of the most scary moments in all the *Doctor Whos*. I have ever watched. When *Fury of the Deep* was sold to Australia their broadcasting board of censors had no hesitation in cutting the scene.

The departure of Debbie Watling from the series caused real problems for my father. Not only had she become a very close friend but professionally an essential part of the successful acting trio. Frazer, Debbie and Dad had all become comfortable with each other both in performance and as people. They knew each other's weaknesses and strengths and were able to support each other as a unit. Dad recalled Debbie's wonderful sense of fun in a postcard,

'Dear Troughton family, filming inserts for Fury down on the south coast at Botany Bay. Beautiful white cliffs but bloody freezing. Debs' birthday. We gave her the bumps! Then chucked her in a huge pile of special FX foam. She came out smiling looking like a snowman. God, I'm going to miss her. Doing her last shot today. Helicopter hired. Hugh wants a lonely Debs on the beach as Frazer and I bugger off in the TARDIS. Will look very sad I think. Hope all is well. Will pop in on way back. Love Dad.'

228

The practical jokes that they all played on each other were evidence of their friendship and an important release of stress during such a tough relentless schedule. On many occasions, 'Leatherlungs' as she was affectionately known, had fallen hook line and sinker for her two male partner's japes. Apart from being thrown into the foam on her birthday, other jokes included false entrance 'Qs' and having her skirt removed rather suddenly just before she was about to start a scene.

'Those few weeks after Debbie left were very depressing. It was a bit like losing a member of your family,' he later confessed.' *We did have such a good time together.'*

Debbie went on to continue a successful career in films, television and on stage. After leaving *Doctor Who* she was immediately cast as a regular character in the seventies soap, *The Newcomers.*

Fury from the Deep was the last of a line of successful, well-constructed and original monster based stories that had made the second year of my father's *Doctor Who* so watchable. From the Cybermen of Kit Pedler to the Yeti of Mervyn Haisman and Henry Lincoln. From the Ice Warriors of Brian Hayles to the foam covered seaweed of Victor Pemberton. All captured their audience. All created suspense. All invited you to wonder what would happen next. My father later agreed that the stories that followed,

'Fury from the Deep' never quite managed to capture the originality, suspense and fun of the period he called 'the year of my monsters.'

By mid-April, three episodes of *The Wheel in Space* had been completed recording at Television Centre. Dad had been hastily granted a week-long holiday by Peter Bryant during episode two after complaints that he felt physically exhausted. I realise now this had been brought on not only by the punishing weekly workload but by the departure of Debbie who had been such a good friend and colleague.

While actor Chris Jeffries took over as Doctor Who's unconscious body during episode two of *The Wheel in Space*, Dad and I spent a glorious couple of sunny days up in Norfolk a riverside chalet he had recently rented. This was a dream come true for both of us. Fishing and sailing from the bottom of your own garden!

I remember we both talked about *Who* a lot during that brief holiday break. However the tone of conversation was not tinged with the usual enthusiastic light-hearted excitement I had become used too. He seemed agitated and quick tempered especially about the recent standard of script and originality of story. He confessed to me,

'We need something new… something creative to happen. The programme's tired and predictable.'

There was an air of desperation in his voice – as if he knew that things were going to become far worse but there was nothing he could do about it. I was very aware of how tired Dad was during this time. I know he had been very disappointed by *The Wheel in Space*, which he described to me as 'dire' and 'the same old tired story bashed out again'. In later years he pinpointed the problem,

'Of all the monsters in the Who *repertoire, the Cybermen had always seemed a real and terrifying threat. But what 'production' did not understand was you couldn't have a Cyberman without a decent story. One was naked without the other.'*

I think he believed that 'production' was beginning to rely too much on tried and tested monsters and not enough on good plots. A copy of the audience research report for the final episode of *The Wheel in Space* that my father kept states,

'One Group enjoyed it fairly well but felt that invention was, perhaps, beginning to flag. The stories are becoming repetitive; the series needs new ideas and new antagonists for Doctor Who rather than Daleks, Cybermen and the like. This was a rather tame adventure, it was said, and there was too much use of pseudo-technical jargon that would be over the heads of most younger viewers.'

* * *

The fifth season came to an end officially with the recording of episode six of *The Wheel in Space* on 12th April 1968. At the end-of-season party my father discussed his worries for the first time about future scripts with Tristan de Ver Cole (director) and Peter Bryant. They had agreed that storylines were lacking in depth and that the new season should focus hard on inventing new directions of plot and original monsters.

Chapter 10
Fluff, Fart and Cough

Although season five had officially ended with the completion of *The Wheel in Space*, production for the new season continued with the first episode of *The Dominators* beginning rehearsals on 10th May 1969. I recall the relief on my father's face when I met him after the read through at his house in Kew.

'Looks like a good one... new monsters, good actors... interesting story. Cross all your fingers!'

The production team had been well aware of the problems with future story lines for the new season and had tried to deal with the same concerns that my father had felt. But unlike my father they still saw the monster-based format as the way forward.

In an attempt to inject new monsters into the series they had commissioned the creators of the popular Yeti, to come up with a replacement for the Daleks. Mervyn Haisman and Henry Lincoln devised The 'Quarks' which were metallic robotic creations with high- pitched voices and a very destructive nature.

However, script editor Derek Sherwin decided that although the monsters were plausible the story was not. Major cuts and rewrites caused Haisman and Lincoln to request that their names be removed from the credits. My father later explained,

'I knew nothing about these troubled scripts and why the original writers had replaced their names with a pseudonym – Norman Ashby. If I had... I would have been very worried. Just what I had feared was coming true.'

After the first recording of *The Dominators* on 17th May my father phoned to invite the whole family to visit the studio the following week. This caused incredible excitement; especially for my sister Jo who had been told that actor Ronald Allen was playing a 'chief baddy' in the story. My sister had suffered from a crush on Ronald for a few years and was speechless at the prospect of meeting him in the flesh. I thought it was all a bit sad! I concentrated on the prospect of being one of the first to inspect that 'all new *Who* monster' – the Quark.

I recall that my third and final visit to TC4 at Television Centre was a bit of a letdown. Maybe I was getting older and less impressed by the magic of *Doctor Who* but as we were greeted at reception, then ushered past security and onwards towards Red Studio area I felt a distinct lack of nervous anticipation that I'd had always experienced with previous visits.

Studio 4 had been chosen because of the immense size of the sets that had been designed by Barry Newbery. The main area consisted of the Dominators' spaceship control room, a ruined war museum with desert exterior, the council rooms of the Dulcians, and a space transport station complete with *Flash Gordon*-lookalike space pod. I recall the sliding door of the pod stuck on many rehearsals and at one point nearly crushed Arthur Cox's (Cully) fingers.

The first scene David and I watched was set in Dulcian council and was rather long and boring. Members of the Dulcian council were discussing the validity of Cully and Zoe's story that a spaceship had landed on an old atomic test site called 'Island of Death'.

The only thing that kept my interest was the extraordinary costumes that the Dulcians were dressed in. It looked as if someone had ripped down five or six metres of velvet curtains from my school dining hall and had then wrapped them around the midriffs of each of the Dulcian councilors. I found it difficult not to laugh out loud when I shared this observation with my brother David, but I think he was too busy staring at the scantily dressed female Dulcians to react.

During the morning coffee break, Ronald Allen and Kenneth Ives talked to us about the costumes they had to endure which consisted of very uncomfortable shoulder enhancing fibreglass armour.

'We feel and look like overweight wood lice!' I remember Ronald explaining to me.

Arthur Cox who was on the next table interrupted with,

'You think you've got problems' and flipped his curtain skirt up to expose his white Y-fronts.

During lunch I got a chance to inspect the Quarks but again a feeling of real disappointment came over me. I had been promised a replacement for the Daleks but all I could see was a rather cumbersome silver painted box like robot which looked as if it was about to fall over every time it attempted to walk. There was no visible weapon, no evil glowing eyes, no terrifying roar. All this monster could offer was a plastic swivelling star shaped head, extending metal arms and a squeaky drunken voice. My father agreed with me that the Quarks were a bit of a let-down,

'They looked like cardboard boxes that had been sprayed with silver paint. I just could not take them seriously. They didn't frighten me in anyway. It was such a shame. The story was pretty good but the realization of it was poor.'

I politely declined an offer from the Ron Oates the visual effects designer, to take a closer inspection and returned to the rest of the family who were sitting outside by the fountain eating cheese sandwiches. Watching the recordings of *Who* were always exciting and thankfully considering how the day had gone up until then that evening was no exception. The most memorable point during the recording of episode two came in a scene between Jamie, the Doctor and the twin evil 'wood lice' Dominators. It was set in an old ruined war museum and my father had been worrying about it all day. In a letter he sent to me the following week Dad explained what we had witnessed,

'A laser gun had to be fired at the wall behind me... of course they didn't use a real one. They put a small charge in a hole some way up the wall. When the moment came the effects team would set it off blowing out some of

the wall. This section of the wall had been packed with something called Fullers Earth and bits of debris so when the charge went off there would be a flash, dust and a small amount of bits flying around. Unfortunately we had run out of time during rehearsals and not managed to test the effect. During the transmission, when the time came for Ronald to point his laser at the wall there was a loud pop, a fizzing sound followed by absolutely nothing. Just as I had feared we had to go right back to the beginning of the scene a reset the charge. The second time round, the effect worked rather too well blowing a large hole in the wall not only taking the actors by surprise but also revealing all the effects team behind. The third attempt was successful, but afterwards the bang was so loud I couldn't hear a bloody thing. So when you watch that bit you now know why it looks as if I am shouting really loudly — like some kind of lunatic!'

Towards the end of that evening's recording there was a wonderful funny moment when as the last Quark climbed the stairs to exit, it tripped and fell very noisily onto the studio floor. Luckily it was just out of shot as the whole head section came off and exposed the embarrassed child actor operator.

Having recently looked at the video of *The Dominators,* the fall of the Quark can be clearly heard off camera and in fact Frazer looks back twice with a slight smirk on his face to see what is going on. I think my father was unaware of what had happened during the scene but as soon as it was over everyone in the studio burst into uncontrollable laughter.

That evening would be the last time I visited the studio and watched my father record *Doctor Who*. It was also the first and final appearance of the 'Quarks'. A dispute over their ownership and licensing rights meant Haisman and Lincoln would never work for *Doctor Who* again. My father said,

'When we began to lose writers like Mervyn and Henry, things were on a downward spiral although I didn't see it at the time. It was a terrible shame. We would never see the Yeti or the Quarks ever again.'

By the end of June, recording for *The Mind Robber* was well underway when Frazer unexpectedly fell ill with the chicken pox contracted from his nephews. The continuing lack of contingency plans for actors going sick was severely tested during the week of the 28th June. Derrick Sherwin hastily rewrote the second episode. Fortunately the story line allowed for Jamie's face to be altered and Hamish Wilson was cast in the part of his look-alike.

During the last few recordings of the production year my father had become noticeably less depressed about the future. I think he felt Peter Ling's script was exactly the type of risky story that they should be attempting to keep *Doctor Who* fresh. After completing the last recording my father met up with Peter in the BBC club and discussed other project ideas.

He told Peter that he was very enthusiastic about *The Mind Robber* which he described as, *'bizarre, but totally in keeping with the ever changing style of* Doctor Who.' Peter then went on to describe a new idea he had about a planet where time went backwards. My father wrote to me explaining,

'Peter has come up with so many great ideas for future stories. You would love him Mike. He is so enthused about science… just like you. Apparently he has submitted a synopsis to Derrick about a world where time is in reverse! I don't know how they could make that one work but, wow!!!!'

Dad had also become good friends with Wendy Padbury (Zoe) and had been able to re-establish that strong actor unit which he felt was so important for his sanity under such unrelenting pressure. In fact he was a little embarrassed and annoyed with himself for being as he put it, *'rather a bad host to Wendy during her first few eps…'*

On the 20th July 1968 the cast were finally released for the summer break. Despite Barry Letts' suggestion of a shorter production week the previous year the physically demanding six-day week had continued relentlessly. Both Dad and Frazer had been working solidly for forty-six weeks and the show was still on air and would be when they returned in September.

When he came over the following Sunday I really noticed a difference in his appearance. God, he looked tired. That kind of

237

tiredness that only shows when you eventually allow yourself to relax after the pressure is off. His face was washed white which was very unlike Dad who generally had a dark tan most of the time. But even so I could see that a weight had been lifted from him and all that pressure had gone now he was on holiday. The worry of script learning, the numbing monotony of routine read-throughs and the never-ending treadmill of rehearsals were over for a short time.

He told my mother that although he was weary he, *'hadn't had the same feeling of total release since being demobbed after the war.'*

'I've been like a hamster on a wheel for nearly a year now'

The plan for the six glorious weeks holiday was to spend three weeks camping in France with his second family and the remaining time with my brother and myself.

It was during this time he made a firm decision to leave the series at the end of season six. In a phone conversation to Peter Bryant in mid-August he made it clear, *'that it was time to move onto new projects.'*

There were many reasons that prompted this inevitable phone call but above all Dad had begun to really fear being typecast. Before being cast as *Doctor Who* he had successfully jumped from one TV character to another, embracing widely different roles. Paul of Tarsus, a crippled dwarf in *The Old Curiosity Shop*, a doctor in *Tale of Two Cities*, a clown in *Give the Clown His Supper*, a hermit in *Jason and the Argonauts* and a Toff in *The Scarlet Pimpernel* were just a few of the hundreds of memorable creations. In a candid letter to my mother he explains,

'The weekly routine of production has become too much like working in the theatre… god forbid! I have found myself slipping into 'easy mode'. Not bothering so much and relying on just getting by. You know how much I detest that. Lazy acting is a crime. I have begun to do that. I must stop now before I become one of those dreadful personality actors. What do you think, Margaret?'

I don't know what she said but I think he felt that he had done as much as he could with the Doctor. There was an instinctive urge that told him to move on not only for the good of his career but for his own well-being as an artist.

'*Three years, no longer,*' he told Peter Bryant on the phone. '*I'll see the season out and leave in the spring.*'

I recall how guilty he felt having to make that call. He must have remembered the kind of problems that Innes Lloyd had faced when trying to find Who Two. He was genuinely concerned that with sliding viewing figures and his departure, *Doctor Who* would not withstand another regeneration. He alone would be responsible for its demise.

Despite this he was determined to have fun and the last three weeks of the holiday I spent helping him rekindle a passion for the game of golf. He had played regularly when he was younger but after the war had never had the time to get back into the routine.

I played most weekends at Northwood Hills public course, which was close to my school and mates. So I was very excited when he announced that he had become a member of the Stage Golfing Society in Richmond Park.

However, playing golf with my father was a bit unpredictable to say the least! He had a temper that would often materialize like the TARDIS – rather suddenly and unexpectedly. It was never directed at any person but usually at an inanimate object. Golf was the perfect catalyst since the frustration of hitting a little white ball with a metal walking stick would often prove too great for him. On many occasions after his shot had finished with a plop in the lake or with a ricochet cracking noise amongst the trees he would shout, curse and jump up and down banging his club against the trolley like a three year old having an inconsolable tantrum. I would walk on smiling politely at any fellow golfer lucky enough to witness the event and pretend that he had absolutely nothing to do with me.

His most embarrassing habit was to urinate at as many locations on the course as possible. This he assured me was because he had a weak bladder but I think he just liked peeing in public. On one occasion while he was in full flow two lady members on the opposite hole could be heard saying,

'What's that man doing?'

'Oh don't worry dear it's not a flasher… it's just Doctor Who going for a pee.'

We played a round on one day with the actor Garfield Morgan who was rather a good golfer and later became president of the Stage Golfing Society. Garfield would always take the piss out of Dad's uncontrollable mood swings, which would only make matters worse. Dad would end up with bent clubs and Garfield would be collapsed lying on the fairway in fits of laughter.

The new production year began on 3rd September 1968 with bad news. My father had learnt that a number of scripts that had been scheduled for season six were in desperate trouble; 'they just can't get interesting stories anymore', he told me.

Scripts such as *The Dream Spinner, The Prison in Space* and *The Aliens in the Blood* had all run into trouble and were close to being aborted. A sense of panic pervaded the production team during this time. Dad's complaints about *Doctor Who* about becoming stale and predictable were finally being recognized. Peter Bryant also complained bitterly about the lack of budget and resources.

'It was for this reason we decided to bring *Doctor Who* back down to Earth again. The money spent on alien planet sets, out of this world filming locations and model special effects could be invested in actors, writers and good solid production values.'

Peter told Dad at the read-through for *The Invasion* that in the future a lot of the stories would occur on earth with real people involved in everyday situations. *The Invasion* was the first step in a deliberate move to bring Doctor Who to a more earth bound location.

The return of Nicholas Courtney who played Brigadier Lethbridge Stewart, the head of UNIT, (United Nations Intelligence Taskforce) pleased Dad. He was keen to see a story with similar settings to *Web of Fear*, which had been such a success. However, he was very disappointed that the Jack Watling's character was not to return. Apparently it had been decided that the part written for Professor Travers was too small to offer to such a well-established actor as Jack and the character was replaced by Professor Watkins played by Edward Burnham.

The first studio for *The Invasion* began on the 20th September. For this sixth production block the suggestion of fewer episodes per season originally discussed between my father and Barry Letts was now implemented. This was an enormous relief to my father and Frazer since it meant pre-filming would no longer cut into important rehearsal time.

They would also have the luxury of six weeks between taping and transmission to cover illness or production problems.

'Starting again was rather like jumping on a running bus. I remember that Monday, Tuesday… Monday we read it, Tuesday rehearsed it, Wednesday rehearsed it, half day Thursday then you were on Friday. We filmed every fortnight, and in the end, Frazer and Wendy and I had a sit-down strike and said 'We're not going to film at the weekends, because we're getting tired irritable'. We had a big conference, Shaun Sutton took us out for a lovely meal, tried to talk us out of it, and we said "No!", and in the end the planners, those chaps up in the sixth floor with their little maps and flags all arrange in lovely patterns but who don't know much about the actual working of a play, they changed their mind.'

At the beginning of October just three episodes into the recording of *The Invasion* my father was told that the next scheduled story called *The Prison in Space* was to be shelved. This made him very uneasy because in the past he had relied on knowing the rough outline of future scripts at least a month in advance. This length of time gave him the option to discuss any worries he had about them and time to implement any changes needed. As Victor Pemberton revealed about his influence on scripts,

'He was quite stubborn, if he didn't agree with something he'd tell someone. He didn't tell me, because I wasn't the director. He knew the chain of command. But he was his own person and he knew what was right and he knew what was wrong.'

241

My father became even more concerned when he learnt that *The Prison in Space* by comedy writer Dick Sharples had got as far as being assigned a director. It had also got to the casting stage and even some design work on a few sets had been completed.

By the beginning of November the troubled *Prison in Space* series had been hastily replaced by a standby story entitled *The Krotons*. The rushed replacement did not impress my father but it was too late to complain. Dad told me,

'I didn't know what was coming next until a few days before we finished the Cybermen story. It was crazy! To close to call for my liking. And the replacement script... well let's put it this way, Krotons are not my favourite alien. Ridiculous nonsense, the whole thing.'

Based on the idea of a primitive god worshipping civilization that was really being controlled by crystalline aliens feeding on their mental energies it relied too heavily on the 'monster format'.

'Production had fallen into the same trap as had caught them during The Dominators. If the Quarks had been simply unimpressive in comparison the Krotons were dreadful!'

Even the writer Robert Holmes was appalled at the design of the Kroton robots calling them 'angry egg boxes'. During the pre-filming in a chalk quarry near Malvern the robots proved unreliable and not very photogenic. My father spent most of the day out of breath not from the energetic escape sequences but from the uncontrollable fits of laughter and giggles caused by the antics of these unwieldy monsters.

'Poor David Maloney. We were very naughty that day but those robot things... they were totally useless! They looked so out of place. They kept falling over... toppling sideways and crashing down the quarry slope. No matter how hard I tried I just couldn't pretend I was terrified of them. But the really funny thing was no matter what anyone did, nobody could make them move because of the rough ground – and they were supposed to be chasing us. At one point when we were filming a chase the front of the robot had to be man handled by some props guys just out of camera. If anyone had looked into the quarry that day they must have thought what a way to earn a living!'

By Christmas my focus had turned from science fiction of *Doctor Who* to science fact. Manned exploration of the moon seemed a lot more exciting. On December 21st 1968 I watched Apollo 8 rise into the sky and leave Earth bound for the moon. The mission was to put a tiny command capsule into orbit around the moon at a height of less than seventy miles. This was no special effects or clever drama script. On board were real astronauts not actors.

Late in the evening on Christmas Eve, my father and I watched in silent amazement as live transmissions were beamed to earth of spectacular views of the lunar surface. I can still remember Colonel Borman's words as he swung his camera around to look back at earth,

'There's a beautiful Earth out there, but boy does it look small.'

I think for Dad and myself, this was a time of change and awakening. For me, the lure of science fact began to offer far more excitement and interest than the false promises in a world of science fiction. For Dad, he had come to realize that time was precious. He needed to move on in his life and that meant leaving *Doctor Who* as soon as possible.

As Dad later explained in an interview,

'You could stay with it, and they wanted me to, for as long as the BBC did it or they got tired of you. That might be at best, one thought, five years. That would have been eight years, and by then one would have been so connected with the character that getting other work would have been very difficult indeed. So that was the main consideration there. Or one could leave. Give up a fortune. And that's what we decided to do'.

On January 7th 1969 the news broke to the press that Dad had decided to leave *Doctor Who* at the end of season six. The TV section of one tabloid reported,

'Doctor Who and Jamie to quit BBC show'
The BBC will lose its Doctor Who actor Patrick Troughton, and his companion Jamie played by Frazer Hines when the TV series reaches it summer break in June.

243

Troughton, who has played the role since he took over from William Hartnell the original time and space Doctor, told the BBC he wanted to leave in March. But producer Peter Bryant said last night: 'He has agreed to stay on until June. I will then look for a replacement.' He added, 'It is a blow to the series because Patrick has proved an excellent Doctor Who.' Hines also asked to be released in March but has agreed to carry on until June. Wendy Padbury, the young mini-skirted teenager Zoe, who accompanies the Doctor on his journeys and his battles against monsters like the Daleks and Krotons, will be the only survivor of the regular *Doctor Who* team when it returns later this year. Why is Troughton leaving the series? 'He wants to do other acting roles,' said a BBC spokesman.'

During these last few months my father began to become edgy and increasingly difficult in rehearsals. I remember on one occasion he had arrived at our house in Mill Hill after completing a producer's run-through for episode two of *The Space Pirates*. He was angry but it was an anger born of frustration more than aggression. As I opened the front door his usual enthusiastic whistle of greeting did not materialize. Instead he gazed straight ahead hardly acknowledging me. He looked haunted and highly stressed. In the tea- time conversation that followed, it became clear that he was not seeing eye-to-eye with either Peter Bryant or the director Michael Hart. I recall him complaining to my mother about how dull and unwatchable *The Space Pirates* was going to be.

'This is episode two and we're still trapped in that bloody awful spaceship set. I told them – people will just turn off.'

In fact Dad was right. People were turning off – viewing figures had dropped alarmingly from over seven million on average to five million during the last few stories. In addition to this, ITV had begun a ratings war transmitting such shows as *Joe 90*, *Voyage to the Bottom of the Sea* and *Land of the Giants*.

Tea-time conversations between my mother and father about the series became a regular weekly routine. She would listen patiently as he vented his frustrations and anger about the way *Doctor Who* was 'sinking into a downwards spiral'. I can recall snatches of it very clearly,

'These new scripts are not professional enough. They're just shoddy. I can't speak poor dialogue… it's just not fair to expect me to. It's like banging your head against a brick wall… nobody will listen.'

The actor Jack May who played General Hermack in *The Space Pirates* told me,

'In rehearsals your father would sound off at the smallest thing. He wasn't the old Pat that I remembered, joking, free, and larking about. He seemed paranoiac and unusually serious about the whole thing.'

Many other actors and directors who I have worked with also confirm that in the last few months of *Doctor Who* my father got a very bad reputation for being difficult to work with. Although not condoning his behaviour, I think this was only a cry for help and a misdirected way of showing how much he cared for the continuing quality and success of the series. He was a perfectionist who faced with the 'far from perfect script' hit out the only way he knew. Frazer remembers a moment where his confidence collapsed during a studio recording and resulted in him 'blowing his top'.

'He blew his top once, with Padders and me, because he had this long speech and he kept fluffing it on the third line. Once an actor starts to corpse, it's very difficult. I said "Patrick, you're paid a fortune to learn these lines, I'm paid to get the girls watching and Padders is paid to stop the Dads doing the gardening, Patrick you're paid to say these lines", so then he did the speech again, he got over the line, he looked at us, then he dried on the next line.'

Dad told me that during the last season the three of them had collected nicknames that referred to what they did whenever they forgot their lines.

'I used to cough just to give myself enough time to think about what I was meant to say next. Frazer just fluffed, laughed and went back. Padders would just release wind when she was nervous.'

245

He had got to the stage where even this was not making him laugh anymore. This kind of behaviour was very unlike my father. As he told me later,

'Towards the end I began to care too much… but most of all, I didn't want to be responsible for killing off Who. *I remember the part just overwhelming me…making me inconsistent and argumentative… almost schizophrenic.'*

A season too far was the way Dad often described this troubled final year as Doctor Who, which saw plummeting viewing figures, poor scripts and budget cutbacks. By mid May 1969 during the recording of episode six of *The War Games*, it had become clear that the ratings had begun to slip once more. In fact by episode eight, figures had reached an all-time low of 3.5 million. My father's time as the Doctor was to end the way he had always feared – with a disinterested public.

Despite these unhappy last few months of season six Dad would always look back on his time as Doctor Who with affection,

'I'd say that Doctor Who was the best working experience of my career.'

For me my father's time as Who was a very special period in my life – a time of change, a time of childhood dreams come true but best of all a time that seeded the inspiration for me to follow in his footsteps.

Chapter 11
Regeneration

A TV critic once wrote about my father,

'I can always sit happily watching Patrick Troughton. Why Mr Troughton is not a celebrated film-star I do not understand; he has a steely virility and hawk like incisiveness, a charm-despising charm, which makes some famous leading character actors look flabby.'

Why my father felt insecure about being able to continue his career after *Doctor Who* is a mystery, especially with marvelous comments like this about his abilities. His biggest nightmare was becoming typecast, but as I told him years later, it was never an option with him because he had a natural ability to be so different in every role he took on – he had the ability to change.

Producers Mark Shivas and Ronald Travers knew this and a week before Pat finished *Doctor Who* they offered him the key role of The Duke of Norfolk in the now legendary colour drama serial, *The Six Wives of Henry VIII*. The truth was, producers and directors were lining up, eager to welcome Patrick back into the exclusive 'TV repertory company' from which he had left so suddenly in 1967.

I can still remember the surprise in dad's face when he was offered work so soon after finishing *Who*. He had felt sure that he was going to be out of work for a good six months and had put aside funds to cover the period of predicted unemployment. Although it was excellent that he did not have to wait for work, unfortunately he was unable to have a good rest after such a punishing three years. Even the holiday that had been planned in Italy with his second family was interrupted half way through by studio recording commitments. Looking at the video of *The Six*

247

Wives of Henry VIII again it is very clear how drawn and tired Dad looks.

He told my mother,

'I was very weary after stopping the Who. It was a bit like jumping off a conveyor belt that had been running for so long. When I stopped...I suddenly realized how tired I was. 'Doctor Theatre' had kept me going because I had to... but afterwards I had time to think and my body had time to take a breath. It was telling me to slow down, but I couldn't. Too many jobs - I couldn't say no to them.'

Patrick as 'The Duke of Norfolk' in the BBC production of *The Six Wives of Henry VIII*

After completing *The Six Wives of Henry VIII*, my father had little time to draw breath. Hammer productions had cast him for the third time in one of their low budget movies entitled *The Scars of Dracula* as Christopher Lee's downtrodden and servile assistant Klove. He reveled in the 'gift of a part' as he described it, which he later called one of his best and most enjoyable performances in the Hammer series.

The film did suffer from a low budget but followed the original Bram Stoker concept very closely including Dracula's ability to fly up walls and appear in bedrooms without a sound. I remember trying to sneak into the Granada cinema in Harrow, London to watch it with some school friends, only to be told I was under age. Even when I told the box office lady that my Dad was in it, she didn't believe me. I had to wait a few more years until it released on video to enjoy such lines as,

'You fools… you think you can destroy my master! The flames will never reach him!'

and,

'It's true, he was here. But he got away. You must get away too. Now! Take her with you. He'll do terrible things to her if you don't. Terrible things. Don't let him. I'll help you to get away. It may be too late. The broth!'

Patrick plays Klove in *The Scars of Dracula* 1970

I worked with the director Roy Ward Baker a few years later on the series *Minder*. He remembered the film very clearly and told me my Dad was wonderful to work with but a little nervous. He told me,

'Pat would always cough when he couldn't remember a line quickly enough just to give him thinking time. He also had the shakes on certain close ups which he would try to disguise with sudden movements of his head.'

He also told me that the film was filled with scenes involving flying rubber bats on elastic wires, which he had constantly tried to make more realistic but had failed abysmally! A young Dennis Waterman played the juvenile lead in the movie and he recalled rehearsing a scene where he grabbed my father by the throat and thought that he had actually hurt him. He apologized straight away, asking whether he was all right. My father gently stopped him and replied '*yes my lad just good acting…*' and then laughed.

This role was closely followed by a TV serialization of *Little Women*, a Playhouse called *Don't Touch Him, He Might Resent It* and a radio version of Evelyn Waugh's *Sword of Honour*. On top of all this work, Dad had been cast as a semi-regular character in the long running ITV serial, *Family at War*.

Set during the dark days of World War II it focused on a lower-middle class family from Liverpool and followed the impact the war had on their lives. Patrick played a character called Harry who had receives a telegram from the War Office, stating that his son John is missing and is believed to be dead. Harry takes to drinking because he will not face up to the news and cannot bring himself to tell his wife Celia and the Ashtons about the letter. In one episode Harry also considers committing suicide by using his revolver to kill himself because he blames himself for encouraging John to enlist.

My mother remembered that Pat found playing the role quite emotionally draining because he had known a friend who had experienced similar problems during the war.

He told her,

It was very odd going into that set and wearing costumes from my past. It felt as if I had been transported back to Mill Hill and your mother's house. All those uncertain feelings of not really knowing what our future held came flooding back. Ghosts from the past - it was very unnerving.'

She agreed that,

'Even just watching Dad on TV transported me back to the war years and brought goose bumps and shivers. A very powerful feeling that a lot of people of our age must have felt while watching the series.'

Patrick plays Harry in *A Family at War*, 1970 © Granada TV

Doomwatch was one of my favourite TV shows and at the age of 16, I never missed a single episode. So, when in 1971 Dad managed to get a role in this BBC science fiction series, I was very excited. Created by the inventors of the Cybermen, Gerry Davis and Kit Pedler had produced an extremely original and innovative drama based around 'The Department for the Observation of Scientific Work'. Their job was to investigate the moral, ethical and environmental implications of the latest scientific research. It was a drama well ahead of its time exploring many issues that are relevant

251

today such as environmental pollution, euthanasia, and genetic engineering.

My dad's episode, *In the Dark,* was the ninth episode of the second season, and was first broadcast on 15 February 1971. He played Alan McArthur who was on life support after contracting a disease that would eventually leave him without the ability to speak, see or move, essentially becoming just a brain in a dead body. I recall Dad explaining,

'I was lying in a plywood box covered with flashing lights and switches for most of the episode. It was so hot and sweaty, especially since I also had a crape bandage wound around my head. The worst thing was though… I couldn't scratch my nose. I had to get the makeup lady to itch my nose many times.'

Patrick encased in his plywood life support machine in an episode of Doomwatch, 1971

Another favourite series of mine was *The Goodies* in which Pat played the dastardly and unloved 'Wolfgang Adolphus Ratfink von Petal' with long black greasy hair and a sly and wicked falsetto voice. One forgets how popular the BBC programme was during the early seventies - actors were lining up to appear with the three stooges – Bill Oddie, Tim Brooke-Taylor and Graeme Garden.

This was the first occasion that Dad had worked with a studio audience and it was a new experience for him. I recall his advice to me when I was about to do my first guest appearance in the sitcom

Bless me Father. He used his performance in *The Goodies,* and explained,

'It is very confusing because at first you don't know who to perform to — the camera or the audience. Your instinct as an actor is to perform to the audience but if you do that, you could end up excluding the viewers at home. On the other hand, if you perform exclusively to the camera the audience will miss a great deal making the performance feel flat due to lack of laughter and reaction. One has to find a half-way house where you are treading a tightrope between both. I found it extremely difficult and nerve racking during The Goodies. *It was worse because I had to be in command all the time.'*

However, with lines such as, 'Just because I'm a mad scientist it doesn't mean I'm not nice!' he need not have worried. The performance was brilliant and I recall gasping for breath through my laughter when I watched it for the first time.

He appeared again in front of a studio audience soon after *The Goodies.* Frankie Howerd, had asked specifically for Patrick to play the evil character 'Tamerlane the Tartar' in his new series *Whoops Bagdad* based on the same format as the highly successful *Up Pompeii.* Pat really enjoyed working with Frankie Howerd who he described as, *'a true professional and naturally funny man who had a stunning presence and control while performing.'*

Patrick as Tamberlane the Tartar in Whoops Bagdad

Work continued to stream into his agent and Patrick had little time to rest between engagements. The early seventies saw him appear as Padre in the TV series *Colditz*, Frederick Owen in *The Main Chance*, Bennett in *Jason King* in which he impersonated Peter Wyngarde, Jim Goody in *The Befrienders*, Count Marceau the aging Nazi in *The Persuaders*, and Ernie Johnson in the police series *Softly Softly*.

In February 1972 Dad arrived home to Mill Hill on one of his hastily unannounced visits and told us that Barry Letts had approached him about appearing in *Doctor Who* again. He showed me the script synopsis for an idea written by Bob Baker and Dave Martin entitled *Deathworld*. The story involved the Time Lords fighting with a Federation of Evil by sending the three Doctors (two from the past) into battle against zombies, dark riders, an evil goddess Kali, and a Cyclops. I remember my Dad dismissing it as a rather contrived idea that may well have been thought up by the fans of the programme rather than the production company. He also immediately went into worry mode regarding his typecasting fears.

'Do I really want the public to see me as the Doctor again after all the hard work I have done to make them forget?'

I told him he should find out what the fee was before he dismissed it! He laughed and retorted,

'I've taught you well!'

About three weeks later he phoned to say he had in principle accepted the offer but that they would have to delay the production until late autumn because he was unavailable until then. They must have offered a large fee for him to commit so early.

During the summer it became clear that Bill Hartnell's arteriosclerosis that he suffered from was worsening and he was now unable to walk very well and appeared rather frail. Hartnell's health would be too poor for him to take an active role in the entire serial. The First Doctor's involvement in the storyline was therefore restricted to brief scenes, which could be pre-filmed, and my father's role was built up. The script was now renamed *The*

Black Hole and the experienced director Lennie Mayne was employed to steer the ship.

My father was contracted officially on 21st September and he began rehearsals mid-November after filming sequences in Denham.

Dad and Jon Pertwee had a professional love-hate relationship. They were the best of friends but had strong personalities with their own very different ideas on acting. Jon described this difference very well,

'He was a magical man, he was a kook, he was strange, he wasn't like other fellows. He was an ad-libber actor. I remember when he came in on my show, and he was a guest, and he was underneath the TARDIS and he was doing something, the cue was

"I can't find the circuit", and he said,

"Oh where is the wretched thing?" and I said,

"What?"

"Come on, I've given you the line"

"No you haven't!"

"Well it's near enough!"

"No it's not, I'm Doctor Who now, I know you did that when you were in it".

He was wonderful, very free, I loved to watch him.'

My father described Pertwee as *'Secure on every moment of his performance. I envy that. Such control over what he is doing. I love him for that. But not dangerous enough for me. I prefer to be more out of control than that. More dependent on emotion than lines.'*

Even before rehearsals had begun, Jon had vetoed ideas to bring back companions from the past such as Wendy Padbury and Frazer Hines because he was concerned that an abundance of old characters might detract from the show's current protagonists.

Not surprisingly Jon was determined that his Doctor should remain the adventure's focus and not be outshone by either Hartnell's or Troughton's.

It is clear that they both thoroughly respected one another but approached performance from very different directions. This

255

difference of opinion seemed to leak into their performances in *The Three Doctors* with wonderfully amusing results. The opening lines of my father's first scene bristles with clipped and cutting exchanges as the two Doctors tussle in a fight for superiority,

JO: Who is he and how did he get in here? He's not one of them is he?
DOCTOR (Jon): One of me to be precise.
DOCTOR (Pat): Oh no no no! I'm sorry my dear, I hate to be contrary but you see he's a little bit confused poor old chap and I do feel you should have the correct explanation. You see Jo… I may call you Jo, main't I? *He* is one of *me*!

Patrick enjoyed that six weeks on *Doctor Who* and looking back never regretted doing it.

'I will always keep my Doctor safe with me in case he needs to be used again.'

For Patrick, it was his last connection with the programme for ten years.

In 1973, I left school after completing my A levels hoping to go to university. Unfortunately, I could not really afford that route although I did ask Dad for help. He told me,

'You have A levels under your belt and that will be enough to get you out of trouble if your acting career doesn't work. Besides, I'm not earning the kind of money that we got on Doctor Who *anymore - and that sent you to private school in Harrow.'*

So with my Dad's help I started work at the Arts Theatre in London with the Children's Unicorn Company as an A.S.M. (Assistant Stage Manager). Dad's friend and college Caryl Jenner who he had met at Amersham Repertory in the 1940's had founded the company, which performed exclusively to a young audience. I had become part of an acting family now that included my brother David. It felt good.

It was about this time that Dad began to drift apart from his partner 'Bunny' for the second time in the thirteen years of their relationship. This time it was Patrick that had met someone new. My mother told me that the woman that had won him over was called Shelagh Holdup. She was a close friend of Bunny's who used to use their garden in Kew to sunbathe and relax during the holidays. She was a perfume technician involved in mixing and testing new fragrances at one of the large cosmetic companies. How they met I am unsure, but by 1975 Patrick had decided to separate from 'Bunny' and marry Shelagh. Yet again he was faced with the unbearable decision of leaving a young family who would miss him terribly. It must have been a gut-wrenching decision to make once but twice? However, make it he did.

I think Shelagh had insisted that they tie the knot because I am sure Patrick would have been quite happy to remain married to my mother Margaret, to whom he had been officially married since 1943.

Dad and Shelagh's long-term relationship had blossomed from affair to full commitment out in Malta where he had been filming *Sinbad and the Eye of the Tiger* during the summer of 1975. Dad had been asked by Sam Wanamaker to play 'Melanthius' an eccentric magician in the new Harryhausen blockbuster after he had looked back over tapes of *Jason and the Argonauts*. Sam was immediately impressed by Dad's portrayal of the *'Harpies'* tormented Phineas. He told me,

'What your father was so good at was playing older than his years. He had a mature edge to him that the audience was drawn too. He also had that enviable ability to disguise himself with such a believable characterization you almost forgot he was acting. I was a real fan and wished I could have used him more.'

Sinbad and the Eye of the Tiger was the third Sinbad film to feature the special effects of Ray Harryhausen. My father had experienced the curious and rather unnatural process of acting to imaginary beings during his short cameo appearance in *Jason and the Argonauts'*. It would be no different on this movie with a sabre-toothed tiger, a big walrus, a huge Troglodyte, a giant mosquito, and the chess-playing baboon-Kassim. Pat's previous natural ability to act to nothing was perhaps another reason that he had been favoured over other actors for the part of Phineas. Sinbad was played by Patrick Wayne (the son of John) with Taryn Power, Margaret Whiting and Jane Seymour starring alongside. This was the first big movie that my father had done where he was in it pretty well all the way through. Up until this moment, he had only ever been offered small character cameos but this was at last a real breakthrough and I remember him saying to me – *'Hollywood next stop!'*

In an airmail letter to me from the unit base in Rabat, Malta he described how the filming was going,

'*NIGRET-A-Flat No.1, New Street, off New Rd, RABAT MALTA.*

Dear Mike,

The telephone number is for the restaurant down the road and not the flat I am staying at. Phoning is very difficult I am afraid – there's always a long delay. You have to pre-book a call and I am generally too late when I return from location. Rather than have your phone going at two in the morning, I'm writing!!

All goes very well indeed and I am 'Blue-eyed-boy number 1'. It's a lovely part and Sam has said nothing but 'lovely' and 'perfect' ever since I started so I naturally think he is a very good director. He shouts at the girls a bit though. Mind you one of them is a bit clueless and it's not Taryn who is very sweet and good. And it's not Maggie Whiting needless to say – she's the 'Blue-eyed girl'.

We left Madrid after a five-hour wait at the hot sweltering airport. Our baggage (filming gear) was difficult to load safely. We eventually had to leave some behind.

The flight was a bit edgy for me as I had a hangover from the last night merriments in the hotel, so I wasn't fortified with my usual scotch! But we saw Minorca, Sardinia and Sicily laid out 45,000 feet beneath us and duly landed at dusk in Malta.

I have had two days off and have now got my bearings and acclimatised. I have a super apartment – very large and airy with a big fridge so at last I can have cold drinks.

Madrid is 3,000 feet up and very hot and sticky – but here we are at sea level and although we are inland at Rabat one feels the sea air and can breathe.

I am hiring a car in 2 days time when Shelagh comes. She managed to squeeze a holiday break and we are going to do a bit of romantic touring on my days off.

We are all mostly grouped around this Nigret nightclub in apartments with the locations near as well.

Patrick Wayne is super and I am sharing No.1 caravan with him – air conditioned and very large. What a star I am turning into!

Hope you are well and work is forth coming. You must meet Shelagh soon. Perhaps not at Mill Hill though.

Smile on your face.

Love and loads of work Dad x'

When Dad returned from Jordan, which was the last filming location, he had reached another turning point in his life – change and renewal was to happen for the third time.

I remember the day my father came over to Mill Hill and asked my mother for a divorce. He didn't beat around the bush. He came straight out with it almost before he had got through the door. He also insisted that the house in Mill Hill should be sold and he should decide how much my mother got. The argument that followed is legendary in our family history. Divorce was acceptable by now for Margaret and she did not object to the idea, but the threat of losing her house after all the time she had spent there bringing up his first family by herself must have really stuck in her throat. My sister Jo recalls,

'It was when Dad returned from filming that he sprang Shelagh on Mum and me - she had been out there with him. He said that although he was going to marry her and divorce Mum, "nothing will change", as far as Mum and all of us were concerned. Then about a week or two later he came over and told Mum he was selling Uphill Road to buy a little 'love nest' for him and Shelagh. He couldn't touch Bunny's house, as I believe she had wisely had it put in trust for her and her children.'

'That's when the iron entered my soul so to speak and I went out and bought 'The Penguin Book of Women's Rights' as I knew Mum was being done over. And that's how the whole saga of the divorce began: *Stay alive in '75* was our slogan for the year!'

It took around a year to drag the rather bitter and unsavory arguments through the courts. A friends of mum's told me,

'When we heard about Pat's attempt to take Margaret's house from her... well we immediately recommended a family lawyer which was a better proposal than the 'Do-it-yourself' variety that was favoured by Pat!'

My mother explained,

'He wanted to sell Uphill Road and then buy me and Jo a small flat somewhere. He would then use the majority of what was left to purchase a new house for him and his wife. Well... I wasn't having that. I had spent my whole life in that house and brought his children up on a shoestring and now he was turning round cashing in on my life. No way! The worst thing he ever said to me that really hurt came out during that dreadful divorce year – he told me 'I had made a very good mother but not a very good wife.' After that I really saw him in a different light.'

The court decision was unanimous and came down very firmly on my mother's side. She was to keep the house and Pat was not to get a penny - when and if she sold it.

From that point on my sister never talked to him again.

In April of the following year my father married Shelagh. The local paper reported,

'A DOCTOR WHO IS CAPTURED!

Actor Patrick Troughton, a former TV 'Doctor Who', happily surrenders to an earth-bound life – with his new bride Shelagh. The couple nipped into a registry office at Richmond, Surrey, yesterday while the Daleks weren't looking. Patrick, aged 56, has just finished making a film with Gregory Peck called *The Omen*. Certainly, his bride's smile augurs well for the future.'

Patrick with his new wife outside Richmond registry office in April 1976

It was such a hastily arranged wedding, that I don't think any of his children were present at the ceremony or gathering afterwards. I remember finding out they were married from an article in the national press.

Just before the wedding, Dad had been working with Gregory Peck and Lee Remick on a major new horror film. *The Omen* was one of Dad's most loved film performances and even now I get asked questions about the filming of 'that sequence' – the one where he gets skewered by the lightening conductor. Pat's son Mark explained,

'Seeing Dad die for the first time in The Viking Queen was pretty alarming. A sword to his perfidious Roman heart. Even though I'd been back stage and seen the (rubber) sword and the carefully prepared bloody slit in the leather jerkin he was to wear, it still was an uncertain moment. "It's ok, it's only a film!" I said to myself (I was only 5 after all). After that, seeing him getting spiked by Damian where the lightning rod falls off the steeple and skewers him to the spot was a piece of cake. Took them all morning to film that, in reverse, with lightning rod going back up invisible wire, (oh, the glory days of pre-CGI!) then played backwards to make it look like a genuine 'brochette au diable'. No expense spared! How times have changed.'

I think the moment I will never forget is the haunted terror in his voice as he whispers those spine-chilling words about Damian to Gregory Peck,

'He will kill the unborn child, then he will kill your wife, and when he is certain to inherit all that is yours, then Mr Thorn, he will kill you.'

Dad thoroughly enjoyed working on the movie and I recall that he fell head over heels in love with Lee Remick who he described as,

'A gorgeous, generous and wonderful woman - a true star in the proper sense of the word.'

Patrick as Father Brennan in *The Omen*

I remember meeting him at the BBC rehearsal rooms a few months later and he could not stop talking about 'how marvelous Lee Remick was' and 'she is so photogenic', and 'I would love to work with her some more'.

I think if he hadn't already committed himself for the third time to Shelagh, then Lee would have been his next target!

By 1976 I had left Watford Palace Theatre where I had been employed as an A.S.M. and had ventured out into the freelance world of TV acting. One of the first jobs I got was an episode of the medical nurse drama 'Angels' directed by a favorite of mine, Tristan DeVere Cole. Alan James had written an episode about a rather loud pushy father and his mentally abused son. Tristan had contacted my father and myself and was very enthusiastic that we should take on the roles. My first proper TV acting job was to be opposite my Dad! Quite a daunting thought at the time. Still I need not have worried. Dad phoned me up and said,

'Do you think we should do this? I will if you will.'

I said,

'Of course we bloody should! You've always told me never turn anything down.'

He replied quickly,

'See you at Acton then'

He said 'goodbye' and that was that.

At the end of August I did a bit of pre-filming for the episode that didn't involve Dad and by September the first rehearsal day had arrived. Read-through days are nerve-racking at the best of times but with your father who was an experienced veteran character actor watching too – well you can imagine.

I recall the scenes we had together were quite disturbing with an undercurrent of real hatred from my character and blundering insensitivity from his. This was the first time that I had ever seen Dad working in rehearsals and it was a surprise to see how nervous he seemed. I am unsure whether this was because of my presence or he was always like it but I noticed an uncomfortable tremor of his head and a distinct tremble in his hands as we worked various scenes.

At lunchtime I had a long chat with him about his way of working in rehearsal and he admitted to me that he found it a pressurized business. He told me that he was the type of actor who needed those nerves to make his character come to life. It was an essential part of the way he prepared for a part and he could not accomplish it any other way. He also told me,

'I envy those actors that can read a book or do their knitting during rehearsals – I can't do that. I have to be focused all the time even when I'm waiting for my scene to start. When I am about to perform, my heart begins to race, my skin begins to glow and I feel myself gently shaking. If I don't feel nervous, I just know that the performance is going to be wrong. It's the way I am made. I expect it will be the death of me one day.'

Looking back at what he had told me – how true were those few words. The amount of nervous tension in his performances, were bound to eventually take their toll on his body. One couldn't sustain that kind of method of working without something giving.

His performance in *Angels* was, as usual, brilliant. It made my job so easy and allowed me the luxury of being able to be the 'reactor', which was a safer place to be for such an inexperienced young actor as I was. His comment on my performance was,

'Lovely innocence, you had the audience on your side right from the start. You have that wonderful ability to make people feel sorry for you. Don't lose it as you get older.'

Working with Dad for that short time I felt I had been let into a secret world that not many people were privileged to witness. My father had showed me his creative vulnerability, his working process stripped bare and the very private method in which he worked.

Just after the premiere of *Sinbad and the Eye of the Tiger,* Dad was asked to play the part of Israel Hands in a high budget Australian and BBC mini-series of *Treasure Island.* Michael E. Briant was directing and was determined to make his version a bit more gritty and realistic. He wrote,

'I was blessed with superb performances from Alfred Burke as Long John Silver, Thorley Walters as Squire Trelawney, Anthony Bate as Dr Livesey and Patrick Troughton as Israel Hands.

Patrick as Israel Hands in *Treasure Island*

Dad filmed at Plymouth, Dartford, Corsica and also at BBC Television Centre at Wood Lane, London. It was the second time he had done Robert Louis Stevenson's adventure story and he was pleased to have a 'baddie' part yet again.

His punishing work schedule continued to increase during the late seventies with numerous productions including, *Yanks Go Home*, *The Sinking of HMS Victoria*, *Van der Valk*, *Warships*, *Edward and Mrs Simpson* and *The Devil's Crown*.

In May 1978 the first episode of a children's drama series called *The Feathered Serpent* was broadcast. It was an impressive and intelligent piece of work set in ancient Mexico, in the pre-Aztec civilization of Toltecs. My father played the chief villain, High Priest Nasca, who plots to murder the Emperor Kukulkhan and take his crown. Diane Keen played the heroine, Princess Chimalma and throughout the series struck up a close friendship with my father. She said of Patrick,

'Working with Patrick was the happiest and most enjoyable time of my career. It was a joy to experience his talent and sheer professionalism, but most of all, I found him a dear, dear friend. We shared many happy times together as friends and artists.

Dad gave Diane one of his paintings as a wedding present. He had recently rekindled his love of painting birds and had also turned his hand to meticulously copying the works of the great painters. I have two of his – a Constable and a Lowry. They are very accurate paintings but could never be mistaken for the real thing. The TV Times wrote, 'If his motives were mercenary and he used canvas instead of hardboard, 'forger' would be a nasty name for him!'

In the eighties he actually exhibited some of his work in Richmond and sold a good few. His Lowrys were the most popular and I think pretty accurate copies of the original style.

My wife Caroline and I went to the private viewing since we only lived around the corner in Twickenham. I recall Dad bounding up to us with two glasses of champagne in one hand and a cheque flapping in the other,

'I've sold my first Lowry for a hundred 'squid'... I've decided to leave acting and become a full time painter! [Pause] *Only joking!'*

Looking back I wish that he could have been serious about leaving the profession. It was very clear to me after having worked with him that the kind of nervous energy that he put into his work was having a long-term effect on his body. The stress and strain that he was putting on his heart was bound to finally have disastrous repercussions.

Despite his doctor warning him about his high blood pressure, Dad continued with a heavy work load which included *Space 1999*, *A Hitch in Time*, *Suez 1956*, *The Onedin Line* and a children's TV series called *The Famous Five*.

By the winter of 1979 Patrick had been booked to recreate his highly acclaimed role of Quilp in a new version of *The Old Curiosity Shop*. I remember him coming over to Mill Hill during the pre-filming of the series and being shocked at how tired he looked. He was also complaining about pains in his legs. He had strapped up both legs with crape bandages for some unknown reason and when I asked him what he had done to them he snorted,

'Don't know. Must have strained them with the bloody stooping I have to do for Quilp.'

At the end of the week I had a phone call from mum to say Dad had had a suspected heart attack during the early morning and was under observation in hospital. I wasn't surprised at all – I had almost anticipated it.

I didn't know what to expect when I visited the hospital the following week. What met my eyes as I entered the ward was typical of dad. He was sitting up drinking a cup of tea ordering nurses and doctors around explaining that he *had* to be better by next week to complete his commitment to the TV series he was doing. I recall at one point he told a nurse that she should be prepared for a large amount of farting because it was always better out than in! I don't think he realized or wanted to admit to himself how close he had come to death. By the end of the following week he had come round to the idea that it was going to take longer than he had first thought recover. Reluctantly he told the BBC that he would be unable to continue and that they must recast the part of Quilp.

One paper reported,

'DOCTOR WHO MAN ILL

Former Doctor Who Patrick Troughton was in hospital last night after recovering from a suspected heart attack. The 58 year old actor collapsed last Friday at his London home. Troughton has been rehearsing for a ten –part dramatization of *The Old Curiosity Shop*, due to be screened at the end of the month. He has now told the producers he will not be able to continue in the series. He played the part of Quilp – one of the major characters.'

Dad's son Mark recalled,

'That was the year [1979] of his first heart attack; well, he does look wretched in *The Omen* and the stress of over-doing it for so many years told. "We have to save for the taxman" was his stock response. The *Who* was punishing - the main reason why mum pressed him to give it up, having encouraged him to take the role in the first place!'

Barry Letts, the producer of 'The Old Curiosity Shop' told me,

'Patrick had fully committed himself to the part both physically and mentally during filming. It really meant a lot for him to do Quilp all over again 'in colour' as he put it! I was absolutely devastated when I heard the news but not entirely surprised. Your father would never just relax when he was working… but that's what made him so good.'

Father and son (author) admire the master's work at his new flat in 1983

Chapter 12
A New Life

Dad was a bad patient – after two months of convalescence and moping around his flat in Ham he was back on the phone to his agent Maurice explaining that he felt as 'fit as a fiddle' and that it had only been a minor blip. Everything was under control.

This was far from the truth. Dad's coronary thrombosis had severely weakened him and his heart had been damaged. It was being treated with beta-blockers to reduce his blood pressure and aspirin to thin his blood but the doctor had warned him about nervous exhaustion associated with his job. Needless to say he took absolutely no notice of this and was appearing on TV in an episode of the hit comedy *Only When I Laugh*, by late spring.

In it, he played a tramp patient called Perkins, who suffers from severe body odour problems and mental instability. He had an invisible dog that he talked to all the time! The comic story line revolved around the main cast discovering that he was unbelievably wealthy and their sudden change of attitude towards him. This was a studio sitcom with a live audience and it must have been a severe test of dad's recovery and state of health at the time.

During the summer of 1980, I visited Dad's new flat for the first time. I had just completed a series called *Testament of Youth* the year before and met my wife to be Caroline who had been a makeup artist on the production. After our engagement, we were invited over to Dad's flat to meet his new wife, Shelagh. When we arrived at the rather modern 1960's two-storey block of flats perched above a petrol station on a busy main road, I recall thinking how quickly Dad's life had changed with a new wife, his illness and the rather claustrophobic residence he now lived in. I felt a little sorry for him.

A tall thin bearded man who introduced himself as Shelagh's son greeted us at the door. The flat was a small two bed-roomed affair with a small kitchen-diner and a sitting room that had a large window overlooking Bushy Park. Dad was sitting in his armchair surrounded by his paintings, which hung on every wall – Lowrys, Constables, Monets and Turners. It was like being in the Tate gallery. I was very shocked at how old he looked. He had suddenly turned grey overnight – not just his jet-black hair but it was his whole face. He got up slowly and greeted us both with,

'Hi Matey, finally I get to meet your gorgeous Caroline and you get to meet my lovely Shelagh.'

The meal we had was a strained affair with many pregnant pauses and embarrassed glances between us. Shelagh's son did his best to lighten the occasion with varying degrees of success. He seemed just as uncomfortable as us. I recall the meal was a hotpot stew with a weird combination of tinned meat such as spam and left over chicken or ham. It tasted pretty bad but we both politely forced it down. Shelagh was quite relaxed and I noticed that she felt the need to mother Dad an awful lot. One of the stories she told us both, made him go bright red. It centered on the fact that before they had met, he had not worn any antiperspirant.

'I changed that straight away by spraying his underarms every morning!'

Dad recovered with an embarrassed smile and told us that the doctor had advised lots of exercise,

'I'm going to get a couple of Labradors. What with the park down there I can walk for miles each morning and get all the exercise the quack insists on.'

I told him about our idea of moving to Twickenham when we were married and he seemed very pleased at the prospect of us becoming neighbours.

Looking back it was a surreal meeting that evening and driving home in silence I reflected on how far apart we had both become. It felt like I was talking to a stranger that evening. He was trying to be someone he wasn't with Shelagh and she was encouraging him. The following morning both Caroline and I woke up feeling

272

dreadful not because of the difficult meeting the night before but because we were spewing our guts up in the bathroom! I think it must have been something we ate?

Apart from playing golf with him at the BBC course in Richmond Park I rarely visited him at his flat from then on. We would meet up at the rehearsal rooms in Acton or he would come over to our house in Twickenham. I preferred to see him by himself when he was more relaxed and more the old Dad I remembered.

My father refused to slow down and if anything his workload during the early eighties increased. A comedy drama series called *Bognar, Nanny* with Wendy Craig, *Shine on Harvey Moon* with Elizabeth Spriggs, *Foxy Lady* with his close friend Dianne Keene, *Kings Royal, Dramarama, 'Jury, John Diamond,* and *The Pigman's Protégé* were just a few of the many TV series and plays he took on.

In 1983 he took a brief role as the Roman soldier named Sextus in episode four of a series called *The Cleopatras.* My wife Caroline was one of the make-up artists on the show and she recalls how professional my father was,

'We were at Television Centre in Shepherd's Bush... I think it was TC8 and anyway he had been waiting all day to do his scene. I think he was some kind of Roman messenger that had to deliver important news to one of the Pharos. Right at the end of the day he was called to *the floor and rushed onto set by the floor manager. We had about ten minutes of VT time left so everyone was a bit stressed out. Patrick walks onto the set and starts to rehearse the scene... "No time for that!" shouts a voice from the control gallery. "Roll VT!" Well, Patrick starts up with this very long speech and almost gets to the end... you can see that he is so nervous, worried he is going to muck up and have to start all over again. Just as he's finishing the speech he fluffs a line and coughs... you know that way he always did to cover up a forgotten line. Back to the start we went, everything was reset. Cue Patrick... and off he went again. I can't tell you how impressed I was with him... so professional. Straight through without a fluff. We just finished in time as the working lights in the studio came on. I was really very impressed.'*

Patrick as Sextus in *The Cleopatras*

The year before - the summer of 1982 - my Dad called to say that he had been contacted by John Nathan-Turner, the series producer on *Doctor Who*, to see whether he would be interested in doing a twentieth anniversary special with all five doctors. He seemed unsure about the whole thing. I recall him asking me,

'Should I do another one? I don't see Tom agreeing... that would pretty well ruin the whole thing. But on the other hand I could ask for a ridiculous amount of money.'

I told him that he shouldn't worry about doing another one. After all, a lot of water had passed under the bridge since *The Three Doctors*. He was hardly going to be typecast after just one special.

274

Jon Pertwee, who had signed up in July must have phoned Dad at some point to persuade him to come on board. There was a problem though. John Nathan Turner had insisted that if Dad did the show he would be obliged to attend the *Doctor Who* Convention to be held at Longleat during the Easter Bank holiday the following year. It wasn't part of the contract but more a gentleman's agreement.

The demands for Patrick to appear in public and talk about *Doctor Who* had become more frequent during the late seventies and early eighties. I was phoned on many occasions by convention organizers and asked to try and persuade my father to change his mind on this matter. Up until this point he would always say no to such appearances, clutching his forehead and mumbling,

'It's all such a long time ago... I can't remember a thing. I would be very boring.'

He still held fast to the notion that there was magic in the mechanics of making TV shows and was determined to decline offers of public appearances to keep the professional secrets, secret. However, for some extraordinary reason I still don't understand, he suddenly abandoned this lifelong rule and changed his mind.

By 2nd August he had signed a provisional contract with the understanding he was to promote the show at the *Doctor Who* Convention in Longleat. Either the BBC had made an offer he just couldn't refuse or Jon and dad's wife Shelagh (who I think was enthusiastic for him to go public), changed his stubborn mind.

Filming for the special began in Wales, a couple of weeks before my Dad's birthday. My Dad loved to tell the story about his friend Jon Pertwee's tantrum that reputedly occurred on location at Manod Quarry when they were filming the Dark Tower sequence. Dad would explain with a mischievous smirk on his face,

'...there was 'Silverfox' Pertwee at the top of this cliff, his cloak flying in the air and crowing at the top of his voice at some poor assistant, "I can't possibly use that ... it's ridiculous. How can I make a glider from this stuff? It's just not believable!" He was a bit like a baby who was throwing his dummy out of

his pram. I couldn't stop laughing at the image when some of the crew told me the story.'

Apparently, Jon had refused to film a sequence in which he was supposed to build a hang-glider out of robot spare parts and his cloak. Then he was to be seen flying towards The Dark Tower. Unfortunately the props that had been supplied looked very unrealistic and John refused to complete the sequence calling it 'preposterous and unbelievable'. The scene was hastily rewritten with Moffatt and Nathan-Turner working together over lunch to come up with an alternative version of the sequence, the Doctor now throwing a line across to the Dark Tower instead.

Dad told me he teased Jon about this moment all through the rehearsals and studio. Some of the wonderfully amusing lines between Jon and Dad in the episode were as a direct consequence of this constant good-humoured barracking between them.

'Fancy pants!'

'Scarecrow!'

The other thing I recall about *The Five Doctors* was Dad's real affection for Nicholas Courtney. They seem so relaxed in those filming sequences in the Welsh caves – a real camaraderie comes over. Nicholas later said of dad,

'My chief memory of Pat was how easy he made my job. He was such a delight to work with. He had a sense of fun and this communicated itself to all the other members of the *Doctor Who* family. As a result, we got on with the job and enjoyed ourselves... I remember us running from the Yeti like we had done in the past. It was a good time. I got to know him and Shelagh even better during the American Conventions where we really let our hair down. He was a dear man and a fine actor'

Patrick did appear at the BBC celebration of twenty years of *Doctor Who* at Longleat House on Easter Bank holiday weekend. It was a great surprise to everyone – his fans, Shelagh, John Nathan Turner and especially me. The event attracted a huge number of people and I remember him telling me he was signing autographs for well over five hours. He also sat on a panel where fans were able to ask questions. He admitted to me that he had really not looked forward to the event and found the prospect of talking to the public very daunting. However, Pat was won over by the generosity and admiration of the fans that weekend and decided from that point on to involve himself more in convention life – besides 'the expenses and hospitality were excellent!' This was the only time he appeared in his own clothes – the following conventions he attended saw him dressed as the Doctor.

Pat appears for the first time at a *Doctor Who* convention

1984 saw my father have another heart scare. This time it was not so serious and went mostly unreported in the press. However, his doctor told him that it was a warning to slow down and that if he carried on with a busy acting schedule he would defiantly have a more serious attack.

I went round to see him after he had returned from a brief visit to Teddington hospital to try to convince him of the wisdom of this advice. I was totally unsuccessful!

'I've just got a splendid children's TV series directed by your friend Renny Rye. He wants me to play the old Punch and Judy man in the adaptation of John Mansfield's The Box of Delights.'

I told him that he shouldn't do it and that rest was the order of the day, but he didn't take any notice and just changed the subject – telling me he was going for a walk with Bill and Ben, his new Labradors and that I was welcome to join him. Marching across Bushy heath at quite a lick with Bill and Ben rushing frantically around after a ball that Dad was bowling to them, I continued to try and persuade him that taking it easy for a while was not a bad thing. I was unsuccessful and left Ham that day feeling I had not tried hard enough – it would be my fault if he fell down dead in a couple of months. Looking back now, I can see that no amount of persuasion would have been enough. Dad was going to do what he loved until his last breath and no one was going to stop him.

Of course, Pat was brilliant as Cole Hawlings in *The Box of Delights* - a very special series that epitomized British children's television at its best. Postcards sent to me during the production revealed how happy he was on the series,

'It feels like we were creating something very special. Of course, it is to be released around Christmas time which will help, but Renee is doing a fantastic job with the special effects considering the budget.'

Filming in Scotland was a bit of a nightmare. January 1984:

'The crew and actors had just arrived at the location hotel and the heavens opened. The whole of Scotland is cut off with blizzards. But it is perfect for the filming... we never got to the locations; Renee decided to film everything in the hotel grounds. Waste deep in snow for three days I was. Bloody freezing but wonderful pictures'

'...got to know Robert Stevens very well and spent a naughty night drinking! Back on the whisky and water. Quack won't like that – don't tell!'

Besides the heavy acting commitments, the phenomenal success of *Doctor Who* in America meant Patrick would always get a warm welcome at conventions across the pond. By this time he had decided that it would be a good idea to develop his convention appearances in America only,

'I don't want to become too associated with the part again in England. But in America, that's different, because I don't appear in anything over there – except in repeats. They don't know me out there like they do here. I can't ruin my career over there because I don't have one.'

Dad made a number of appearances in America including the Twentieth Anniversary Celebrations in Chicago. He would always appear in costume as the Doctor rather than himself, insisting it was what the fans wanted to see. Besides, he was far more at home acting a part than revealing his real self to an audience. It gave him the excuse to act the clown and be disruptive which is exactly what his fans wanted. I recall one famous appearance involved him materializing from the TARDIS draped only in a bath towel and nothing else, shouting that Jon Pertwee had stolen his costume. On another occasion Jon and Dad would perform a mock duel with water pistols. He later described how he felt about these conventions to John Peel for Fantasy Empire,

'It's an ego trip. They love you so much. When I was on the show, you didn't have time for such things. You didn't have time to do anything but to go home and go to sleep. I went to bed at nine o clock every night for three years! I couldn't have existed otherwise.'

It had taken almost fifteen years for Dad to embrace the cult status of *Doctor Who* and to have finally embraced it without fear of it damaging his career. He even started attending a few British conventions. It was no surprise then, that when he was contacted about doing another *Doctor Who* special he said yes without even reading the script.

Originally called *The Kraglon Inheritance, The Two Doctors* was the last time Dad was to appear on TV as the 'time-travelling hobo'. Filming began in August in the height of the Spanish summer. A postcard sent to the family from Seville explained,

'Spent the first two days sunbathing and swimming in the pool. They'd lost my eyebrows and some wigs en route! They say that one of the actresses is proving rather difficult about her costume as well. Still filming nearly done now in temperature of 104° F. All our make-up is running and the glue to wigs is un-sticking. Sea fog today, thank heavens. Colin sends David his love. Dad xx'.

After working with my Dad on *The Two Doctors*, Colin Baker described Pat's doctor as,

'A walking junk heap of disorganized mayhem, self-deprecating, affecting those delightful moments of utter dismay and panic, he lurched through space and time, not so much as the 'cosmic hobo' but more as an unlikely cross between Don Quixote and

Machiavelli. It was a stunning characterization, which at once made his successors' tasks much easier and much, much more difficult. Easier because Pat had established the concept of regeneration instantly, by virtue of his great talent and commitment and had accordingly been accepted by the viewing millions – but more difficult because, to coin a cliché, 'Follow that!'

Of the man himself he said,

'My impression of Pat then was and remained that of a 'gentle' man in the true sense of the word. A kind man, of strongly held principles, who felt no need to dominate others but was secure in himself, thereby of course drawing others to him like a magnet. He could also be wicked in the nicest possible way – and often was. You only have to ask Debbie Watling or Frazer Hines what it was like to work with Pat to be regaled with the most amazing and outrageous stories. Having worked with Pat and Frazer on *The Two Doctors*, I believe them!'

Colin's articulate words offer a warm and touching description of dad's final appearance as the Doctor, words that the family have kept in his scrapbook and will continue to do so.

Apart from *Who* conventions, the last connection Dad had with the Doctor is shrouded in mystery and a little uncertainty. During the summer of 1986 it seems that he could have been contacted by Sydney Newman regarding the possibility of taking over the role of Doctor Who for a short 'caretaker' period – possibly one season. It is alleged that Newman had contacted Michael Grade because he knew that the series was floundering and close to being axed. In a letter to Grade, Newman urged the controller to temporarily reintroduce Patrick Troughton to steady the TARDIS and pave the way for the most radical change in the show's 23-year history - that at a later stage Doctor Who should be metamorphosed into a woman. How much of this is true still remains unclear but I do know that my father would never have considered taking on the role again – no matter what the fee.

One of the last parts that Dad played rather ironically was that of a super-fit grandfather in the sitcom *The Two of Us* with Nicholas Lyndhurst and Janet Dibley. He told the TV Times in November 1986 that it,

'...is the first time since 1938, that I have ever played myself. The series is about a young couple thinking of marriage, and I am the grandfather to whom the boy, Nicholas Lyndhurst, comes for advice. The character is a slightly cranky old man, one who goes in for fads and enthusiastic exercise. I do nurse a slight grudge though for the four hours the makeup girls spend greying up my hair – I am still pretty dark and it's all my own!

He adds, 'He's not really a dead ringer for me but I have reached the stage of totting up my grandchildren on my fingers.'

Patrick had a quite a few grandchildren by now. His son David and wife Alison had given him Sam, Jim and William, Caroline and myself had added Matthew and Sally, Peter and his wife had produced Tierney and Florence, Mark the youngest son and wife Jane had delivered Tom, Eleanor, Rebekah, Beatrice and Charlotte and my sister Joanna had added Jack and Harry. There may have been more from his daughter Jane.

By this time, Dad was on pretty good terms with all his children apart from his first born, Joanna. She had never really forgiven him for the way he had treated our mother Margaret over the divorce. In a letter to her he shows how desperate he was to remedy the breakdown in relations,

'My dearest Jo, Should you wish, at any time, to break the silence between us – then the usually way this is done is to talk about what we have in common. Painting perhaps. This way there is no embarrassment and one's pride does not stand in the way. I'd love to know what you are painting recently and how it's going. I'd love to tell you what I've been painting. Sitting room looks like the National Gallery! Please contact me. Love Dad xx

A curiously formal letter, which lacks emotion but is heavy on wanting reconciliation. Jo had not spoken to Dad since 1976 and it remained that way until his death. Jo's children never met their grandfather.

Early 1986 was busy for Patrick which saw him complete series such as *Yesterday's Dreams, Inspector Morse, Super Gran,* and *Knight of the Gods.* By the Autumn he told me,

'I am gloriously free to play golf and paint. My only other commitment is a Doctor Who *convention in Chicago.'*

I didn't see Dad that Christmas. The New Year came and went and I kept reminding myself to give him a call and invite him over but life was busy for me with a new baby and a TV series called *The New Statesman*. I had one postcard from him in February updating me on how things were going. I noticed how spidery and shaky his writing had become and I worried about his health. He wrote,

'Dear Mike, Thought your performance in The Mill on the Floss *was brilliant. He was such a touching character. Bill and Ben are still ruling the roost here. Not working this week. Have a 'Who' convention coming up in Columbus, Georgia. Hope Caroline, Matthew and baby Sally are well. I will come over soon to meet the new addition. Love Dad xx*

He never did get to meet our daughter - those were his last words to me before his fatal heart attack at the Magnum Opus Con II science fiction convention in Columbus, Georgia.

Mark recalls,

'I was with mum when the phone call from the US came to say that Dad had died of a heart attack in his bedroom in the hotel in Columbus, Georgia where he was doing yet another *Doctor Who* Convention. Eleven years had passed since he'd left home so there was some attenuation to the impact of the sad news. But your Dad is your Dad - even if you happen to share him with two other families.'

My wife Caroline told me the news. I had just driven back from London after working all day on an advert. I opened our front door and Caroline immediately blurted out,

'I've got some bad news I'm afraid… you'd better sit down.'

I listened as she told me that my mother had phoned earlier in the day to tell me Dad was dead. I wasn't shocked by the news. I think I was expecting it to happen soon.

The first phone call I got that day was from Annie Morrish. After passing on her sympathy she finished by saying,

'He was far too young to die. He had so much more to give. I can't believe he is dead. Death is so final.'

Those words have stayed with me to this day.

Afterword
by Colin Baker

When I was starting out as an actor in London in the early 1970's, a girl that I was sharing a flat with brought her boyfriend back one night. His name was David Troughton (the brother of the author of this book) and he was just embarking on a career in theatre too. I naturally asked him if he was related to the famous actor whom I had always admired and who had recently played Doctor Who with great distinction – Patrick Troughton. He was his son it transpired. I was impressed.

David and I became great friends and when he married his wife Ali in the summer of 1973, I was honoured to be invited to be his Best Man. This led to meeting Patrick for the first time, briefly, outside the Church in North London where the wedding took place. It was a high spot for me, as long before Patrick had played the second incarnation of you know Who, I had been captivated by many of his roles on television and film, and in particular his definitive 'Quilp' in *The Old Curiosity Shop* on the BBC back in 1962, a superb performance which is remembered to this day with great clarity and affection by all who saw it.

Unfortunately, I was working in the theatre on the day of David's wedding, so had to rush back for the matinee at the Theatre Royal, Windsor immediately after the marriage ceremony, so I missed out on the opportunity to meet Patrick during the less formal elements of the wedding. Perhaps that was just as well. I was young and would have been a tad in awe of the great man and would, in all likelihood, have committed the crime of the inarticulate gush and alienated him for ever.

So, it was not until 1984, when I was playing the Doctor myself that we met again at the BBC rehearsal rooms in Acton to rehearse *The Two Doctors*. I must confess that I was still a bit in awe of him. For me he was the 'guvnor' among Doctors. He was the man who gave the rest of us the opportunity to have our moments in the Tardis. Had he not seized the opportunity offered by the first regeneration so firmly and so beguilingly, it would possibly have been a case of 'Tom Who?'

Just think what we would have missed! All those scarves lying unloved at the bottom of wardrobes, the blue police boxes long-forgotten and children sitting comfortably on sofas instead of scurrying behind them in terror for the last forty-five years. Patrick's genius really did set a different time line in motion in more ways than one.

Any small anxieties I may have had about performing my version of the Doctor in his company were soon dispelled. Patrick was relaxed, professional and very friendly. If he had any opinions about this brash young upstart who had moved in on his territory, then he did not show it; and I certainly did not, I hope, offer any 'young lion marking out his territory' behaviour to suggest that I did not respect and honour my predecessor. Indeed, it is quite probable, although I cannot remember now exactly, that I did do a bit of modified gushing. But what the heck; he deserved it.

We got to film in Seville for a week or so, which was for me a rare treat. We had a splendid time. He, Frazer, Nicola and I got on extremely well and it was probably the best experience of my acting career in many ways, professionally, socially and artistically. The abiding memory I have is of evenings spent in the hotel swimming pool, with Patrick who was twenty odd years my senior and only a few years younger than I am now as I write this, tolerating amiably the frolics of us younger ones and joining in some of the silly games that carefree people play in the sun in swimming pools, when the pressure is off. We did work hard too, I hasten to add.

Acting is so much easier when you are working with people like Patrick. He slipped back into his character with the practised ease of a true master of his art. The scenes when we finally met in *The Two Doctors* were wonderful to film and he was kind enough to indicate that he was enjoying the process as much as I was. We had a great time.

Every other time I met Patrick was at a convention, either here in the UK or in America. After initial reluctance and uncertainty, he had taken to the *Doctor Who* Convention circuit with something approaching relish. He and Jon Pertwee worked out a wonderful shtick that they performed in panels, involving insults, sarcasm and water pistols. He had great fun and was a convivial and generous companion at these events; and he had endless time for fans too.

But above all else he was a superb and very clever actor, who truly inhabited every role he undertook; a true character actor, and a true character.

Also available from www.hirstpublishing.com

BLUE BOX BOY

A MEMOIR OF DOCTOR WHO IN FOUR EPISODES

MATTHEW WATERHOUSE

Also available from www.hirstpublishing.com

THE FLIGHT OF THE
BUDGERIGAR

THE AUTOBIOGRAPHY OF
JOHN LEESON

LIFE BEGINS AT 40

BY CHRIS NEWTON
AND MARK CHARLESWORTH

Also available from www.hirstpublishing.com

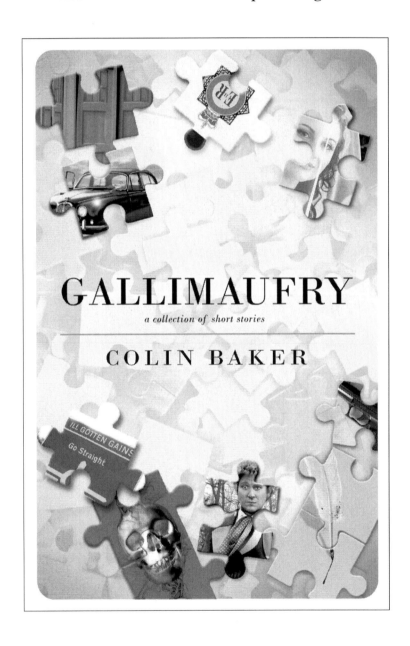

GALLIMAUFRY

a collection of short stories

COLIN BAKER

Also available from www.hirstpublishing.com

Single White Who Fan

The life & times of *Jackie Jenkins*

as featured in Doctor Who Magazine –
includes exclusive new material.

Foreword by Gary Gillat

Also available from www.hirstpublishing.com

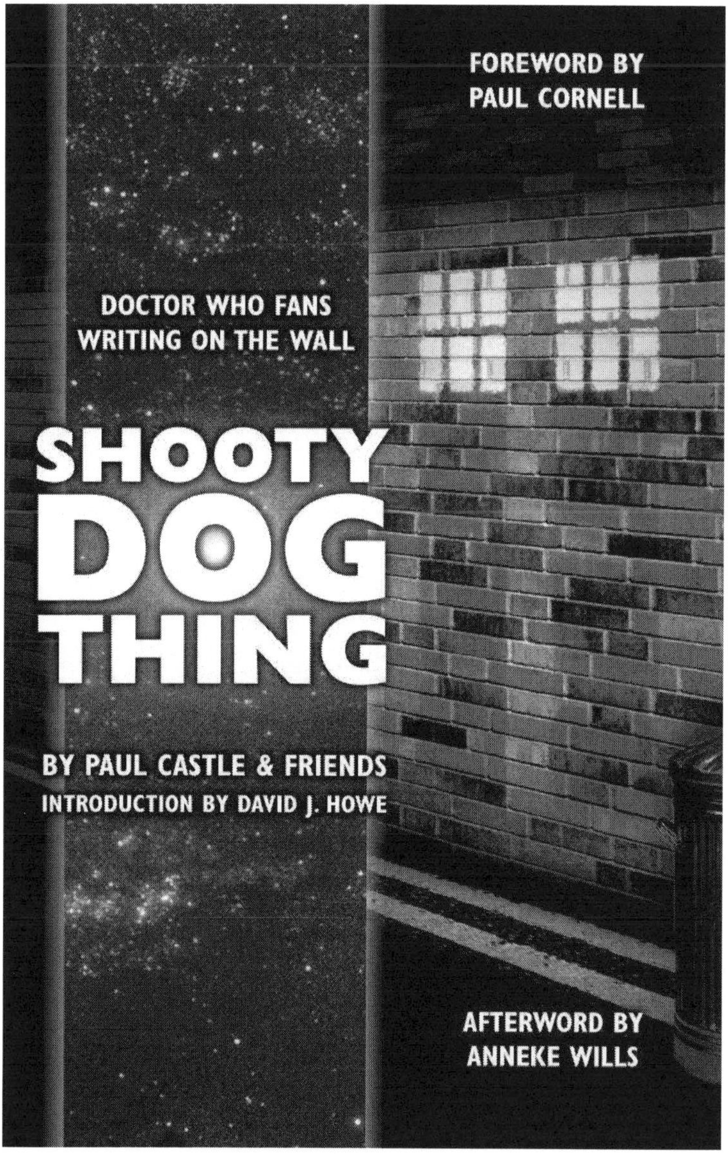

FOREWORD BY
PAUL CORNELL

DOCTOR WHO FANS
WRITING ON THE WALL

SHOOTY
DOG
THING

BY PAUL CASTLE & FRIENDS
INTRODUCTION BY DAVID J. HOWE

AFTERWORD BY
ANNEKE WILLS

SHOOTY DOG THING

2th & CLAW

EDITED BY PAUL CASTLE
AND JON ARNOLD

Also available from www.hirstpublishing.com

YOU · AND
WHO

edited by J R SOUTHALL

The author and publisher wish to thank the following people for pre-ordering this book:

Richard Abela
Brian Adams
David Adler
Kevin Aitchison
Barry Aldridge
Tristan Alfaro
Kade Allen
Edward Allison
Matthew Almond
Tony Amis
Paul Arnall
Kevin Ash
Michael Atkinson
Julie Augustin
Anne Austin
Joseph Backes
Mark Bailey
Keith Baldock-Grimes
Gary Bates
Antony Bellows
Steven Bennett
Paul Bensilum
Cinnabarre Bertelsen
Matt Betts
Paul Bevan
Gareth Bevan
Darren Bibby
Stephanie Black
Philip Blackman
Nicholas Blake
Roger Bolton
Josslyn Bond
Gareth Bowley
Scan Brady

Ian Branch
Michael Brandt
Rod Brown
Derek Buchanan
Shaun Butcher
Roger Byrne
Stephen Candy
Melissa Cane
Chris Cane
Michael Carr
Mark Caul
Adam Chamberlain
Darla Chambers
David Checkley
Stuart Clark
Neil Clarke
Paul Clifford
Alan Clyde
Mark Cockram
Lorraine Coles
Phil Collinson
Shane Cook
Martin Cook
Mike Cook
Barry Cooper
Robert Cooper
Ralph Corderoy
Blaine Coughlan
Jeremy Cravos
Sarah Crotzer
Michael Crouch
Joseph Culp
Andrew Cummins
Oliver Dale

Ian Darby
Simon Davies
James Dean
Jon Dear
Barry Delve
Michael Dennis
Margaret Deutsch
Tracy Devereux
Steven Dieter
Mark Dimon
Trevor Donnelly
Paul Dunn
David Durham
Adam Dymond
John Eccles
Jason Eckard
Carl Ellis
Steve Emmerson
Paul Engelberg
Glyn Evans
Kent Evenden
David Ewen
Jeffrey Farrell
Chris Fenn
Cody Ferrell
Morvyn Finch
Stuart Flanagan
David John Forbes
Scott Fraser
David French
Paul Gardner
Jeffrey Garrett
Kevin Gauntlett
David Gay
Nicholas George
KristianGerdes
Karl Gibson
Paul Gilbert

Sal Giliberto
Paul Goodison
David Green
Ian Greenfield
Paul Griffin
Kris Griffin
Stephen Griffiths
James Guthrie
Sarah Hadley
Stephanie Hamilton
Hayden Harris
Roger Harris
Simon Hart
Peter Hastings.
Jo Healy
Colin Hendry
Tim Hicks
Matt Hills
Edward Hipkiss
Martin Holmes
Stephen Hoy
Chris Hoyle
Rodney Hrvatin
Darren Hughes
Mark Humphrey
Helen Hunter
Robin Huntley
Karen Hurren
Linda Isele
Paul Jackson
David Jackson
Gavin Jarvis
Tom Jennings
Lesley Jones
Sterling Jones
David Jones
Linda Jones
Iain Keiller

David Kelly
Neil Kenny
Derek Kettlety
Michael Kincaid
Steve King
Adam King
Chris King
Gary Knowles
Jack Kusler
Ceri Laing
Jim Lancaster
Adrian Last
Christopher Leather
Rob Lee
Shaun Ley
Jonathan Light
Simon Lloyd
Glynis Lovell
Chris MacAllister
Joseph G MacColl
Steve Mackenzie
Eleanor Maddocks
John Main
Vinny Mainolfi
Sean Marsh
Alison Martin
Kenneth Mason
Stuart Masterman
Steve Matthewman
Emrys Matthews
Ben McClory
Ciara McConkey
Mark McDonnell
Roddy McDougall
James C McFetridge
Mark McGeechan
Ian McLachlan
Joe McGill

Joe McIntyre
David McKinlay
Steven McNicoll
Andrew Meadows
Andrew Melling
Nick Mellish
Gary Miscandlon
Christine Mounser
Erol Muhammed
Patrick Mulkern
David Mullen
Christopher Murfin
Tim Neal
Gordon Nicholson
Paul Norman
Katy Oakes
Mark Oliver
Mike Osborne
Antoinette Palmieri
Gavin Parfitt
Malcolm Parkinson
Matthew Partis
Stephen Pasqua
Rob Pearson
Alister Pearson
David Perry
Thomas Phillip
Emma Potts
Farzaneh Pourmasoumi
Jon Preddle
Robert Preston
Graeme Pritchard
Nicky Pugh
Carl Purkis
Curtis Pyles
Billy Rees
Robert Reeve
Jason Rhodes

Peter Rich
John Richardson
Neil Roberts
James Robertson
Robert Robinson
Peter Rosace
Phil Rosenbach
Gordon Roxburgh
Martin Sawyer
Andew Scott
Peter Scott
Chris Sedman
Kathleen Sennott
Michael Shakesby
Joseph Shanks
Colin Sharpe
William Shawcross
Alexandra Shewan
Jenny Shirt
Bryan Simcott
Robert J.E. Simpson
John Sissons
Katrina Slater
Johnathan Smith
Russ Smith
Martin Smith
Mark Snyder
Chris St.Pier
David Stevens
Andrew Stocker
Anthony Swan

Michael Swart
David Sweeney
David Tamblyn
Simon Taylor
Robert Taylor
Randall Thomas
Paul Thomas
Jeffrey T Toschlog
Jason Vaught
Gary Vernon
David Vincent
Antony Wainer
Martin Wakefield
Stephen James Walker
Jeffrey Walker
Angela Walker-Scott
Alistair Wallace
Liz Ward
Paul Webster
Gillian Wen
Chris Westbrook
Alex White
Simon Whitehead
Peter Wilcock
Jonathan Wilkinson
Sean Williams
Ian Woodhouse
David Woodley
Paul Wrzesinski
Matt Zitron
Roberts Zubeckis

www.hirstpublishing.com

www.michaeltroughton.co.uk

www.facebook.com/hirstbooks

Hirst Publishing on Twitter: @hirstbooks

Michael Troughton on Twitter: @mwtroughton